"Until the modern, or postmodern era, education was about character formation and virtue ethics for leaders. When education was radically democratized in the twentieth century, which brought both virtue and vice to the campus, so too was character formation—and this democratization became thin and now virtue ethics have become rare or non-existent. This book pleads with Christian university leaders to make character and spiritual formation central to what happens on the campus. God bless this book."

—Scot McKnight, Karl A. Olsson Professor in Religious Studies, North Park University

"As one who cares deeply about Christian spiritual formation on the college campus, I found this book to be a treasure of insight and information I have been longing for. How can the campus be a place of formation? What role does the university president play in spiritual nurture? How do you hire the right faculty? The authors of these fine essays answer these questions, and many more. This book is a valuable resource for me and my staff."

—James Bryan Smith, director of the Aprentis Institute for Christian Spiritual Formation, Friends University and author of the *Apprentice* Series

"If you are ready to consider faith integration in a fresh, holistic, comprehensive way that connects with students on Christian college campuses, you will want to read *Building a Culture of Faith: University-wide Partnerships for Spiritual Formation*. Cary Balzer and Rod Reed have brought together voices from all areas of campus life to address the spiritual formation of students who seek to follow Christ in a rapidly changing culture. The authors are campus-influencers both inside and outside the classroom and their essays will provoke life- and work-changing dialogue for those who are called to serve the cause of Christian Higher Education."

—Kina Mallard, Provost and Vice President of Academic Affairs, Carson-Newman University

"As a Christian educator/administrator, nothing stirs doubt in me as much as the question: 'Is my institution accomplishing what our mission statement says we do in the faith lives of our students?' Knowing that educational shops resist change, the authors address the process needed to correctly construct a faith-encouraging culture. Cary Balzer and Rod Reed have put together an outstanding group of authors and their thoughtful essays addressing this challenging subject. I eagerly await the book's release in order to place a volume into each of our faculty member's hands."

—Loren Gresham, President, Southern Nazarene University

"What is spiritual formation, really? And does it matter that we—presidents, staff, perhaps especially faculty—participate personally in the ongoing, life-giving discipline of spiritual formation? I am encouraged by the self-searching honesty of these thoughtful essays, important reading for those of us who care deeply that spiritual formation remains at the vital center of our Christian universities."

—PHILIP W. EATON, President, Seattle Pacific University and author of *Engaging the Culture, Changing the World: The Christian University in a Post-Christian World*

"What do the word's 'spiritual formation' mean for today's Christian college or university? This collection of essays explores not only what it means, but more importantly, why it matters—for students, faculty, administrators, alumni and those who invest in our work. Reed and Balzer have gathered together a rich team of experienced and deeply committed leaders who challenge the reader to think, learn and live out the call to be faithful followers of Christ. This work will both challenge and inspire those who work and serve in Christian higher education to be active participants in building a culture of faith."

—RONALD P. MAHURIN, Vice President for Professional Development & Research, Council for Christian Colleges & Universities

"The pioneering contribution of this book is laying out a holistic vision of spiritual formation across the range of campus life. This engaging vision is accompanied by specific strategies for implementation, including 'soul projects' for the classroom, suggestions for administrators, and examples of what universities are presently doing. A rich feast for all Christian college and university personnel."

—DARRYL TIPPENS, Provost, Pepperdine University

BUILDING
A CULTURE
OF FAITH

BUILDING A CULTURE OF FAITH

University-Wide Partnerships for Spiritual Formation

CARY BALZER & ROD REED

EDITORS

Abilene Christian University Press

BUILDING A CULTURE OF FAITH
University-Wide Partnerships for Spiritual Formation

ACU
PRESS

LIBRARY OF CONGRESS CATALOGING-IN-PUBLICATION DATA
Building a culture of faith : university-wide partnerships for spiritual formation / Cary Balzer & Rod Reed, editors.
    p. cm.
Includes bibliographical references and index.
ISBN 978-0-89112-300-2 (alk. paper)
1. Christian universities and colleges--United States. 2. College students--Religious life--United States. 3. Spiritual formation. I. Balzer, Cary, 1961- II. Reed, Rod.
LC427.B85 2012
378'.071--dc23

2012021254

Cover design by Rick Gibson
Interior text design by Sandy Armstrong

For information contact:
Abilene Christian University Press
1626 Campus Court
Abilene, Texas 79601

1-877-816-4455 toll free
www.abilenechristianuniversitypress.com

To the faculty and staff at Seattle Pacific University,
the University of Sioux Falls, Asbury Theological Seminary, and Bethel
Theological Seminary. While attending these schools,
we began to learn what a culture of faith could be.

ACKNOWLEDGMENTS

We would like to express our thanks to everyone at John Brown University for encouraging projects such as this. The university's Professional Development Grants and the donor-funded McGee Chair of Biblical Studies supported our research and writing. JBU student Esther Carey provided invaluable help with proofreading and editing. We are also thankful to our authors who applied their wisdom and an unmistakable passion for spiritual formation to this project. Our editors from Abilene Christian University Press, Leonard Allen and Jennifer Day, worked diligently to make this book a reality. Most importantly, we would like to thank our wives and families: Tracy Balzer, Kelsey Howard, and Langley Balzer; and Michelle, Connor, Zachary, Kaden, and Zoe Reed. They cheered us on and supported us as we pursued this project.

TABLE OF CONTENTS

Section Three
Implementation, Praxis, and Models

INTRODUCTION

Cary Balzer

I met Dayhe Kim, a new undergraduate student from Korea, at John Brown University's international host family reception. My wife, Tracy, had requested that we become her host family after the two of them met at a new student orientation event earlier in the semester. Dayhe encouraged us to call her "Sarah," the American name she had chosen. Over the next year and a half we attended Friday night high school football games, our small-town Christmas parade (complete with church floats and Santa atop the fire engine) and the pre-prom red-carpet event downtown where my daughter Langley and her friends appeared in their gowns and tuxes. In addition, our oldest daughter and her husband moved to South Korea in August to teach English in the public schools and during Christmas vacation they had dinner together with Sarah's family in Seoul. In the short time we have known Sarah, we have experienced many memorable events together. We could not have guessed that visiting her in a neural trauma intensive care unit would be part of those memories.

Sarah was involved in a serious accident as she crossed a busy street near our campus. She sustained life-threatening injuries and was airlifted to a regional trauma center where she lay in a coma. Over the next seven weeks we witnessed the work of an incredible medical team who worked together to slowly reconstruct Sarah's life. Doctors diagnosed critical injuries and performed lifesaving surgeries, nurses administered medications and cared for everyday needs, and translators communicated news to Sarah's father, who had flown from South Korea within days of the accident. Members of the Korean church in Northwest Arkansas sat with Sarah every day and cooked welcome Korean meals for her father. JBU administrators, faculty, staff, students, and friends kept vigil, brought meals, and offered help of all kinds.

Over the course of several weeks, Sarah gradually emerged from her coma and small movements turned into deliberate actions. One week she blinked her eyes and squeezed our hands. A week later she opened her eyes and made meaningful hand signs. Late the following week I answered the phone and heard Sarah's voice for the first time in over a month and the next day we walked into her room, found her sitting up—laptop in hand—updating Facebook. Less than eight weeks after her accident, Sarah left the hospital and she and her father returned to Korea.

I tell this story of tragedy and recovery to point out two key observations. First, progress—like Sarah's journey from the ICU to her return to Korea—can be a complicated and frightening process, but ultimately it is a fulfilling journey filled with hope. This concept is true whether we are discussing physical healing from a traffic accident or discussing academic achievement or spiritual maturity. Within these pages, we seek to expand the conversation of how Christian higher education can support and encourage spiritual formation. It may be complicated and, at times, frightening, but ultimately it is a worthwhile, fulfilling journey of hope.

Recent books, such as *Beyond Integration* by Todd Ream, Jerry Pattengale, and David Riggs[1] or James K. A. Smith's *Desiring the Kingdom: Worship, Worldview, and Cultural Formation*,[2] examine the process of Christian higher education from a fresh perspective. *Beyond Integration* seeks to reflect upon Christian higher education and move the discussion beyond the traditional Reformed model of the integration of faith and learning. Smith's book attempts to re-vision Christian education as a formative process that redirects our desires to the highest ends for which we were created. In the pages that follow, the authors of this volume will also push us to consider a broader understanding of the role of Christian higher education in the process of faith maturity. It is our contention that the integration of faith and learning is a noble goal, but that in itself it falls short of God's highest and best calling for Christian educators in the university. This project will pursue a larger vision for the Christian university by promoting a culture that fosters spiritual formation among the faculty, staff, and—ultimately—in the lives of our students.

Second, Sarah's recovery reminds me that complex and difficult projects are best accomplished by teams representing a wide array of gifts, talents, and experiences. Just as Sarah's recovery utilized the attention of an array of skilled professionals and a supportive community, so too the tremendous task of holistic Christian education requires a university-wide partnership. To influence the whole student—"head, heart, and hand," as our mission at JBU states—will require the work of the whole university, from the president to the chaplain, faculty, residence directors, coaches, counselors, administrative support, and grounds crew.

In February 2010, Rod Reed and I, along with a small team of colleagues from John Brown University, presented a paper entitled "Building a University-wide Partnership for Spiritual Formation" at the International Forum on Christian Higher Education in Atlanta, Georgia. Sometime after that presentation Rod and I considered how we might continue the discussion and decided to include others within the higher education community with similar approaches and stories. This book is the result of that process and includes seventeen authors from twelve different institutions. The two-fold purpose of the book is to promote a broader view of Christian learning that moves beyond integration to holistic spiritual formation and to discuss the ways in which various parts of the university might contribute to this formation process. The following pages briefly summarize the fourteen chapters, and the three sections into which they are organized.

Section One
Institutional Influences on Spiritual Formation

Contemporary Christian universities claim that students grow spiritually while enrolled, yet very little work has been done to explore the influences of various parts of the university on student spiritual formation, including the impact of faculty. We suggest that spiritual formation is more than just addressing cognitive issues of worldview and faith integration. It is also more than chapel and small groups. This section will address the unique setting available at a university for spiritual formation.

Chapter 1: "Setting the Tone for Spiritual Formation on Campus: The President's Role"

Bill Robinson begins the journey by looking at the role of the most influential person on a college campus: the university president. He encourages presidents to pay attention to both the important and the seemingly insignificant choices they make, as both areas set the tone for the entire campus environment. Bill states, "Even when they are not trying, presidents set tones. The challenge is setting the kind of tone that inspires and instructs students to become imitators of Christ."

Chapter 2: "Mapping the Christian Higher Education Genome"

Steve Moore calls Christian universities to incarnate the "Character Chromosomes" of humility, hospitality, incarnation, reconciliation, and imagination. He emphasizes the importance of these attributes in creating the DNA of a spiritually alive, globally aware campus. Steve states, "To seek the highest experiences of scholarship and model the highest expression of what it means to be a Christian educator requires courage and a commitment . . . far beyond what is typical in higher education."

Chapter 3: "Historical and Contemporary Approaches to Spiritual Formation in the University"

Contemporary Christian universities need to learn from the successes and mistakes of the past. In Chapter Three, Rod Reed provides an overview of approaches to spiritual formation in four overlapping eras of American higher education history. At various times, universities have relied on campus ethos, student initiative, the chaplaincy, or faith integration to carry the spiritual mission of the university. He contends that contemporary universities must intentionally incorporate each of these approaches in an integrated way to help students grow spiritually.

Chapter 4: "Leaving a Mark: The Role of Faculty in University-Wide Spiritual Formation"

Cary Balzer highlights the influence faculty have in the spiritual formation process. Universities influence student spiritual formation as they hire and develop faculty who see ministry to students as part of their responsibility. As a result, Cary demonstrates the importance of the institution's involvement in faculty's spiritual growth, utilizing several examples implemented at John Brown University. He states, "[an] investment in the lives of faculty members sets the tone for and expectation of spiritual formation in the context of the larger life of the university."

Section Two
Exploring Spiritual Formation

Spiritual formation is a term that is widely and often indiscriminately used in contemporary Christianity. Section Two provides a framework for understanding spiritual formation—specifically as it is practiced in the Christian university—and addresses the ways that an academic setting influences the goals and processes of spiritual formation.

Chapter 5: "A Theology of Christian Spiritual Formation"

In this chapter, Steve Harper focuses on the theological foundations of spiritual development. He explains the importance of formation with regard to the three areas of trinity, tradition, and trajectory. Formation in this way provides us and our students with identity, vocation, and hope. The process is not easy, but the academy has the opportunity to be actively involved in helping students learn to live this challenging task.

Chapter 6: "The Power of Context: Spiritual Formation in the Christian University"

Rod Reed contends that Christian universities offer a unique context for educating the whole person. Because the Christian university has a different mission and culture than the local church or para-church ministry, the goals and processes of spiritual formation of students should look different as well. Because Christian universities claim to influence their students spiritually as well as academically, it is essential for them to create an environment that encourages spiritual formation in ways that are consistent with their mission.

Chapter 7: "Who Are We to Form Students? The Importance of Remembering Who We Are"

Perry Glanzer issues a call to Christian faculty and student-development personnel to return to a truly Christian understanding of their role in developing students spiritually. Such understanding requires having a biblical view of humanity, particularly as it relates to loving one another. He especially encourages faculty and staff to "practice love in various identity contexts" by mentoring students.

Chapter 8: "Invitation to an Academic Journey of Spiritual Formation"

Robert Mulholland dispels the idea that the academy must be divorced from the realm in which spiritual formation can occur. He asks, "Is it possible to integrate their life in Christ with their academic discipline in a way that has integrity for both?" Robert calls faculty and staff to "engage in a spiritual journey into God for the sake of the world," particularly the students we serve.

Section Three
Implementation, Praxis, and Models

Responsibility for spiritual formation in the Christian university is often delegated to student development or campus ministries departments. However, for a

Christian university to fully invest in the spiritual formation of students, members of all parts of the community must fulfill their role. This section will provide practical models for the role of faculty and staff in the spiritual formation of students.

Chapter 9: "On the Lookout for What Would Be Revealed: Faculty and Spiritual Formation"

Keith Anderson tells the story of faculty members who helped him to pay attention, stating that "spirituality is learning to pay attention to the presence of God in everything." Because education "is inherently sacred," he offers five paradigms for faculty involvement in student spiritual formation. These paradigms call faculty members to pay attention to their own spiritual formation so that they may be able to help students who are very much in process spiritually.

Chapter 10: "Conversation Creates Culture: Student Development and Spiritual Formation in the Christian University"

Susan Reese discusses the importance of student-development personnel taking the time to invest in students' lives through conversation. Just as faculty contribute to a culture of spiritual formation through relationships and the curriculum, so student-development professionals help create culture through providing space for meaningful conversations. Reese explains that students need people to walk and talk with them as they are frequently passing through thresholds during their college years. She states, "Students are seeking mentors and conversations to decipher their true beliefs."

Chapter 11: "Strengthening a Christian College as a Faith Mentoring Environment through *Knowing—Being—Doing*"

Bob Yoder provides a case study of how faculty at Goshen College seek to create a "faith-mentoring environment" for their students. Yoder explores two years of student and faculty survey data to discuss how Goshen is working to build a culture that fosters student spiritual formation. He suggests building a framework that incorporates *Knowing—Being—Doing* to facilitate spiritual growth.

Chapter 12: "Soul Projects: Class-Related Spiritual Practices in Higher Education"

A team of faculty from Wheaton College presents a model for facilitating student spiritual formation. This model involves including "soul projects" in various classes. The group of authors provides helpful descriptions of several sample soul projects, as well as offering reflections on pedagogy and suggestions for grading these projects. They suggest that these projects help students "enter into the academic life in a spiritually transformative manner."

Chapter 13: "Tour Guides, Translators, and Traveling Companions: How Faculty Contribute to the Spiritual Formation of Students"

Greg Carmer presents three metaphors for faculty influence in spiritual formation: tour guides, translators, and traveling companions. In so doing, he addresses the obstacles that faculty face in their desire to influence students, as well as the promise of partnership with other departments on campus. In each of these metaphorical roles, faculty have the opportunity to help students navigate unfamiliar territory in their spiritual journeys.

Chapter 14: "In Partnership with Communities: Spiritual Formation and Cross-Cultural Immersion"

Cynthia Toms-Smedley addresses the spiritual formation potential that comes as part of cross-cultural experiences. When students are exposed to new ideas outside of their typical environment, they have the opportunity to grow in new ways and areas of their lives. She challenges leaders of cross-cultural experiences to provide opportunities for theological and spiritual reflection for students during key moments of their participation. She states, "Theological reflection offers a place where tradition and experience intersect, a place where experience and religious tradition converse with each other."

———

As you read these chapters, we hope this book encourages conversation and cooperation across universities that foster the spiritual formation of our students. If Christian universities are to fulfill the claims that they make regarding student spirituality, such intentional partnership is required. The university must be a place of integration that is greater than cognitive understanding. To truly integrate faith and learning, all parts of the university must work together to build a culture of faith so that students are influenced spiritually in the classroom, in the residence halls, in their work-study jobs, on their athletic teams, and wherever they study around the world.

Introduction Notes

[1] Todd C. Ream, Jerry Pattengale, and David L. Riggs, eds., *Beyond Integration?: Inter/Disciplinary Possibilities for the Future of Christian Higher Education* (Abilene, Tex.: Abilene Christian University Press, 2012).

[2] James K. A. Smith, *Desiring the Kingdom: Worship, Worldview, and Cultural Formation* (Grand Rapids, Mich.: Baker, 2009).

Institutional Influences on Spiritual Formation

SETTING THE TONE FOR SPIRITUAL FORMATION ON CAMPUS

The President's Role

Bill Robinson

How do presidents set the tone for spiritual formation on campus?
The short answer is "by everything they do." Even when they are not trying, presidents set tones. In fact, it would be wise for Christian college presidents to assume they never stop setting the tone for spiritual formation. Everything counts—what they say, what they do not say, what they do, what they do not do, and generally how they go about their jobs. Setting a tone is not the challenge. The challenge is setting the kind of tone that inspires and instructs students to become imitators of Christ.

Most presidents realize their campuses are listening and watching. But sometimes they miscalculate what is being seen and heard. In my early years as a college president, I frequently

- overestimated the impact of *what* I did, and underestimated the impact of *how* I did it;
- overestimated the impact of the big things I did, and underestimated the impact of the little things I did;
- overestimated the impact of resource-building, and underestimated the impact of culture-building.

Presidents never stop creating the culture of their university. I picked up litter when I walked around campus. Our facilities people would say my direct efforts were just an eyelash above worthless in the annual reduction of stray wrappers. But an email from a new faculty member seemed to say my litter obsession was setting a tone: "Bill, just about the time I thought I had no more room on my plate, I looked out the window of my subterranean office and there you were giving me one more job. If you're picking up litter, it's my job too."

I pick up litter when I am alone in the woods. When I pick it up on campus, I do not try to set a tone for the faculty any more than I try to set a tone for the squirrels in the woods. But it is the *presidency* that creates a ripple effect, so the folks who occupy that position need to remember they are walking, talking tone-setters. When they stop to greet a campus tour, it sets a tone; when they walk past a campus tour and smile, it sets a tone; when they ignore a campus tour, it sets a tone.

I recall making two big decisions that set two very different cultural tones. Early in my first presidency, I made a swift, courageous, data-driven move. It was also one in which I flunked listening, asking, and communicating. As a thirty-six-year-old rookie, I thought the right decision would erase any process mistakes. I was wrong. My cavalier tone was heard throughout the college. In my second presidency, I faced another agonizing decision. For this one, I spent close to a year asking and listening before making the call. A very different tone accompanied this approach—one of respect for both people and processes.

Because presidents do influence campus culture in both healthy and unhealthy ways, it bears noting that we are not the best judges of the tones we set, especially for spiritual formation. When we talk about the effective ways we influence campus climate, it sounds self-congratulatory. For that I apologize in advance, but the spiritual formation tones with which I am most familiar are the ones I set. Ultimately, how well a president shapes a university's faith-related efforts is best evaluated by the students, faculty, and staff. And that leads to my first suggestion for how presidents can set a good tone for spiritual formation.

Sit Down, Listen, and Ask Questions

A couple of months ago, I was reading Luke 2 before my morning prayers. I always chuckle at the thought of Mary and Joseph losing Jesus and not figuring it out for three days. Calling 911 to report losing the Son of God for a few days is the call no parent would want to make. Fortunately, Mary and Joseph realized he was missing and went back to Jerusalem where they found him "astounding" the religious leadership in the temple. But for the first I time noticed the verbs Luke used to describe what Jesus was doing. Luke says Jesus was sitting, listening, and asking.

Listening and asking represent one of the few areas where presidents get worse with experience. Early in their presidencies, they ask questions all over campus.

They want to know the place that has welcomed them so enthusiastically. But the more they learn, the less they ask. And when they do ask, they ask consultants and presidential colleagues. To be sure, fresh ideas can and should be imported. But it is not very deep into their tenures when presidents think they have tapped their campuses. When that happens, they look past their best resources for knowing how to shape spiritual formation: their own people. Presidents should work closely with several groups:

- Spiritual life (and other student life) leaders. Do we have a common understanding of "spiritual formation?" What are the themes and strategies we are using this year? What can I as president do to support your efforts?
- Students. What can our college, in general, and I, in particular, do to help you become more conformed to the image of Christ for the sake of others? Where do you feel least supported and least knowledgeable? Where are we currently doing well in nourishing your spirituality?
- Faculty. In what ways can the administration support your efforts to do faith-learning integration in your classrooms? What empowers or impedes your efforts now? Do you feel the university values your efforts to support the spiritual growth of our students?
- Alumni. What enriched your spiritual development while you were in school? What could have added to that enrichment?

Understand What Is Meant by Spiritual Formation

If presidents on Christian college campuses are responsible for the tone, it will help if they know the words to the music. And, alas, the lyrics change somewhat according to the differing theological traditions of our campuses. Before evangelicals started talking about "spiritual formation," both the term and concept were common among Catholics. Drawing on such classics as *The Imitation of Christ* by Thomas à Kempis and *Spiritual Exercises* by Ignatius of Loyola, the Catholic Church has accented the contemplative life as essential in spiritual formation. Their notion of integration echoes the writings of Ignatius when he lifts high Christ's "divine majesty in his presence, power, and essence"[1] in all things.

Similarly, presidents of Protestant colleges should understand and reinforce the ways in which spiritual formation is influenced by the theological and ecclesial traditions of their institutions. In Washington, for example, Seattle Pacific University's Free Methodist origins will probably give a Wesleyan shade to its practice of spiritual formation. Across the state, Whitworth University's approach to spiritual formation bears the marks of a Reformed influence that stems from its Presbyterian roots. The differences can surface in assumptions about human nature, creation, the fall, redemption, and the activity of Christ's Holy Spirit. And although these distinctions may lie beyond the grasp of the average college sophomore, that sophomore's president should be able to tell a board of trustees how the university's understanding of spiritual formation reflects its theological roots.

My push for understanding spiritual formation comes from the fear that when a term or a concept takes on a rather sudden popularity, as this term has, we are all guilty of throwing it around as if it only has one meaning, and we all know what it is. I am quick to admit we did not all agree on the meaning of spiritual formation's forebears—sanctification, spiritual maturity, and spirit-filled, for example. But it is still worthwhile for a president to have a theologically informed answer when asked, "How would a student well along in the process of spiritual formation at your university look?"

Think Integration

If spiritual formation is about anything it is about integrating the partitions of our lives into a Christ-imitating whole. A president's own life can and should reflect this integrity. That is easier said than done. When I served as president, I failed to accept my own spiritual formation as an essential part of doing my job. I led a fragmented, achievement-driven life. I longed only for the kind of communion with Christ that would hold everything together. In my heart and on the surface, my desire to imitate Christ was clear. My daily duties, however, proved a formidable enemy of all things spiritual. In the final years of my presidency, my spiritual integration efforts improved, largely because I relied more intentionally on morning prayers, communion, and personal liturgies. But still, I never stopped battling the entropic forces of the president's centrifugal life.

A parallel impediment to spiritual integration for students is the way virtually all universities are structured. Commonly, institutional divisions correspond to the partitions we ask our students to integrate. Student life and academic affairs are led by different vice presidents who do not meet structurally until they reach the president's office or, in some cases, the provost's office. These divisions extend into another set of offices with the spiritual life program dangling out there one branch removed from the presidential vine. If presidents hope to see students live integrated spiritual lives, perhaps they could explore organizational structures that unite divisional efforts in faith-building areas.

In my second year at Whitworth, I created a dean of spiritual life position that reported both to the president and the vice president of student life. Further, the position carried a non-tenure-track appointment in the theology department. Technically, Dr. Terry McGonigal, who still holds the position seventeen years later, served student life, academic affairs, and the president's office. But in practice, we all served him and the spiritual needs of our students. To this day it remains a structural mess that works beautifully, which is a tribute to the current president, Beck Taylor. Beck understands that Terry's job is to make spiritual formation everyone's job.

Interdivisional cooperation can bring together a campus in various ways. For instance, in my last ten years at Whitworth, my opening convocation kicked off a spiritual theme woven throughout the spiritual, academic, and residential lives of our first-year students.

My remarks this morning are prompted by the book all of our first-year students read over the summer—*Mountains Beyond Mountains*. I still have ninety pages left, but basically the book chronicles the life of a man named Paul Farmer, a professor of medical anthropology at Harvard. After a rather bizarre and economically deprived childhood, Farmer graduated from Duke University and worked for a year in the central plateau of Haiti, probably the most impoverished and disease-ridden nation in the Western Hemisphere. In a nutshell, this raw-boned kid decided to take on the health of Haiti, and while he was at it, to change the way the world in general and the United Nations in particular thought about infectious disease and poverty. So he headed for Massachusetts and completed the rather challenging task of graduating from the Harvard Medical School while simultaneously picking up a PhD in anthropology. He excelled in both programs, in spite of missing a ton of classes because he was busy saving lives in Haiti. He was and is, as they say in Boston, "wicked smaht."

Maybe some of you "undecideds" are thinking, "Hey, grab a couple of doctorates, build a hospital that treats 350,000 patients annually, improve the health and welfare of a small nation . . . I'll do that." You might want to test the waters with a less ambitious health project. Like flossing.

What do we do with Paul Farmer? Like all of us, he is a flawed human being. But his towering intelligence and furious moral resolve just tear the limits off what we expect from one single life. You don't want to bump into this guy at a party. "Hi, my name is Paul and I've pretty much changed the health picture of Latin America; what have you been up to?"

Most of you are in the process of finding your vocation. Your gifts have begun to direct you. During Orientation I heard freshmen speak of becoming teachers, accountants, physicians, attorneys, curators, and businesspeople. . . .[2]

Consistent invitation to similar spiritual themes in multiple venues encourages student engagement with significant material. Beyond a shadow of a doubt, I know the core-curriculum discussion groups gave durability to the points I tried to drive home in my opening convocations.

Recently, I mentioned to a former college president that I had to prepare to speak at several universities. He replied, "Don't work too hard on it; the students won't be listening." Maybe not, but the odds rise if the contents of the speech get reinforced in several different areas of their academic lives. The day after I announced I was stepping out of the presidency, I received this deeply gratifying note from an alumna who had just graduated from Princeton Theological Seminary. She attended Whitworth during the time when a Lilly grant on vocation gave extra staying power to our thematic school year openings:

Bill, your opening convocation message about Truth and Grace has been the backdrop for basically everything in my life since then. It is still the refrain that guides my choices and relationships. Whitworth will miss you no doubt, but you will leave an indelible mark on its identity as a school, just as you have on those thousands of us you have known by name over the years. Thank you, and God bless you and your family.

Miranda[3]

Give Centrality to the Themes of Spiritual Formation

The seeds of Miranda's recollection of grace and truth were sown on December 24, 2000, long before Miranda showed up for college. On that night, John's description of the incarnate Christ, being filled with grace and truth, hit me with a new, indelible force. For the next decade, I tried to make grace and truth a part of everything I said and did. Whether I was speaking at convocation, the Governor's prayer breakfast, or a publicly-held utility company, I spoke of grace and truth.

Whether my fixation on our need for Christ's grace and truth in our lives served as a cause or effect to the centrality of spiritual formation at Whitworth does not matter. What matters is the impact a president can have when she or he reinforces the university's thematic work of spiritual formation in students' lives. In other words, presidents set a tone for their campuses not only in form but in content. In form, presidents use their lives to model for students (and faculty and staff) a life growing in Christ. In content, presidents communicate in ways that reinforce the substantive themes of what spiritual formation means on their campuses.

Dwell Among

In both form and content, the story of Christ's incarnation has served as the North Star for the way I thought about my role as college president. Eventually, I wrote a short book about its influence on my understanding of leadership.[4]

When John introduced his leader to the world in the first chapter of his gospel, he shifted tenses from third person to first person in the fourteenth verse. "And the word became flesh and dwelt among us . . . ." The first thing John had to say about the word becoming flesh had nothing to do with a big miracle. Or maybe it did. Maybe for John, Jesus' biggest miracle was his home address: "He dwelt among us."

The tone for spiritual formation that college presidents set from a distance will be different than the ones they set up close. Tones from afar will probably be too soft for students to hear in the noisy lives they lead. Remote control tone-setting relies on the hope students will listen to us on those rare occasions when we are within earshot, or that other spiritual leaders on campus will set the right tone. Being distant geographically and relationally represents a massive opportunity lost for presidents to influence all things tonal. But when presidents do dwell within their communities, they can set a spiritual tone without even knowing it. A few years ago, I got the following note:

> Hey Bill,
>
> I was just talking to my friend who was ragging about how her college president drives a massive SUV and her professors drive gaudy convertibles and I was recalling how you would bike to campus every day.
>
> Whether it was for simplicity or environmentalism, or just convenience, I really appreciate now the message you chose to NOT send to me and other students by not driving the latest and sexiest sports car. I am really growing in my understanding of God as the creator/re-creator as well my understanding of what it means to be a godly and compassionate world citizen and it is a huge joy to see examples in people for how to creatively pursue that.
>
> Gregory[5]

I wrote Gregory back and told him it was for convenience, because it was. But my suspicion is his impression was influenced by more than just the bike. My attempts, often feeble, to dwell among the students had allowed Gregory and me a few opportunities to peek into each other's lives. And I am sure that changed the lens through which he saw me cruising around campus.

Presidents get misled about the danger of being too close to the folks God has given them to lead. Jesus did not worry about being too close to people. Presidents receive early warnings not to become friends with students and faculty. Is that the picture we get of Jesus in the upper room with those he explicitly called his friends?

The wager presidents place when they dwell among their students and faculty is that proximity will create more impact rather than less respect. They bet on people's ability to differentiate. Not long after I clicked on send with my resignation announcement, an English professor replied, "I am stunned, thinking of you not being our president, leader, and friend. . . ." I do not think "our friend" is a bad thing. I believe the odds are overwhelmingly in favor of most students and faculty being able to maintain respect for the offices presidents hold while standing alongside of the occupants as friends.

Imitate Jesus

During my years as a college president, as mentioned previously, I worked far too little on my own spiritual formation. Privately, I either thought or hoped my abundant efforts on behalf of others would make up for my own spiritual negligence. I worried more about the spiritual formation of our students than I did about my own spiritual formation. Ultimately, the campus probably suffered from not having a leader who lived in the awareness of Christ's presence and the fellowship of his Holy Spirit.

Presidents get tangled up in the relentless demands of their noble jobs. Privately, they scoff, albeit enviously, at all things contemplative. I had a trustee tell me he was tired of hearing how busy I am. Huh? That was my badge he was talking about. I did my best to lead and to operate in ways that were faithful to Christ's teaching. I worked hard at making sure "right" won the battles with "expedient" whenever the two conflicted. I was professionally self-righteous and fiercely disciplined, but I was the one defining discipline. For me and for the people to whom I projected my spirit-depleting values, discipline meant non-stop activity. Using a metaphor borrowed from our students, discipline meant pulling all-nighters.

In my final years as a college president, I started to redefine discipline in more spiritually mature terms. Henri Nouwen says it best:

The word *discipleship* and the word *discipline* are the same word—that has always fascinated me. Once you have made the choice to say, "Yes, I want to follow Jesus," the question is, "What disciplines will help me remain faithful to that choice?" If we want to be disciples of Jesus, we have to live a disciplined life.

By *discipline*, I do not mean control. If I know the discipline of psychology or of economics, I have a certain control over a body of knowledge. If I discipline my children, I want to have a little control over them.

But in the spiritual life, the word *discipline* means "the effort to create some space in which God can act." Discipline means to prevent everything in your life from being filled up. Discipline means that somewhere you're not occupied, and certainly not preoccupied. In the spiritual life, discipline means to create that space in which something can happen that you hadn't planned or counted on.[6]

College presidents create the culture for spiritual formation on their campuses. They are well positioned to shape and support efforts that deepen the spiritual lives of their students. But I wonder if college presidents should be expected to set the *example* for spiritual formation. What if Christian college presidents' reputations centered on the extent their lives imitated that of our strong and humble Savior? For certain, a president will not serve his or her campus well if direct ministry with students becomes a top priority. But living a life that projects a disciplined longing to grow in Christ's spirit could ripple through faculty and staff straight into the hearts of our students.

In countless ways, my relationship with the triune God grew during my years in the Christian college presidency. For that I am grateful to the Whitworth community for teaching me and inspiring me. I do, however, wish I had created more elbow room for the movement of the Holy Spirit and the nourishing presence of Christ.

Conclusion

In their strengths, in their weaknesses, and in the voice of their positions, Christian college presidents set tones. When listening presidents with informed intentions, integrated teams, and spiritual disciplines stand in the middle of their campus communities, I am confident a tone will be heard—a tone that gives beauty to the words of the Apostle Paul, "Let this mind be in you which was also in Christ Jesus" (Phil. 2:5 NKJV). Surely, these presidents will give vitality to a pervasive spiritual formation, with the beneficiaries including students, faculty, staff and, yes, the presidents themselves.

Chapter 1 Notes

[1] *Letters of St. Ignatius of Loyola*, selected and translated by William J. Young, S.J. (Chicago: Loyola University Press, 1959), 240.

[2] Bill Robinson, opening convocation address, Whitworth University.

[3] Personal communication to the author.

[4] William P. Robinson, *Incarnate Leadership: 5 Leadership Lessons from the Life of Jesus* (Grand Rapids, Mich.: Zondervan, 2009).

[5] Personal communication to the author.

[6] Henri Nouwen, "Moving from Solitude to Community," *Leadership Journal* 16, no. 2 (Spring 1995).

MAPPING THE CHRISTIAN HIGHER EDUCATION GENOME

Steve Moore

We must learn to speak the truest truths of the universe
in a language the whole world can understand.

Steve Garber[1]

I love Google Earth. I hope you have discovered this great wonder on the Internet. Aside from Internet joke sharing and YouTube, Google Earth may be one of the most used functions of the World Wide Web. With Google Earth one can view the globe from satellites—zoom in on locales as specific as your or my address, and zoom out to view a block, a neighborhood, a city, or a state.

In some ways Google Earth is also a metaphor for thinking about Christian higher education. People everywhere who have access to technology are able to have an experiential frame of reference for the world in which we live and

- view the world as a whole;
- connect with others around the world and function as a community from all over the world;
- zoom in on a historical event and experience it as a shared memory.

With Google Earth we see clearly the interconnected and diverse world of which we are a part.

Increasingly, higher education must realize that an important part of the learning experience is understanding we live in an interconnected world, within a single social space, marked by competing world views—and we must learn what it means to navigate these realities as Christians.

Of course, as I hinted earlier, we must also understand that the "Google Earth perspective" is by far not everyone's experience in this world! In fact, two-thirds of humanity is mostly concerned with eking out their daily existence of food, shelter, and clean water. That means that those of us privileged to experience higher education have good reason for humility and a responsibility for this gift of learning. Nonetheless, everyone who inhabits the planet is touched and impacted by the reality of living in an increasingly global village. It is everywhere we go.

My father lives in a small West Texas town in the center of one of the largest cotton production centers in the world. A significant part of its harvested cotton is exported to India, Pakistan, or elsewhere for refinement and turned into products that are then exported around the globe for sale. My dad's favorite restaurant in this small town is Thai takeout, owned by a Cambodian family. The nicest motels in town are run by immigrants from India. The nine new dairies in the area are run by recent immigrants from Holland. In some ways, what is happening in this small West Texas town is a microcosm of what is happening around the world: a kind of cultural mixing, changing, and shifting.

Not only is there massive cultural shifting, but we have also seen the economic center shifting. And for those who are a part of the Christian faith, there has also been a shifting of leadership, growth rates, and styles of worship. This point has been well documented and well articulated by Lamin Sanneh, Philip Jenkins, Kwame Bediako, Vinoth Ramachandra, and others who help us understand that the center of gravity of world Christianity has shifted from the "Christian West" (Western Europe and North America) to the "global South" (Africa, Asia, and South America).

It comes as no surprise—perhaps a restatement of the obvious—that ours is a day of shifting and changing alliances, partnerships, linkages, and connections. The opportunity for mutuality, interdependence, partnerships, and such has never been greater, and the Christian university is poised to both envision what it means to be interconnected and to model how our living in these new realities should and could look to navigate a future that is full of new realities and unexpected challenges.

We must discipline ourselves to step back and look at the big picture . . . to develop the Google Earth practice of zooming in and zooming out as we discern how the experience of higher learning from a Christian perspective would and could look.

It is important to note at this point that scholars, businesspeople, and politicians are quick to invoke the idea of globalization, almost obsessively, to describe the post-Cold War, twenty-first-century world in which we live. Yet the word *globalization*, as with *culture, tolerance,* or other catch-all, in-vogue words, needs to be carefully defined or unpacked.

For some, globalization might mean expanding markets, increasing realization of human rights, or greater opportunity for people around the world to improve their life conditions. For others, globalization might suggest the spread of scientific, technological innovation, national prosperity, and unprecedented human freedom liberated from the restraints imposed by religion, family, or culture. For still others, the idea of globalization leads to economic imperialism and raping of natural resources, the loss of local cultures, the spread of global disease, growing groups of rich and poor, international terrorism, and environmental degradation.

Globalization means different things to different people in different places— and it is not always a positive thing. Being clear about what we mean and from what vantage we are speaking becomes critically important to the conversations we have, and an important first step is moving beyond global mania, on the one hand, and globalization phobias on the other. We have to move beyond impassioned polemical rhetoric against the spread of KFC and Golden Arches as well as starry-eyed celebration of ground-breaking technological developments as simply a new means of evangelism or the spreading of pop culture.

Understanding globalization and its implications is a critical step because that understanding will shape our forthcoming actions within Christian higher education. However, rather than attempt to predict what shape some of these external circumstances and contexts might take in the future, or attempt to project political and economic realities, I suggest we start from a different place altogether. I would instead encourage the cultivation of virtues that must become a part of our educational DNA in order to live and thrive into our globalized future.

Mapping Our DNA

If Google Earth is a metaphor for informing our perspective and guiding our navigation, then mapping our DNA is an equally important task—the DNA of our thinking, teaching, learning, practices, and the way we live in community. What we value at the core of who we are will ultimately shape the paths and practices we take and the relationships we value.

The work of identifying, celebrating, affirming, and nurturing our distinctives is the ongoing work of every institution. It must be an alive, ongoing conversation, not simply a sterile paragraph in a school catalog or handbook or an occasional special event. "Integrating faith and learning," "engaging the culture," and "preparing global citizens" are the catch phrases that fill advertisements, recruitment talks, and websites of most Christian colleges. It is only when these and other values and commitments are embodied in the trustees, faculty, and staff—the "living curriculum"—that students experience the educational formation that has the potential to be life-giving and world-changing. What we teach is initially important. How we teach and learn together is equally important. The temptation to disconnect these two and emphasize one or the other continues to be one of our greatest challenges. Ensuring the DNA of our curriculum, co-curriculum, and the life of the campus community is an ongoing work of art and science!

The most important task of any group of trustees is the stewardship of the distinctive in the context of the mission of the college or university of which they are a part. And the most important task of the faculty, staff, and administration is fleshing out these distinctives in a dynamic and organic way in the unique educational experience of the students and the life of the campus community.

Therefore, let me attempt to identify the DNA code of our thinking and practices that have particular relevance to our conversation about Christian higher education going forward. These "character chromosomes" are essential for healthy, vibrant, and faithful experiences of learning. Their absence, or presence in a defective form, will lead to corresponding deficiencies for student learning. They are: humility, hospitality, incarnation, reconciliation, and imagination. And as we cultivate them we must also ask ourselves three questions that emerge from the Gospels as we work out each distinctive:

Are *we* living the story?

Who is *our* neighbor?

Where is God at work in *our* world, and how is God compelling *us* to join him?

To paraphrase Bishop Lesslie Newbigin, where the Christian university is faithful, the powers of the Kingdom are visibly and tangibly present and the people who encounter such a body will be compelled to ask the questions to which the gospel is the most compelling answer.[2]

Humility

We must remind ourselves that Christian institutions of higher learning in the West have exhibited an amazing ability to be co-opted by values of the secular academy. One thing history shows us quite clearly is that the road to becoming secular is well-traveled by Christian colleges and universities.

Most historians agree the world's first educational institution in the West was in Bologna, Italy, in the eleventh century, followed by Paris in the twelfth century—both thoroughly Christian then, both thoroughly secular today. The medieval universities rose in England and Scotland: Oxford, Cambridge, St Andrews. Shortly after, and with the Protestant Reformation, things really took off. In North America, Harvard was launched in 1636, Yale in 1701, Penn, and Princeton—all founded as Christian universities—with Dartmouth, Rutgers, and Brown following. These institutions were all begun by clergy who were also the activist faculty seeking to build institutions dedicated to *uni*–one, *veritas*–truth—the pursuit of the one truth of Christian faith.

Clearly, all of these universities have moved to become thoroughly secular, modeling a trajectory that has been repeated over and over in many institutions in American higher education up until the present day. In all humility we have to ask: What are we doing differently today? What have we learned to insure a different trajectory? Do we really want to export what we are doing to other places?

In 1989 at Lausanne II, an international gathering of Christian leaders, a plea came forward from a president of an American seminary lamenting the fact that "our definition of Christian higher education has the tendency to identify with the North American system, with a few stringers from Europe, not all of which is positive."

He pleaded to make Christian higher learning truly global: "We must learn from others around the world." But when recently asked of their attempts to respond to this plea, a group of current college presidents gave their institutions failing marks. "If we are really honest," said one president, "we are more concerned with our *U.S. News and World Report* standing than our standing and contribution in the world." We allow our insecurities and our drive for approval and acceptance to determine our course rather than our vision and calling, just as our students often do in their pursuit of good grades. Andrew Walls, an astute observer of both the Western Academy and the non-Western majority world, noted, "The Western Academy is sick and we can no longer afford to do business as usual, and if we are not careful we could infect higher learning elsewhere."

Do we really want to export what we have done? Are we prepared to say what we do well and what we do not do well?

If we want to live into twenty-first century-higher learning, we must shift from an industrialized, commodification-exporter mentality to being active conversation partners in global learning. We must help create and enter the Christian higher education conversation with the realization that we all have something to contribute *and* we all have ethnocentrisms that need to be challenged in light of the cross. We all bring some good, we all bring some baggage . . . and what can be created could be revolutionary for the future.

We must enter as learners with a spirit of humility. Genuine humility has nothing to do with downcast eyes, a misty voice, and noble stories of sacrifice. Humility is living courageously in a spirit of radical, intentional connectedness with others, enabling us to see ourselves as God sees us. True humility enables us to love fiercely and to extend strong love and dignity to others and to all we encounter. It is essential for our DNA in higher education that calls itself Christian. Over the centuries the church has seen humility as the first virtue of the Kingdom values. As one historian remarked, "When the church attempts something and doesn't start from humility, it very quickly goes bad."

Hospitality

It is interesting that when one reads the earliest history of Christians in the world, the thing they are known for is their hospitality. How those Christians loved one another was what caught the attention of the first-century world.

When I have had the opportunity to travel, I am often amazed and over-whelmed at the spirit of hospitality elsewhere in the world. I am also aware we spend millions of dollars and enormous amounts of energy on short-term mission trips each year (and, frankly, I want to argue we should be spending more). But I am embarrassed by the fact that a majority of international students who come to North America to study are never invited into the home of an American family, much less a Christian family! We must recapture hospitality as a Christian virtue and practice it in our institutions. Julian of Norwich sometimes called it cultivating the courtesy of Christ. It is certainly not the vacuous "May I help you?" of American customer service (though I've been to some campuses where that would have been welcome!). I have come to believe that hospitality is a foundational component of the teaching and learning of higher education that calls itself Christian.

Ed is a professor, often teaching large sections of entry-level classes in his discipline. A few years ago he introduced a simple change that he says revolution-ized his classes. On the first day he asks students to sign up in groups of three and four to have coffee with him. Then during a subsequent class he tells his personal story in an honest but professional way. "When we have coffee," he mentions as a follow-up to his students, "I want to hear *your* story." Looking back, Ed observes, "Once I've had coffee with about 25 to 30 percent of the students in the class, the class changes. We have more lively, thoughtful discussions, and students get to class early and stay around after. People come prepared and ready to engage." Hospitality sets the stage for the kind of learning community we value and reinforces the kinds of learning to which we most aspire.

If we want to be truly radical and life-giving to the understanding of how Christian higher education might look, we must recapture and live out radical hospitality. In our classrooms, in our student centers, in our residence hall construction, in our worship, in our recruitment and admission processes, in our ceremonies and major events, in our boardrooms or faculty and staff offices, hospitality must be foundational to the experience of all students who encounter an education claiming to be Christian. But hospitality must also work itself into the way we engage ideas and viewpoints of those with whom we radically disagree. Hospitality should mark our pedagogies, our town–gown relationships, and our faculty meetings.

I recently learned of a school that each year made sure every new staff and faculty, as well as students, have a "move-in" team ready to support new arrivals in the campus community. They also make sure that visitors to the campus are welcomed with enthusiasm, not with a voice-mail directory or poor campus signage.

Incarnation

One of the central and most critical components of what must shape our understanding of Christian learning is the incarnation. In one sense, everything hinges on this. It is the heart of the gospel. It is the heart of true education. We must move beyond the conception of Christian mission that polarizes into saving souls around the world, or righting social injustice in every setting, or being most concerned with global warming and the rain forests. The old battles of the fundamentalist/modernist clashes of the last century have consumed enough time and resources.

I love Tom Wright's observation that "what finally changes the world right now is flesh—words with skin on them! Words that hug you and cry with you; words that play with you and love you; words that rebuke you and eat with you. Words with flesh on them remain the most powerful force in the world!"[3]

This is why a work such as E. Stanley Jones' *Christ of the Indian Road* was so powerful and is a model for us on these contemporary global roads. It is why the great stories of Chaim Potok's Orthodox Judaism, James Joyce's Ireland, or Dostoevsky's Russia keep drawing us in and drawing us back. It is in the particular—the sacred ordinary of day-to-day living—that we see the world and its challenges. It is also in the particular that we see ourselves. It is why the story of a Jewish man who lived in the Middle East over two thousand years ago is so compelling. The word became flesh and dwelt among us.

Incarnation means embracing the constraints of a particular place, a particular people, and a particular educational community. "He is the visible expression of the invisible God," say the Scriptures (Col. 1:15 PHILLIPS). And that is not just a truth, it is a calling. You and I are to be visible expressions in the world in which we live and learn and love and work. All of our thinking about education, in general, and engaging the cultures of our world, in specific, must be formed by a renewed biblical understanding of incarnation. We are to be a living curriculum, the persons and places where the mission comes to life in visible, everyday kinds of ways for all members of the learning community. The genius of the incarnation resonates deeply with us. When we are invited to come and see, we learn at levels that are life-changing.

My family was fortunate to often live close to campus. It was not unusual for us to invite students into our home for spontaneous dinners. Students often offered to help with projects, babysitting, or would stop by and visit about things happening on campus. We often would say, "We can't stop what we're doing, but if we can talk while we work, we'd love to visit with you." To this day we get former students dropping by and saying, "Thanks for inviting us into your lives and into your home. My experience of learning was changed by just being invited in to see and experience the ups and downs of your family's life."

Believe me, we were not perfect. And students often were the ones who helped us survive the crazy schedules and unexpected crises of family and campus life. But we chose not to put on a façade or insulate students from the reality of growing a marriage or raising a family. We were simply seeking to be incarnational—to live out what we believe.

The thinking about Christian higher education that is going to reseed the whole world of learning with the fruits of life-giving transformation is going to have to start in a particular place and time with ordinary people. In places such as Siloam Springs, Arkansas; Spring Arbor, Michigan; Abilene, Texas; Wilmore, Kentucky; Vancouver, Washington; Cochabamba, Bolivia; or Nairobi, Kenya, with people such as you and me in words with flesh.

Reconciliation

It should be so obvious to us. Reconciliation is central to the gospel. That we experience brokenness, alienation, or separation comes as no surprise. What does come as a repeated surprise is how we shy away from the hard work of reconciliation. The difficulty is compounded in North America by our quick deferral to litigation. But truth be told, our institutions and our individual lives are desperate for authentic reconciliation.

Recently, while in China, I asked the leader of one of the large house-church movements what he saw to be some of the greatest challenges for Christians in China. He quickly identified the hard work of reconciling those who had been a part of the underground church—who had suffered deeply—with those who had been part of the state church, those who often betrayed those in the underground. That is the reality of reconciliation.

From the beginning of the Book of Acts we see the same. We desperately need creative, good thinking given to the work of reconciliation, and we need it modeled in higher education. If changing the world is to be more than a buzz phrase, Christian higher education must nurture this in its understanding, work, and practice.

Many of us are familiar with the work of Rick Warren and the "PEACE Plan" launched a few years ago. He initially framed it as Planting churches, Equipping leaders, Assisting the poor, Caring for the sick, and Educating the next generation. I took notice when Rick later came out with PEACE Plan 2.0. Why? Because in his new plan he changed the directive from Planting churches (a worthy goal) to Promoting reconciliation. Here is what he said:

> Two years ago, I did this 46,000-mile trip in 45 days. We literally went around the world. [What] I saw in every single country were conflict and broken relationships. In the Philippines it was between the two major evangelical networks. In Seoul it was between the charismatics and the Presbyterians. In the Middle East it was between Arab and Jew. In Rwanda it was between Hutu and Tutsi. Everywhere I went there were broken relationships. Everywhere we went, we had to be bridge builders, moderators, and peacemakers. Get right with God and get right with each other.
>
> When I looked at the PEACE Plan, church planting was the only [point] that had a prescribed method. We are still doing church planting, but now we put it under partnerships with the local church. We don't expect government and business, the other two legs of the stool, to do church planting. But there are biblical principles of reconciliation that apply to everybody. If you listen before you speak, you are going to have better relationships, whether you are a believer or not.[4]

Reconciliation is a central part of the DNA of higher learning that seeks to be Christian.

An Awakening of Imagination

Abraham Kaplan, an astute observer of American higher education, once remarked:

> My fear about American higher education today is not that there is a values crisis. It is not a concern of people whoring after false gods but that they don't worship at all. Our crisis today is the academy's overwhelming absorption with the narrow, the immediate, and ever petty concerns. Students and faculty are preoccupied and self absorbed with the mundane, the trivial, and the latest fad. . . . [W]hat we really have is a crisis of apathy, self absorption and moral indifference.[5]

When asked if he thought there might be an American contender for the Nobel Prize in literature, the chair of the Nobel Prize Committee (secretary of the Swedish academy) remarked, "The U.S. literary world is too isolated, too insular; they don't participate or particularly understand the big dialog of literature in the world. Their ignorance is restraining."

He was speaking of literature, but the same could be said of almost any academic discipline in Christian higher education as well as most of the world of theological education. Those of us who work in philosophy, theology, biblical studies, missiology, spiritual formation, and related areas should be leading the way in thinking about Christian higher education and the distinctives that should be shaping and guiding it. Unfortunately we, similar to many other academic disciplines, can all become enamored with the acceptance or approval of the guild within which we operate, and our creative thinking suffers because of it. But it is just as true in the sciences, social sciences, and humanities, where fear often dominates and challenging the dominant ideological viewpoints is rarely attempted. In most disciplines peer review can sometimes be more of a call to conformity along the latest social cause or trend than an invitation to creative innovative thinking. Every discipline tends to have a sociology—uniquely pushing to be homogenous—and with self-interests that seek to preserve the status quo.

To seek the highest experiences of scholarship and model the highest expression of what it means to be a Christian educator requires courage and a commitment to imagination—far beyond what is typical in higher education.

Dare We Do Things Differently?

From 1394–1460 there lived a man named Henry the Navigator, whose home was a small coastal town on the eastern shores of Portugal. The interesting thing about Henry is that he never captained a ship or sailed on a voyage of exploration. What he did do was read every account he could get his hands on of others who sailed. He thought about what they said, sought to reconcile different accounts, and let his mind march around new ideas of how things must be and what must be explored, tested. He calculated, drew maps, wondered, and imagined. Thirty years after he died, explorers were able to test his ideas. When they did, they found them incredibly accurate!

As a result, Portugal took the lead for the next one hundred years in exploration and discovery of lands that were unknown to Europeans. Others held back, worrying about spending resources in that way, doubting and questioning Henry's ideas, trusting only in the known part, unwilling to step out into the uncertain future. Many believed what was often written on the maps of that day. In the fourteenth and fifteenth centuries, when mapmakers got to the edge of the known world, they often wrote, "Beyond here there be dragons!" That day is not unlike our day. The world as we know it is changing right before our eyes, right underneath us. All of our securities are proving not so secure. We all feel the strains and pressures of upheaval, shifting, and change.

Will we follow the old maps, avoiding the dragons, or will we navigate by the stars of kingdom values? Will we invite the Spirit to genetically re-engineer the DNA of our campus communities, exponentially increasing the transformational learning experiences of our students, or will we settle for the safer status quo in the history of higher education?

Only time will tell.

Chapter 2 Notes

[1] Steve Garber, *Fabric of Faithfulness: Weaving Together Belief & Behavior during the University Years* (Downers Grove, Ill.: InterVarsity Press, 1996).

[2] Lesslie Newbigin, *The Gospel in a Pluralist Society* (Grand Rapids, Mich.: Eerdmans, 1989), 119. Bishop Newbigin's original quote was referring to the church in general.

[3] N. T. Wright, *The Crown and the Fire* (Grand Rapids, Mich.: Eerdmans, 1989), 61.

[4] Rick Warren, "After the Aloha Shirts," interview by Timothy C. Morgan, *Christianity Today*, October 2008. Available online at: http://www.christianitytoday.com/ct/2008/october/16.42.html?start=1.

[5] Dennis L. Thomson, ed., "Moral Values in Higher Education," in *Moral Values and Higher Education: A Notion at Risk* (Albany, N.Y.: SUNY Press, 1991), 11.

HISTORICAL AND CONTEMPORARY APPROACHES TO SPIRITUAL FORMATION IN THE UNIVERSITY

Rod Reed

As we explore how various parts of the Christian university work together for the common goal of student spiritual formation, it is important to learn from the successes and failures of past attempts in the history of American higher education. While many have explored the secularization of the American university and chronicled the history of contemporary Christian universities,[1] none have focused on institutional approaches to the spiritual formation of students.

In this chapter, I briefly identify three overlapping "eras" in American history and describe approaches to spiritual formation in each of those eras. Each era's methodology represents approaches to spiritual formation that are important, but alone were not comprehensive enough to sustain the holistic mission that American universities claimed. The current era of Christ-centered higher education, especially as represented by the schools of the Council for Christian Colleges and Universities (CCCU), exemplifies the latest efforts to match holistic rhetoric with comparable methodology. I will describe how CCCU schools incorporate approaches from these historical eras as I highlight five contemporary themes shared by many, if not all, the CCCU membership. I will use the term "spiritual formation" throughout each era for the sake of consistency, recognizing that the term is anachronistic in many places. The following chart offers a visual representation of these eras and their methodologies.

Historical Approaches to Student Spiritual Formation

Era	Primary impact period	Approach
Early American colleges	1636–1865	Institutionalized ethos of piety
Student movements	1806–1920	Student enthusiasm and initiative
Chaplaincy	1900–1970	Institutional pastoral leadership
Christ-centered higher education	1945–present	Institutionally integrative intentionality

Era 1—Early American Colleges

Primary Impact: 1636-1865
Approach: Institutionalized Ethos of Piety

Charting the course of intentional efforts in the spiritual formation of American university students necessarily begins by examining the earliest efforts in American higher education—pre-colonial colleges such as Harvard, Yale, and Princeton. In many ways, contemporary Christian universities desire to emulate the ideals, if not the practice, of higher education articulated by early American educators, whose goal was "the education of the whole person, morally and spiritually as well as intellectually."[2] These schools sought to educate holistically through developing what I call "an institutionalized ethos of piety." They created this ethos by surrounding the classical, essentially pagan, Greek education of the day with Christian people and practices that would influence students' lives.

Most pre-colonial and colonial college presidents were clergy, and therefore brought spiritual concern for students to academic endeavors. "Presiding at regular, perhaps daily, convocations of the whole college, the president of the church-founded schools played the role of both spiritual and academic leader."[3] Faculty played a similar role on a more personal level. They taught students in the classroom, attended chapel together, and, if unmarried, sometimes lived with them in dormitories, desiring spiritual, as well as intellectual, development. These faculty and presidents incorporated academic and student development roles that are now separated in contemporary universities. From their beginnings most of these schools assumed that a core element of their mission was "nourishing the piety"[4] of their students in all areas of life. Founding churches expected it, and the broadly Christian culture of the seventeenth and eighteenth centuries seemed to support that purpose.

Given the rhetorical emphasis on the spiritual development of students, one might expect the curriculum of early colleges to reflect that aim. However, the spiritual aspirations of most early American colleges remained structurally separated from academic programming. Especially after Puritan influences waned, colleges addressed the intellectual and spiritual lives of students in different ways, and even in different places. For example, James Burtchaell notes of Dartmouth in the 1850s, "It was piety, not religious learning, that sustained the college's religious identity. Piety . . . had a life of its own and was not amalgamated with a program of learning."[5] Faculty and presidents desired that their students would grow spiritually, but they did not see the curriculum playing a major role in the intentional development of piety.

While many schools required divinity classes or Saturday Bible classes, these activities were not integrated into the rest of the curriculum. Therefore, although historian William Ringenberg claims that students at early colleges studied Scripture as much as students at "seriously Christian liberal arts colleges today,"[6] the fact that those studies were structurally separated from the curriculum inherently relegated them to the realm of personal piety—which was rapidly diminishing as a primary concern of mainstream academia. To influence students spiritually, therefore, colleges created an "extracurriculum"[7] that operated independently of the curriculum. This extracurriculum was intended to foster a Christian environment within which classical education resided.

Historian George Marsden notes, "The medieval pattern of surrounding pagan elements with the Christian environment allowed most of University education to be freed from the direct concerns of theology."[8] In other words, education happened in the sphere of the classroom and formed the mind, while spiritual formation happened elsewhere and formed the soul. Since most students lived on campus, they were assured of being surrounded by spiritual influences. Because they were required to attend daily chapel services and Sunday church services, and were taught by pious teachers, students were immersed in religious activities. In creating such an approach to education, early college leaders assumed that the environment itself, as opposed to the curriculum, was the primary spiritual influence. Therefore, the ethos of the college had to carry the weight of the spiritual goals colleges had for their students. Within a culture that affirmed a common Christian worldview, this approach made sense. Students were so surrounded by spiritual influences that to structurally incorporate spiritual concerns and address them explicitly within the curriculum seemed superfluous.

Ironically, however, this approach inevitably separated the academic and spiritual goals that the founders had envisioned and ensured that one would take priority over the other. By assuming that the primary locus for addressing the spiritual lives of students was outside the classroom, early college founders ensured that those concerns would become increasingly marginalized. Marsden summarizes the point, "So the potential was already there for the distinctly Christian aspects of the intellectual enterprise to be jettisoned, or broadened into vestigial platitudes, without threatening any of the fundamental functions of the educational enterprise."[9]

In essence, the early colleges' educational structures impeded their holistic goals for student growth. The early American colleges created an institutionalized ethos of piety that surrounded, but minimally influenced the academic mission of the colleges themselves, and assumed that student faith would be the natural consequence. The historical record demonstrates the wishful thinking of that assumption. Students of these colleges, however, recognized early on the inadequacy of this approach and initiated programs that addressed their own spiritual needs, including the need to serve.

Era 2—Student Movements

Primary Impact: 1806-1920
Approach: Student Initiative and Enthusiasm

A cursory glance at the role of student Christian movements in the history of American higher education would seem to indicate that these movements arose in reaction to the secularization of the academy in the nineteenth century. While this perspective has some validity as it relates to the most famous intercollegiate student movements, history shows that students started forming their own societies for spiritual and theological development within mere decades of the founding of the schools they attended. In the perceived absence of sufficient institutional attention to student spiritual formation, this era of higher education history highlights the importance of *student initiative and enthusiasm*. Clarence Shedd, the early chronicler of American college student movements, observed, "Christian Student Societies are indigenous to the religious and educational life of American colleges."[10] Donald Shockley adds, "Student Christians took the initiative in developing programs which were designed to serve their own spiritual needs when they determined the institutional responses in such matters were inadequate."[11]

By the early 1720s we find brief mentions of student societies that shared much in common with the activities of the local church, gathering together for Scripture reading, prayer, singing, times of sharing, and encouragement for godly living. Some student societies, however, also addressed theological issues in addition to personal piety. Harvard's late eighteenth-century *Adelphoi Theologia* society, for example, sought to "attend with fervor and assiduity to the exercises of devotion amidst the constant pressure of academical avocations, and to preserve principles pure and untainted from the contagion of laxity in morals and skepticism in religion."[12] These societies provided students opportunities to discuss theological and spiritual issues in ways that were not available to them elsewhere on campus. The shape and scope of these societies, however, changed dramatically as the eighteenth century ended and the nineteenth century began.

In reaction to spiritual decay in the colleges of the late eighteenth century, a series of movements swept the nation's colleges. Many students began to initiate student Christian societies in the century's first decade, including the *Religious Society of Dartmouth* (1801), the *College Praying Society* (Brown, circa 1802), and the *Saturday Evening Religious Society* (Harvard, 1802), among others.[13] On a broader scale, the early nineteenth century revivals of the Second Great Awakening touched virtually every college in the nation. The most enduring spiritual movements affecting college students, however, were the international, intercollegiate missionary and Christian fellowship movements. These societies of the mid- to late-nineteenth century challenged students to see the world as their mission field. The forerunner of these intercollegiate movements began in 1806, when Samuel Mills—a Williams College freshman—along with four others, took shelter under a haystack during a thunderstorm. As the rain came down, these students, who had gathered together for prayer, dedicated their lives to missionary service—an act that would influence generations of college students, including such prominent missionaries as Adoniram Judson, Samuel Nott, Jr., and Samuel Newall.[14] The most significant consequence of this movement arose fifty years later.

In 1856 the first two college chapters of the *Young Men's Christian Association* (YMCA) were founded at Cumberland University and Milton Academy.[15] In the twenty years following the establishment of these chapters, more than forty other campuses formed YMCA chapters. The YMCA movement would grow even more dramatically as the nineteenth century neared its close, spawning a related organization—the *Student Volunteer Movement* (SVM)—which mobilized students for overseas missions. The SVM saw itself as heir to the earlier societies, especially those arising out of the Haystack movement. Luther Wishard, one of the first full-time student secretaries of the YMCA, noted, "What they [Mills and the Williams College students] had done was ours to complete."[16] The SVM movement unified and catalyzed the nation's college students in ways never before seen. As a result, by 1902, nearly eight hundred colleges, universities, and seminaries had some sort of SVM presence, and collectively had sent 1,953 students to foreign missions assignments.[17]

One reason for the massive response to the student missions movement was the quality of its student leaders. Samuel Mills and the other Haystack leaders had a vision for foreign missions and were personally affected by that vision, but their impact was more focused on key individuals and schools than on an intercollegiate network of schools. The student leaders of the late nineteenth and early twentieth century, however, saw the necessity of connecting the nation's students to change the world. For example, by their own initiative, students took responsibility for forming missions societies, even though they faced the reality "that there was then no missionary society on this continent [North America] which had a station on a foreign field."[18] These students were so convinced that what they were doing was ordained by God that they persevered and largely inspired the American foreign missions movement, despite concern from family and faculty, some of whom "felt that highly competent people should not be 'wasted' in foreign lands...."[19] In fact, many of the brightest American students answered God's call to become foreign missionaries, with the foremost example, John Mott, eventually winning the Nobel Peace Prize for his ability to mobilize the world's students.

The dominant characteristic of the student movements was the role of student initiative. Students recognized needs and responded to God's call to meet those needs. These responses tapped into and capitalized on the enthusiasm of idealistic students. Such enthusiasm was contagious and spread quickly on individual campuses and around the country. Contrary to the institutionally-created ethos of piety of the early colleges, student societies operated independently of their schools, a status that was largely affirmed by college faculty and administrators of the late nineteenth century. One college president stated, "I believe, first of all, that we ought to maintain this as a purely student movement. Any help of the faculty ought to be not official, but by way of personal touch."[20] Such independence did bring unintended consequences, however. Because these movements functioned primarily as para-institutional ministries and student leaders were accountable to external organizations (e.g., the YMCA or SVM), their loyalty and energy were often directed to those organizations as opposed to their schools. Even in the Haystack case, some students planned to transfer to another school to help spread the "gospel" of foreign missions. While student loyalty to their schools suffered, the benefit of such external connections was the relatively consistent patterns and quality of ministry that developed across the country. For example, the stated goal of the college YMCA during its rapid growth period (1890–1915) was "to win college men to Christ, with all that that implied."[21] This goal pervaded American college campuses, as did the "watchword" of the Student Volunteer Movement: "the evangelization of the world in this generation." Students responded to these clear, focused calls to action and radically transformed the spiritual culture of American colleges and universities through the early decades of the twentieth century.

Over time, the schools in which these associations operated began to desire more control over religious programming as they observed their success and the largely positive impact on students. However, some schools also demonstrated concern for the quality of religious life organized by some associations. W. H. Morgan noted, "In some cases disappointment has been expressed in the existing religious agencies from the standpoint of problems peculiar to the institution . . . [and] has sometimes seemed to be so unfortunate as to demand some action on the part of the institution. . . ."[22]

Even when the quality of the program was high, the fact that leadership for religious programming was located outside of the school's control inevitably led to concern and eventual institutionalization of the associations' services. Consequently, between 1920 and 1940 more than two hundred student associations disappeared as colleges appointed campus ministry personnel and denominations initiated ministries on most American campuses.[23]

Era 3—University Chaplaincy

Primary Impact: 1900–1970
Approach: Institutional Pastoral Leadership

The growth and impact of the student movements was a significant factor in motivating colleges and universities to become more intentionally involved in the spiritual lives of students. This era is characterized by the *institutional pastoral leadership* of the chaplains, who brought together the evangelistic, discipleship, and service emphases of the external organizations under the umbrella of the educational mission of the universities. Merrimon Cuninggim noted in 1941 that this growth of the chaplaincy arose as "the colleges . . . recaptured much of their lost concern for the religious development of their students and have increasingly assumed responsibility for such nurture."[24]

The history of college chaplaincies originated in 1755 when Yale appointed the Rev. Naphtali Dagget as the Livingston Professor of Divinity and the first American college chaplain. This appointment was hardly precedent-setting as fewer than twenty American colleges employed chaplains prior to the turn of the twentieth century.[25] However, in response to calls for more explicit spiritual leadership on campus, the number of chaplains increased dramatically, growing from one hundred to two hundred between 1928 and 1948.[26] One reason for the development of the chaplaincy was the desire for religious leadership on campus to keep pace with the increasing quality of academic instruction. As universities specialized, Smith notes, "Faculty members and college presidents found themselves unable to meet the demands of a consistently satisfactory chapel program."[27] While chapel was not the only area of spiritual leadership needing improvement, it was often the most visible example of need. Consequently, many universities determined that professional, specialized leadership was required for the spiritual life of students as it was in other areas of administration. Fortunately, models of effective ministry were present on many campuses in the form of the student associations, and the chaplaincy movement gained strength as colleges placed greater emphasis on institutional leadership for students' spiritual lives.

As chaplaincies developed, it became apparent that this form of ministry required a certain set of skills and sense of calling that was unique to the university context. To adequately fill the chaplaincy role also required significant institutional commitment, as Cuninggim asserted: "The first need, then, is for the colleges to become convinced that the leadership of its religious life is no part-time, secondary job; that in the small as well as the large institution at least one full-time director of the religious program, by whatever title he may be called, is a necessary administrative officer."[28]

Seeing the chaplaincy as a viable, full-time vocational calling required a different institutional priority on spiritual leadership. Early chaplains, such as Naphtali Dagget, filled the role as a supplement to their full-time faculty responsibilities or local church pastorates. Later chaplaincies were modeled after the student association secretariats, which were necessarily temporary positions. The first wave of full-time, vocational chaplains elevated standards of credibility for spiritual leadership on campus, one example of which is seen in their academic credentials. Seymour Smith's study of 150 chaplains in the early 1950s revealed that twenty-five percent of those surveyed had earned doctoral degrees, a percentage even more impressive when compared with the thirty-five percent of doctoral degrees earned by teaching faculty in church-related colleges at the time.[29]

As the chaplaincy matured, the context in which it operated changed dramatically. From 1950 to 1975 the college-going population increased by four hundred percent, with the diversity of that population growing as well.[30] The changing nature of American higher education following World War II gradually forced chaplains to broaden the scope of their ministry. By the 1970s and 1980s, the chaplaincy on most campuses had shifted from a central, institutional focus on the spiritual development of Protestant students to an auxiliary service that coordinated interfaith exploration. The primary role shifted from pastoral leadership of a Christian community to interfaith coordinator at institutions that often view religion and spirituality with suspicion.

The example of Yale University is instructive. In a 2005 study of religious belief and activity at Yale, Kathrin Day Lassila comments on the culture shift that has taken place: "There is no hegemony of belief any more. Only 150 people, out of 10,000 students and 10,000 faculty and staff, regularly attend Congregationalist services at the official university church, the Church of Christ in Yale."[31]

Minimal chapel attendance is but one indicator, but it signifies the chaplains' changed role in the culture of mainstream academia. Contemporary chaplains commonly work with an advisory group or council of chaplains from various religious and non-religious groups to provide optional services for students from varied backgrounds. For example, the Harvard chaplain coordinates the activities of thirty-five chaplains from twenty-five different religious traditions, including Baha'i, Buddhist, Hindu, Humanist, Islamic, Jewish, and Unitarian Universalist.[32] Clearly, the changing context in major American universities has greatly altered the form of the chaplaincy in these schools. However, the centrality of spiritual life and spiritual leadership still characterizes certain segments of American higher education. Member schools of the CCCU, for example, have attempted to maintain a commitment to spiritual formation as a core element of educational mission in the face of the same cultural forces that have sidetracked efforts in the majority of American colleges and universities.

Era 4—Christ-centered Colleges & Universities

Primary Impact: 1945–present
Approach: Institutionally Integrative Intentionality

The fourth era of approaches to spiritual formation is represented by member schools of the Council for Christian Colleges and Universities (CCCU). While many of these schools were founded in the nineteenth and early twentieth centuries, the development of an *institutionally integrative* approach to Christian higher education did not become prominent until the latter half of the twentieth century.[33] In contrast to the methodologies of the other eras that relied on ethos, student initiative, or the pastoral leadership of the chaplaincy, member schools of the CCCU strive for philosophical and organizational integration in the spiritual formation of students. This integrative approach incorporates key characteristics of the first three eras in American Christian higher education in addition to emphasizing the spiritually formational role of the classroom. I will address the theory that underlies this approach in Chapter Seven, but will address research into the praxis of spiritual formation on contemporary campuses in this chapter.

To better understand this praxis, I have analyzed *Campus Ministry Program Assessment* reports from fifteen CCCU schools that were assessed between 2002 and 2008, and that offer a representative sample of the membership of the CCCU. They represent every time zone of the continental United States, and include schools from urban, suburban, and small town areas. Numerically, they range in size from some of the smallest CCCU schools to some of the largest. Theologically, they include schools from Anabaptist, Baptist, non-denominational, Pentecostal, Reformed, and Wesleyan traditions, as well as schools from smaller theological movements. To protect the confidentiality of the assessment process, I refer only to the school's theological tradition when quoting a student or employee from a particular school. My research into these universities focuses on five primary themes that characterize the schools as a whole:

- Shared responsibility for spiritual formation
- The role of chapel in contemporary Christian universities
- The importance of student-led ministries in contemporary Christian universities
- The role of the chaplaincy in contemporary Christian universities
- Conflict regarding spiritual formation

Shared Responsibility for Spiritual Formation

Most CCCU schools claim that the whole campus is involved in the spiritual formation of students, and virtually every school assessed reports some level of shared responsibility for spiritual formation. Eleven of fifteen indicate that this partnership motif is central to their identity, including Anabaptist, Baptist, non-denominational, Pentecostal, Reformed, and Wesleyan schools. This ethos pervades campuses in a variety of ways. As one student at a Pentecostal university stated, "Coming in as a freshman, I was surprised about how God is in everything here." A faculty member at a non-denominational university commented, "One of the things we do well is every faculty member is deeply committed to Christ and committed to helping students grow spiritually." Comments such as these arose at virtually every campus studied and seem to indicate that spiritual care, encouragement, and challenge happen across campus at most CCCU universities. In particular, an ethos of shared responsibility often results in faculty and staff serving as primary spiritual influences for many students.[34] These faculty and staff often exert more significant influence than many of the traditional programs that schools develop for students.[35]

The Role of Chapel in the CCCU

Every school that was assessed reserves a privileged place in its weekly academic calendar for chapel services, whether chapel attendance is required or voluntary. The perceived value of chapel, however, varies significantly from school to school. Strong chapel programs typically have a fairly clear sense of purpose (whether implicit or explicit), fit the mission of the university well, are integral to institutional culture, and provide good-quality music and messages. Programs that received mixed responses are lacking in one or more of these areas, and weak programs exhibit significant deficiencies in multiple areas. Interestingly, the attendance policy for chapel does not correlate with the perceived strength or prominence of the program. While it is true that the strength of the program is often tied to a well-respected chaplain, it is even more connected to a clear sense of priority by the university. In other words, if students and faculty clearly understand that chapel is valued by administrators and trustees, and the program is led with sufficient quality in a way that is consistent with the academic mission of the university, its status as required or voluntary is relatively unimportant.

Comparing two voluntary chapel programs is instructive. Both schools employ long-term, respected chaplains, and have developed a style and quality that most students appreciate. The Baptist university examined offers one voluntary chapel service per week that is recognized as being part of the fabric of the university, and regularly attracts a majority of students. Conversely, the Reformed university attracts less than seven percent of its students to a typical chapel program. An analysis of each culture indicates that the variance in attendance signifies the different priority that the institution places upon chapel services.

The different roles that chapel plays in CCCU schools provide an example of changing expectations for this cultural icon. Whereas chapel used to be a unifying place and time for a college community, the growing diversity of these universities calls for a different shape of chapel. However, as mentioned previously, chapel looks very similar across most CCCU campuses. The contemporary worship movement characterizes most chapel programs, yet there are consistent student voices calling for a broader representation of worship styles. For example, students at one Wesleyan university expressed appreciation for "a more inclusive kind of worship which requires a progression of worship styles." One Baptist university's students, conversely, expressed frustration with their chapel experience because of the lack of diversity in worship. This issue is not merely one of musical preference; it is also an issue of representation and justice as the university strives to minister effectively to the significant percentages of African American and Catholic students it recruits. Some frustration is also symbolic of the growing expectation that chapel will play an educational role for students, in addition to its traditional inspirational role. This type of educational perspective recognizes that chapel is set in the context of a university and needs to reflect its academic commitments by contributing to students' education, not just their piety.

The Role of Student Leadership in the CCCU

Current CCCU schools rely on the enthusiasm and initiative of idealistic student leaders in much the same way that earlier generations did. At most schools, some of the strongest programs are led by students. The range of these programs is found on virtually every campus and can be categorized in two ways: student-initiated (and staff-supported) and staff-guided (and student-led).

Student-initiated ministries typically arise because a student or group of students perceives a spiritual need and decides to do something about it. Many of these programs are informally supported by staff from the chaplain's office who provide counsel and/or limited resources to enable enthusiastic students to put their ideas into action. If these ministries persist over time, they may become part of the second category: staff-guided, student-led ministries. The mission program at one non-denominational university is a prime example of this. In 1995, in response to the lack of cross-cultural missions opportunities, students initiated their own missions trip to Mexico. This fledgling effort grew substantially until the university decided to hire a staff person to lead and manage the program. Once ministries become institutionalized in this way, the chaplain's office typically invests more time and effort into the selection, training, and accountability of the student leaders. The quality of these leaders and their programs generates praise for their contributions to the spiritual formation of students. One university administrator articulated a theme that is common across the CCCU, "I don't know who is training these students, but they're like having mini-pastors spread all over campus." The impact these students have on their peers and others is quite remarkable.

Unfortunately, a majority of schools reports significant dissatisfaction and frustration from student leaders regarding the level of preparation, support, and accountability they receive. This is true of schools with both long and short histories of the chaplaincy. At one Wesleyan university, for example, there exists "a general consensus that expectations for student ministry leaders are greater than existing supervision, training, and support." This situation results in "many stories of fatigue and loneliness" on the part of student leaders. The primary reason for this deficit appears to be an imbalance in the amount of professional staff compared with the number of student leaders. The sheer volume of programs and student leaders makes it very difficult for a limited staff to provide the type of supervision, encouragement, and accountability students need. This imbalance, combined with increasing expectations for the chaplain's office, often means that student leaders are asked to provide more pastoral care and program leadership for their peers than they are equipped to give. Remarkably, many of these student leaders rise to the occasion of leadership and provide significant spiritual growth opportunities for their peers and those to whom they minister. This peer ministry augments the institutional pastoral leadership provided by the chaplain's office.

Chaplaincy in the CCCU

CCCU schools have hired chaplains to provide institutional leadership for spiritual formation and desire that this leadership would be comparable to the quality of education in the classroom. A typical job description calls for chaplains to develop "an integrated spiritual life program." Fulfilling this requirement, however, ends up being a much more complex task than it may appear to be. One significant barrier to fulfilling this requirement is the lack of educational preparation for the role. Only three of fifteen chaplains at assessed schools had experience with university students prior to coming to their school, and none of the fifteen had graduate education focused on ministry to university students in a Christian university context. Given this lack of contextual preparation, it is notable that the majority of these leaders are well-regarded on campus by students, faculty, and administrators. In fact, a common theme from the assessment reports is that most universities see their chaplains as respected institutional leaders, and many desire their chaplains to have a stronger voice in the institution outside the area of student ministries. The president of one Baptist university spoke to the respect for its chaplain by stating, "There's nothing we do here that exceeds the reach of campus ministry."

Several other schools articulated similar sentiments regarding the potential for a larger institutional leadership role for the chaplain. One Wesleyan university reports that there exists "a clear desire for [the chaplain] to give more intentional spiritual formation leadership to the faculty." As universities grow and diversify, the need for respected, unifying voices in crucial missional areas increases. If given the opportunity, it is apparent that a well-regarded chaplain who understands university culture has the potential to be one of those voices.

Unfortunately, not every school exhibits such a high opinion of its chaplain. The status of the chaplaincy at the assessed schools can be categorized in one of three ways—respected, conflicted, and transitional—based upon the overall responses of students, faculty, and administrators (see chart below).

Historical Approaches to Student Spiritual Formation

Perception of the chaplain	Number of schools	Traditions represented
Respected	7	Baptist, small denomination, non-denominational, Pentecostal, Reformed, Wesleyan
Conflicted	5	Anabaptist, small denomination, Wesleyan
Transitional	3	Anabaptist, Baptist, Wesleyan

Seven of the fifteen schools have chaplains who are well respected by students, faculty, and administrators. They are seen as providing effective leadership to the spiritual formation program at their schools. Collectively, these chaplains average nearly twelve years of service at their universities. Members of the university recognize room for growth, typically in areas of strategic planning, leadership development, and assessment, yet are basically satisfied with the form and content of spiritual formation programming on campus. The chaplains on three campuses could be described as being in a transitional state, having recently come to their roles. They are generally well regarded by students, faculty, and administrators, but the scope of their role is still being determined.

On five campuses, however, the chaplaincy could be described as conflicted. On these campuses, one or more of the major groups on campus (students, faculty, or administrators), and sometimes all three, expressed dissatisfaction with the chaplain's leadership. An analysis of these situations reveals similarities in the conflicts. One of the common sources of conflict is confusion surrounding the role of the chaplain, often beginning with frustration over the hiring process. Conflicting expectations are exaggerated when the chaplain comes to the university inadequately aware of the unique context of the university. Although each of the "conflicted" chaplains was recognized as caring deeply for students, conflicts arose because of an inability or unwillingness on the part of the chaplain to minister in ways that were consistent with the academic ethos of the university. Similar potential for conflict centered on the ability of the chaplain to develop a comprehensive, balanced spiritual formation program. Many schools, including some with respected chaplains, seem to "provide a cafeteria of programs [that] are not widely understood as an integrative system for spiritual formation." This critique is true of chapel, as well as other spiritual formation programs. At these schools, students have plenty of opportunities for involvement, but neither students nor staff have a clear understanding of how involvement in the various programs contributes to a holistic faith. In the academic context, where students and faculty are very aware of curriculum, learning outcomes, and assessment strategies, such perceived randomness seems incongruous.

Conflict Regarding Contemporary Spiritual Formation

One of the primary challenges many CCCU schools face in the early twenty-first century is maintaining a clear sense of identity and mission. As schools have grown numerically and qualitatively, they have diversified beyond their original constituencies. Such diversity often creates tension regarding spiritual formation, both at denominational and non-denominational schools. At one Baptist school for example, a faculty member commented that "it's hard for many to even envision what such a common vision [for spiritual formation] would be, if it could be agreed to at all." A faculty member at a Wesleyan school articulated a similar sentiment, stating, "We now have a diverse campus, but our willingness to talk about faith-learning integration has evaporated. We don't have a shared vision for spiritual formation across the campus." While diverse opinions rightly characterize a university, many schools are struggling to find consensus regarding the spiritual formation they desire. Assessors typically recommend that chaplains and other leaders on campus initiate intentional conversations among faculty, staff, and administrators to create a common language for spiritual formation that can help foster some state of consensus in this area.

A different problem also creates conflict at some schools. While most campuses are diversifying, many seem to develop a primary approach to spiritual formation in the co-curriculum that appeals to the majority of students, but does not intentionally expose students to the breadth of Christian expression. Many students respond positively to these programs, but a significant percentage of students feels marginalized by this approach. This tension between a unifying vision for spiritual formation and the diversity of the campus is characteristic of most of the CCCU schools we studied.

Conclusion

In the university context, spiritual formation is recognized to be more complex than merely providing lively chapel services, ministry options, and student-friendly pastoral care. There is an implicit understanding that the university needs to help students grow spiritually in ways that are consistent with its academic mission. When chaplains and others do not minister in contextually appropriate ways, and have not developed a comprehensive approach to spiritual formation, conflict often arises. It is easy to interpret these conflicts as controversy over the place of spiritual formation within the university. However, this does not appear to be the case. In fact, these conflicts can legitimately be interpreted as recognition of the importance that faculty, staff, and students place on the centrality of spiritual formation in the CCCU. Most CCCU schools are keenly aware of the centrality of spiritual formation to their mission, and are working to maintain their commitment to Christ-centered higher education. They seek to learn from the past and provide approaches to spiritual formation that involve the whole university in ways that are consistent with the mission of the university.

Chapter 3 Notes

[1] E.g., George Marsden, James Burtchaell, Robert Benne, Williams Ringenberg, as well as individual histories of many of the schools of the CCCU.

[2] Leland Ryken, "Reformation and Puritan Ideals of Education," in *Making Higher Education Christian: The History and Mission of Evangelical Colleges in America*, eds. Joel A. Carpenter and Kenneth W. Shipps (Grand Rapids, Mich.: Christian University Press, 1987), 43.

[3] Donald G. Shockley, *Campus Ministry: The Church beyond Itself* (Louisville, Ky.: Westminster/John Knox, 1989), 27.

[4] Mark A. Noll, *Princeton and the Republic, 1768–1822: The Search for a Christian Enlightenment in the Era of Samuel Stanhope Smith* (Princeton, N.J.: Princeton University Press, 1989), 20.

[5] James Tunstead Burtchaell *The Dying of the Light: The Disengagement of Colleges and Universities from Their Christian Churches* (Grand Rapids, Mich.: Eerdmans, 1998), 17.

[6] William C. Ringenberg, *The Christian College: A History of Protestant Higher Education in America*, 2nd ed. (Grand Rapids, Mich.: Baker Academic, 2006), 70.

[7] This term is used by Rudolph (1962), among others to describe the variety of organized extracurricular activities in American colleges in the mid-nineteenth century. I have applied the term to pietistically-oriented programming that was present in all of the early colleges.

[8] George M. Marsden, *The Soul of the American University: From Protestant Establishment to Established Nonbelief* (New York: Oxford University Press, 1994), 35.

[9] Ibid., 99.

[10] Clarence P. Shedd, *Two Centuries of Student Christian Movements, Their Origin and Intercollegiate Life* (New York: Association Press, 1934), xvii.

[11] Shockley, *Campus Ministry*, 12.

[12] "Constitution of the Adelphoi Theologia," 1785, Records of Adelphoi Theologia and The Society for Religious Improvement, 1785–1847, HUD 3120, Harvard University Archives.

[13] Shedd, *Two Centuries of Student Christian Movements*, 38–44.

[14] Gardiner Spring, *Memoir of Samuel John Mills*, 2nd ed. (Boston: Perkins and Marvin, 1829), 37.

[15] Charles Howard Hopkins, *History of the YMCA in North America* (New York: Association Press, 1951), 37.

[16] Ibid., 280.

[17] John R. Mott, "Progress of the Volunteer Movement: Report of the Executive Committee of the Student Volunteer Movement for Foreign Missions, 1898–1902," in *World-wide Evangelization: The Urgent Business of the Church; Addresses Delivered Before the Fourth International Convention of the Student Volunteer Movement for Foreign Missions, Toronto, Canada, February 26–March 2, 1902*, Student Volunteer Movement for Foreign Missions (New York: Student Volunteer Movement for Foreign Missions, 1902), 44.

[18] Ralph Winter, *Student Mission Power: Report of the First International Convention of the Student Volunteer Movement for Foreign Missions, 1891* (Pasadena, Calif.: William Carey Library, 1979) 219.

[19] Ibid., 166.

[20] R. C. Hughes, "How May We Wisely Promote Missionary Interests?" in *World-wide Evangelization: The Urgent Business of the Church, Addresses Delivered Before the Fourth International Convention of the Student Volunteer Movement for Foreign Missions, Toronto, Canada, February 26–March 2, 1902*, Student Volunteer Movement for Foreign Missions (New York: Student Volunteer Movement for Foreign Missions, 1902), 569.

[21] Hopkins, *History of the YMCA*, 627.

[22] William Henry Morgan, *Student Religion during Fifty Years* (New York: Association Press, 1935), 169–170.

[23] Hopkins, *History of the YMCA*, 655–656.

[24] Merrimon Cuninggim, *The College Seeks Religion*, vol. 20, Yale Studies in Religious Education (New Haven, Conn: Yale University Press, 1947), 1.

[25] Shedd, *Two Centuries of Student Christian Movements*, 11.

[26] "Bits of History: 1948–1975" Archives of the National Association of College and University Chaplains and Directors of Religious Life, Record Group No. 167, Series 1 Administrative Records, Yale University Library, 1.

[27] S. A. Smith, *The American College Chaplaincy* (New York: Association Press, 1954), 32.

[28] Cuninggim, *College Seeks Religion*, 283.

[29] Smith, *American College Chaplaincy*, 125.

[30] "Bits of History: 1948–1975," 4.

[31] Kathrin Day Lassila, "Gods and Man at Yale," *Yale Alumni Magazine*, May/June 2005. Available online at http://www.yalealumnimagazine.com/issues/2005_05/religion.html.

[32] Harvard Chaplains, accessed December 26, 2010, http://chaplains.harvard.edu/chaplains.php.

[33] CCCU historians James Patterson and William Ringenberg note the shift from focusing on survival to focusing on identity and definition following World War II.

[34] When asked, "Who would you turn to for spiritual guidance?" students typically name one or more faculty or staff members, in addition to their peers, as those they would trust for guidance.

[35] Todd W. Hall, "Furnishing the Soul: The Five Relational Dimensions that Guide Spiritual Transformation" (presentation, 2010 International Forum on Christian Higher Education, February 26, 2010). Results from Hall's research project rank faculty and staff influence higher than programs such as chapel, missions trips, and small group Bible studies.

LEAVING A MARK

The Role of Faculty in University-wide Spiritual Formation

Cary L. Balzer

Bang your shin or stub your toe in public these days and someone is bound to exclaim, "That'll leave a mark!" Many of us wish the response to a Christian education were as automatic. It is, after all, our goal to influence the lives of students and to do so in a holistic way. As David L. Smith and James K. A. Smith observe in *Teaching and Christian Practices*, the mission of Christian universities involves "more than the transmission of information—the spiritual and moral as well as the intellectual formation is in some sense at stake."[1] At John Brown University we use the phrase "Head, Heart, and Hand" to describe the multidimensional nature of Christian higher education. We want to leave a mark on the way our students think, the way they love God and neighbor, and the way they serve Christ in the church and the world.

The goal of this chapter is to discuss the important role that faculty play in a university-wide partnership for spiritual formation and therefore the crucial role the university plays—and specifically the faculty development program—in the spiritual formation of faculty members. I will also describe various methods of faculty spiritual formation practiced today, share the results of a limited study of ten sister institutions, and discuss implications thereof.

Paul Hoon wrote that the "spiritual development of the student begins with and depends upon the spiritual formation of the faculty."[2] While Hoon wrote this forty years ago about faculty in a seminary setting, the truth of his bold statement is no less true today in the undergraduate environment. Is the task of spiritual formation any less important in our setting—especially if our claim is to prepare students in every discipline to be Christlike ambassadors ready to serve in any vocation? Are faculty any less integral in our institutions? Hoon goes on to say that "spiritual formation is by definition community formation . . . community is the matrix of growth . . . and the vertebrae of the community are the faculty."[3] The goal of this chapter is not to argue that faculty are more important than presidents, chaplains, or residence-life directors in the process of student formation, but rather that faculty should take their rightful place in a university-wide partnership of formation. Hoon calls for institutions who champion "not *just* a teaching faculty nor a social-action faculty nor a professionally oriented faculty," (nor, I might add, *just* an academically-rigorous faculty), "but a collegium of men and women intentionally committed to helping students be formed into a measure of the fullness of Christ."[4] I agree and would urge our institutions to champion this pursuit in every discipline.

The crucial role of faculty in the faith development of undergraduate students was recently affirmed by Todd Hall's "Furnishing the Soul"[5] study which surveyed nearly two thousand Christian college students. It reveals that out of nineteen factors studied, faculty were cited in four of the top ten "spiritually transformational influences"[6] for these students. Faculty influence ranked higher than chapel programs, service learning and outreach, student leadership opportunities, and other ministry programming.

These results raise a number of important questions:

- If these professor-student relationships are critical in student faith development, what role does the faith development of the *faculty member* have in the faith development of the student?
- What responsibility does the university have for fostering the spiritual formation of its faculty?
- What efforts are currently underway in our institutions to encourage this formative process in the lives of our faculty?
- Which of these initiatives are most effective?

In order to begin the process of answering these important questions I contacted colleagues at ten sister institutions and asked each a series of questions regarding his or her school's role in nurturing the spiritual formation of their faculty and the role of faculty in the spiritual formation of the students. I then collected and categorized the responses and in some cases contacted the respondents to ask follow-up questions. Several interesting sets of responses emerged.

Fostering a Faculty Environment Conducive to the Spiritual Formation of Students

This environment includes faculty members who are growing in Christian maturity, who are familiar with the process of spiritual formation, and who are willing to participate in the ongoing formative process with their students. The majority of participants in our study agreed that it is the university's responsibility to encourage the spiritual formation of its faculty. One such participant replied, "Because character is foundational and because teaching is incarnational, the Christian university is well advised to partner with the Holy Spirit in the formation of its primary front-line representatives." Another said, "We must minister to those who are spending time with our students and who our students are following." Still another said, "We hire faculty who demonstrate/articulate the formation of appropriate spiritual beliefs. This said, we believe that it is helpful for the university to encourage and create opportunities for faculty and students to deepen their faith and develop their understanding of their roles in the body of Christ."

On the other hand, a participant representing the minority view disagreed, stressing that the "spiritual formation of the faculty member is the responsibility of the local congregation." Yet another expressed a mediating point of view by agreeing with and yet qualifying the assertion, saying, "Not solely, since most faculty find this need met in their local faith communities." Finally, another interviewee asserted that:

> Spiritual formation (essentially one's sanctification) is primarily the responsibility of the believer and the community/local church that they are a part of/members of. However, if the university moves in the direction of a comprehensive framework and curriculum for spiritual formation, the faculty must be equipped so that they can teach what they have learned and lived out. It should be noted, that some faculty do not have (or do not engage) the resources needed for their own spiritual formation which causes concern and a need for fostering the spiritual formation education and praxis of our faculty.

I would contend that we must encourage such an environment on our campuses for several reasons. While we partner with and support the ministry of the local congregations, and may require faculty to participate in a local church, the Christian university cannot assume that formation is a priority in every local church. In addition, it is not appropriate to expect that most local churches are equipped to offer the kind of training specific to the tasks of higher education. We should not be surprised that the integration of faith and learning, theories of moral development, and strategies for student faith formation rarely appear on the radar screen of most congregations, though there are notable exceptions. However, if we value faculty members who are growing in Christlikeness, integrating faith and learning, and encouraging students to do the same, then the university needs to participate in the process.

As director of the Office of Faculty Development at John Brown University, I have had the opportunity to include elements in the faculty development curriculum that are designed to nurture the spiritual formation of faculty, promote university-wide academic discussion and exploration of spiritual formation, and encourage faculty to consider the ways in which their teaching influences students' spiritual formation. At JBU we, similar to many of our sister schools, have created a number of structures designed to encourage a faculty environment conducive to the spiritual formation of students. The spiritual formation of students and faculty should be a critical concern addressed in the hiring process, the professional development of faculty, new faculty orientation, and summer workshops.

The Hiring Process

Last week I met with seven of my colleagues to consider over ninety applications for one religion and philosophy position. Those of us on the search committee take this responsibility seriously because we recognize that the faculty we hire today will become the defenders of the institution's mission tomorrow. James Burtchaell points out the important link between faculty and mission, saying, "Whatever presidents and trustees do, whatever the market forces imposed by those who pay (students and benefactors), the inertial force of these institutions is in their faculty (and staff)."[7] As we met to ponder this critical task and faced this mountain of vitas, letters, and applications, we expressed thanks for our jobs and voiced our excitement about the possibilities for the future of our division buried somewhere in the stack. At the same time we felt overwhelmed by the amount of work represented by all those applications: hours spent by nearly one hundred applicants painstakingly preparing their materials and countless hours and significant resources committed by our institution.

Clearly, hiring represents an enormous commitment of time and resources. Kina Mallard, provost at Carson Newman University, writes, "Administrators involved in hiring recognize the reality that a new hire is the most expensive investment made and, hopefully, suggests a long-term commitment to the university."[8] In light of the crucial role faculty play in the ongoing mission of the institution and the significant investment represented by the hiring process, it is imperative to create and sustain structures to ensure the mission fit of those considered for faculty positions. In our study all respondents agreed. When asked what steps are taken in the hiring process to ensure the "spiritual fit" of potential faculty members, the largest group of participants indicated that a committee interview performs this task and that the candidate submits a statement of faith and a statement of agreement with the university's doctrinal statement. A majority of participants require a statement on the integration of faith and learning. Several observed that an interview with the president or an appropriate vice president fulfills this function. One participant commented, "The process documents theological fit extensively, but I think the spiritual fit is more an intuitive judgment made from the interview process. . . . There's not really any attention paid specifically to the faculty member's understanding of formation and ability to articulate that, as is the case with their theological fit." Clearly there is consensus on the need for theological fit and mission agreement. Specific expectations regarding spiritual formation, however, are more difficult to identify.

As an evangelical Christian university, JBU seeks to hire faculty who support the mission of the school and are in agreement with the school's statement of faith. All candidates must submit a statement of agreement with the university's statement of faith and an essay on the integration of faith and learning. Each candidate for a faculty position must meet with the president or the vice president of academic affairs, the search committee, and a representative from human resources, have lunch with a group of students from the appropriate major, share a meal with other members of the division, and teach a class session attended by members of the search committee. In addition, every candidate brought to campus for an interview meets with the faculty status committee to ensure that potential new faculty members do, in fact, affirm the faith statement of the university, support the mission of the school, and that they will be a good spiritual fit for the school. This committee sends each candidate four questions prior to the campus visit:

1. Please describe your conversion story and the current status of your Christian life.
2. How would you respond to a student who asked how to become a Christian?
3. How would you integrate faith and learning in the classroom?
4. Who has acted as a role model for teaching and the integration of faith and learning in your career?

While these questions may not serve the intended purpose at every institution, they have equipped us to pursue those candidates most likely to succeed in our spiritual environment. One member of the faculty status committee noted that the questions function not to illicit specific desired answers but to give candidates the opportunity to describe their understanding of an authentic Christian life and articulate the relationship between faith and their particular academic discipline. To put it another way, the questions serve as a filter that helps our university hire only those faculty who will advance our mission and serve our students.

Each candidate interview begins with the introduction of committee members and an explanation of the committee's purpose. The candidate is then asked to address each of the standard questions. After the candidate has answered the questions, there is an opportunity for members of the faculty status committee to ask follow-up questions and the candidate is given the chance to ask questions about our institution. After the candidate completes the interview and has been excused, the committee discusses the various responses. A score[9] given to each candidate reflects a scale similar to that used in our promotion and evaluation process (1 - does not meet basic requirements, 2 - needs improvement, 3 - meets basic requirements, 4 - exceeds expectations, and 5 - exceptional candidate). This information is sent to the vice president of academic affairs and the president.

Is it problematic that our questions do not specifically contain the words "spiritual formation"? While your institution may include questions using that terminology, our current questions do tell us a great deal despite excluding this important phrase. For example, the response to the first question usually gives the committee valuable insights into the person's understanding of growth and the Christian life. The second question often prompts responses that reveal a great deal about the candidate's attitude toward students and their understanding of the nature of the student-teacher relationship. The third question, while it asks specifically about integration, provides an opportunity for the candidate to make connection between integration and formation. And the fourth question allows the candidate to tell the committee about someone who was influential in his or her life and career.

This approach guarantees that every candidate for every faculty position is examined in light of the university's concern for spiritual formation. It does not preclude the need for spiritual formation issues to pervade other aspects of the hiring process. Position descriptions in every discipline should reflect appropriate expectations of the faculty member's role in the spiritual formation process of students. Division chairs and search committees should discuss these expectations prior to evaluating applications and interviewing candidates. If a university-wide partnership for spiritual formation is to become a reality then it must be a part of the institution's culture at every stage—and this initial stage, the hiring process, is tremendously important.

Faculty Development Initiatives

A second critical factor in the development of a culture of spiritual formation is the attention given to the ongoing process of faculty development. The purpose of a faculty development program is to nurture faculty on a variety of levels: pedagogy, scholarship, service, and spiritual formation. Some may resist the inclusion of spiritual formation in this list. As stated earlier, we at JBU expect our faculty to be engaged members of local churches, and thus to be the recipients of the preaching and teaching ministries of the local church. It is not the goal of the faculty development program to replace or repeat the ministry of the local church. However, the ministry of the local church does not usually provide specialized instruction for those involved in the academic enterprise, such as how to apply the great truths of the Christian faith to teaching biology, philosophy, or art history. At JBU we have the responsibility to help our faculty grow in Christ and, more specifically, to help them think through the ways in which the Christian worldview informs every discipline.

One of the primary goals of this study in particular is to provide a list of the kinds of initiatives used in Christian higher education to promote the spiritual formation of faculty. When asked "What programs or initiatives at your university are designed specifically to encourage faculty formation?" the following responses were listed in order of popularity:

- new faculty orientation
- book studies
- faculty mentoring
- summer workshops
- faculty small groups

Other responses included:

- faculty retreats
- mission trips and service projects
- faculty chapels
- workshops
- faculty development events

- annual faculty gathering event
- prayer lists
- spiritual direction grants
- new faculty assignment on spiritual formation

When asked which of these were most effective, summer workshops was the most popular answer, followed by faculty mentoring and a three-way tie between faculty chapel, new faculty orientation, and faculty small groups. One respondent from a West Coast school described programming that was specifically designed to equip female faculty in soul care and spiritual formation:

> For the last couple of years I have participated in our female faculty retreat, where we engaged in extensive discussions and seminar sessions that related to relational transformation, spiritual formation, and embracing our God-given strengths. We had some in-depth group talk regarding how we, as female faculty, are modeling our faith with our students, in the classroom and beyond. We were guided in a *lectio divina* exercise, and then sent into a time of solitude and retreat. This all led to some rich group processing afterwards. Some of the questions we engaged with dealt with how our tendencies as faculty may lead toward an imbalance of rest and work, and what parts of our work may have the potential to endanger our souls. Several of my colleagues have indicated that it was spiritually nourishing, and increased their motivation to be mindful of how they are modeling their faith and shaping students spiritually. From my standpoint, it was the solidarity we experienced through processing together our common challenges that made it so formative.

Surprisingly, answers such as "unsure," "difficult to answer," and "none" were more common than any particular program. Several of those in this category instead wanted to emphasize the informal nature of spiritual formation in their community. One such participant from a Midwestern institution emphasized informal channels, saying that "people support one another informally." He went on to tell the story of one division's "tea time:"

> Our campus is comprised of four academic schools, each with several departments. One school of faculty gathers each day in the break-room for tea and conversation. This initiative began over six years ago following renovation of some building space in which a "break/conference room" was provided and some departments re-shuffled their locations. Also, a

new faculty member who spent over twenty-five years on the mission field in Northern Ireland simply made tea each day and invited others to join.

This same participant went on to emphasize that these informal channels, though valuable, were not enough on their own and voiced his desire to increase intentional programming to nurture faculty formation. While some schools have a moderate amount of intentional programming designed to encourage spiritual formation, others seem to be lacking, as demonstrated in this response: "Other than an optional chapel, I don't know of things that are consistently done to foster the faculty. We use our faculty to lead some small groups but do not have small groups for them."

New Faculty Orientation

Faculty orientation is one of the most common forms of faculty development and should be one of the most influential opportunities for encouraging an environment conducive to faculty spiritual formation. Before the school year starts at our institution, orientations take place for new faculty, adjunct faculty, and concurrent[10] faculty.[11] In our context, the needs of these different groups of instructors warrant separate events, but the orientations convey a common set of priorities and principles. The goals of these orientations are to help new faculty understand the purpose of the university and obtain ownership of that purpose; to understand the mission of the university, that is, what the institution does to live out its purpose; and to invite the new faculty members to understand and affirm the core values that shape the ethos of the university. Three texts are provided for the new faculty and used during the orientation and the New Faculty Institute: Roger Olson's *Mosaic of Christian Belief*, Steve Beers' *Soul of the Christian University* and Linda B. Nilson's *Teaching at Its Best*. Finally, the orientation equips the new faculty with the practical information they will need to begin teaching. The three-day event for new faculty members includes seminars on topics such as:

- Teaching at JBU
- History and Vision
- Creating a Great Syllabus
- Technology at JBU
- JBU Facts and Personnel Essentials

In addition, all new faculty members receive one course release for their first semester and are required to attend the fourteen-week Faculty Institute. These one-hour weekly sessions examine the important qualities of our institution that new faculty need to know about. Sessions include:

71

- JBU's mission, vision, and values
- The essentials of evangelical theology
- The integration of faith and learning (a session led by our president, Chip Pollard)
- Students at risk (led by Dr. Tim Dinger, the director of Counseling Services)
- Christian formation for faculty and students (led by our University Chaplain, Rod Reed)
- Pedagogy for today's students

This initial investment in the lives of new faculty members sets the tone for and expectation of spiritual formation in the context of the larger life of the university and has resulted in long-term rewards.

Summer Workshops for Faculty

Our Summer Institutes began in 2000 with a Teagle Grant that helped defray the costs in the early years. The university has subsequently built these costs into the operating budget. These annual summer workshops provide thirty-five to forty of our faculty members with the opportunity to read, reflect, learn, discuss, write, and experience best practices in Christian higher education. Faculty members apply for the institute, attend seminars for twenty-five to forty hours per week, and receive a stipend for participation. The institute, led by outside experts or key faculty members, usually takes place in August prior to the beginning of the contract year for most faculty members. Participants are required to complete readings, attend all sessions, write a pre-seminar reflection paper, and complete a practical project that applies the principles learned to some aspect of the faculty task: course revisions, lesson plans, syllabus changes, student learning outcomes, etc.

These seminars help promote the best practices among our faculty by exposing them to the works of respected educators and encouraging them to discuss ways to implement these practices in our particular environment. The seminars also encourage cross-disciplinary faculty collegiality and teamwork as teachers from various subject areas interact, share perspectives, and wrestle with the multi-dimensional priorities of university life. It is also a wonderful opportunity for new faculty to mingle with seasoned veterans. The inevitable confluence of youthful enthusiasm and the sage perspective of experience creates a dynamic environment that benefits those at all points along the spectrum. The required practical project also motivates even the most abstract thinkers to apply the principles learned to concrete practices in the classroom. These proposals to update a research project, alter a set of grading rubrics, or reorganize student outcomes are usually presented to other participants around their tables or in brief presentations to the larger group.

In recent years, Summer Institutes have featured these titles: "Engaged Learning: What the Best College Teachers Do"; "Assessment: Connecting, Grading, and Learning"; "Engaging Learners through Research and Creative Projects"; "StrengthsQuest: Utilizing a Strengths Approach to Learning"; and "Invitation to a Journey: A Roadmap for Spiritual Formation."

The next few paragraphs will briefly describe those institutes that focused intentionally on issues related to spiritual formation and then focus on a more careful account of the most recent institute.

Essentials of Evangelical Theology workshop explored the faith we are called to integrate and examined the key Christian doctrines, including the authority of Scripture, the Trinity, the humanity and divinity of Christ, humanity as created fallen and redeemable, the role of the Church, the end of history, and the return of Christ. This seminar is especially important in our interdenominational context, and helps us explore both the essentials of faith as well as the issues upon which we agree to disagree.[12]

The Integration of Faith and Learning workshop examined common misunderstandings and provided models, strategies, and tools for faith integration. Integration is not merely programming spiritual life activities, facilitating prayer or other practices in the classroom, adding biblical or spiritual materials as examples, or even modeling Christian values and morals. None of these practices, though valuable, represent a robust model of faith integration until the Christian scholar holistically engages the course. Several integration strategies and course tools were explored and practiced.[13]

Invitation to a Journey: Spiritual Formation for Faculty. At JBU we often describe Christian formation as the "process of becoming more like Christ for the glory of God and for the sake of others." If faculty members are to model, promote, and lead students in Christian formation, they themselves need to understand the process and be participants in the process. In these seminars we explored various models of formation and spiritual practices that can be used both in and out of the classroom.[14]

The most recent Summer Faculty Institute focused on the spiritual formation of faculty. Led by the University Chaplain, the Director of Christian Formation, and the Director of Faculty Development, the institute featured Robert Mulholland's classic text *Invitation to a Journey: A Roadmap for Spiritual Formation*. The first two days explored Mulholland's definition of spiritual formation: "the process of being conformed to the image of Christ for the sake of others."[15] The third day featured a presentation on the book *Sacred Pathways*[16] and a discussion of the different ways in which traditionalists, sensates, naturalists, intellectuals, activists, and caregivers experience God. On day four we explored a variety of practices designed to help faculty engage in and think about prayer, silence, and reflection. These included a silent retreat, a *lectio divina* exercise, "Praying in Color"[17] and "Making Crosses."[18] And, finally, day five highlighted our faculty book studies as a means of promoting spiritual formation in the context of an academic community.

One of the chief benefits of prolonged workshops during the summer or a "J-term" is the availability of time for reflection and process. With this sacred time set apart, we determined two goals for the workshop: (1) expose participants to spiritual practices and (2) help our faculty define spiritual formation. In the post-workshop evaluation, comments such as this one were common: "I believe it was great to get the opportunity to stop and really spend time thinking about spiritual formation." Another workshop participant said, "It was a great experience of taking time to draw near to God." Still another mentioned enjoying "spending time not just thinking and talking about spiritual formation, but more importantly spending time experiencing and practicing spiritual disciplines."

Also in the evaluation, faculty were asked to provide a definition of spiritual formation. These are some of the resulting definitions:

- "Allowing the Holy Spirit to repair the damage caused by sin and transform us into the whole person that God intended"
- "A continuous unveiling of who I am in Christ and how that influences others towards Him"
- "The jagged, recursive process of being transformed into Jesus' likeness"
- "The process of being conformed to the image of Christ for the sake of others"

The last definition most closely reflects Mulholland's text, but each shows familiarity with the concepts discussed and, in some cases, ownership and creative rephrasing.

These summer workshops offer tremendous opportunities for spiritual formation but are not the only venue for these discussions. At JBU we also utilize our fall faculty workshops, semester-long faculty book studies, regular faculty lunch colloquia, monthly "Teaching Tuesdays," and other faculty development events to encourage the spiritual formation of faculty. The fall faculty workshops welcome the faculty back to campus every year and feature an all-employee worship service, the president's State of the University address, practical workshops, and a series of addresses and seminars by nationally recognized authors and educators. Last year the event featured Andy Crouch, author of *Culture Making,* and this year Kina Mallard, provost at Carson-Newman and CCCU Faculty Development Senior Fellow, addressed our faculty on "Finding Joy in Christian Higher Education." Two faculty book studies this fall highlighted the work of James K. A. Smith: *Desiring the Kingdom*[19] and *Teaching and Christian Practices.*[20] Each of these opportunities provided rich environments for learning and discussion.

Conclusion

The goal of this chapter was to discuss the important role that faculty play in the spiritual formation of students and to highlight the role of the university in the spiritual formation of faculty members. A broad range of initiatives used to encourage faculty formation were listed and various methods explored. Most of those interviewed believed the university was to some degree responsible to foster the spiritual formation of the faculty, and there was some degree of consensus around the popularity of certain methods. Interestingly, there was no consensus on which methods were most effective. Clearly what remains to be done is a broad-based study of CCCU schools to measure the effectiveness of these practices on faculty and subsequently on the students they teach and to provide research that answers the following questions:

- Which initiatives currently utilized by universities most influence the positive faith development of the faculty?
- What instruments can be utilized to measure the effectiveness of these university initiatives?
- What role do campus leaders (i.e. presidents, division chairs, chaplains, etc.) have on faculty faith development?
- What is the role of faith development of the faculty on the integration of faith and learning?
- What is an appropriate means of including spiritual formation issues in the process of evaluation and promotion?
- What is the role of faculty faith development in the faculty member's ability to maintain and promote the university's mission and vision?

Research reflects that faculty are among the primary influences on the spiritual transformation of our students. The spiritual formation of the faculty themselves must, therefore, become a priority for the Christian university and must become a key element in recruiting and hiring new faculty, ongoing professional development, orienting faculty, and training workshops. Surely these are crucial ways to meet the needs of our constituencies, remain true to our mission, distinguish ourselves from secular institutions, and provide evidence of the student outcomes we promote for the accrediting institutions. By effectively nurturing a faculty environment conducive to the Christian formation of students, we will leave a lasting mark on those we are called to serve.

Chapter 4 Notes

[1] David I. Smith and James K. A. Smith, *Teaching and Christian Practices: Reshaping Faith and Learning* (Grand Rapids, Mich.: Eerdmans, 2011), 3.

[2] Paul Hoon, "Report of the Task Force on Spiritual Formation," *Theological Education*, Autumn 1972, 45.

[3] Ibid.

[4] Ibid.

[5] Todd W. Hall, "Furnishing the Soul: The Five Relational Dimensions that Guide Spiritual Transformation" (presentation, 2010 International Forum on Christian Higher Education, February 26, 2010).

[6] Hall, in "Furnishing the Soul" presentation. A list of impact items listed under "School Impact on Spirituality" includes: #3 Bible /Theology Courses, #5 Academic Courses, #9 Mentoring with Faculty, and #10 Integration of Faith and Learning Courses.

[7] James Tunstead Burtchaell, *The Dying of the Light: The Disengagement of Colleges and Universities from Their Christian Churches* (Grand Rapids, Mich.: Eerdmans, 1998), 828.

[8] Kina Mallard, "Finding and Sustaining Joy in your New Role" in *The Soul of the Christian University: A Field Guide for Educators*, ed. Steve Beers, (Abilene, Tex.: Abilene Christian University Press, 2008), 127.

[9] Several members of the faculty status committee regularly resist the idea of "reducing" an interview to a number, but our vice president of academic affairs argues that it helps bring some order to the process.

[10] The concurrent program includes teachers at affiliated high schools across the country who teach high school courses in which students can potentially earn college credit. These teachers and administrators travel to our campus for this event to attend and participate in orientation seminars and meet supervising faculty in their discipline.

[11] The orientation for new faculty in the graduate programs and degree completion programs follow a different calendar reflecting the needs of adult learners, a cohort model and, in many cases, online delivery systems, but the priorities reflected in those orientations

are consistent with those of the orientations discussed above. See *Systems of Excellence* for a discussion of an orientation program designed for an adult learning environment.

[12] The main text for this workshop: Roger Olson, *The Mosaic of Christian Belief* (Downers Grove, Ill.: InterVarsity, 2002).

[13] The main text for this workshop: Stephen Beers, *The Soul of the Christian University* (Abilene, Tex.: Abilene Christian University Press, 2008).

[14] The main text for this workshop: Robert Mulholland, *Invitation to a Journey: A Roadmap for Spiritual Formation* (Downers Grove, Ill.: InterVarsity, 1993).

[15] Mulholland, *Invitation to a Journey*, 5.

[16] Gary Thomas, *Sacred Pathways: Discover Your Soul's Path to God* (Grand Rapids, Mich.: Zondervan, 2000).

[17] Sybil MacBeth, *Praying in Color* (Brewster, Mass.: Paraclete Press, 2007).

[18] Ellen Morris Prewitt, *Making Crosses: A Creative Connection to God* (Brewster, Mass.: Paraclete Press, 2009).

[19] James K. A. Smith, *Desiring the Kingdom* (Grand Rapids, Mich.: Baker, 2009).

[20] Smith and Smith, *Teaching and Christian Practices*.

Exploring Spiritual Formation

A THEOLOGY OF CHRISTIAN SPIRITUAL FORMATION

Steve Harper

Christian spiritual formation has been misrepresented as being theo-
logically weak. It has been caricatured as a "touchy-feely" enterprise. Unfortunately, it has sometimes borne those characteristics, but a more accurate look at the discipline shows these stereotypes to be false. In fact, it may be argued that spiritual formation actually is "more theological" in that it draws upon and contributes to biblical, historical, systematic, and practical theology. It cannot exist as an isolated discipline. For that reason, many Roman Catholic, Orthodox, and a few Protestant seminaries have placed the discipline in their theology departments.[1] There is an ecumenical awareness that knowledge and piety must be conjoined. The discipline of spiritual formation is one way in which it is done in educational institutions.

Any exploration of a Christian topic begins with its theology. What we believe about something inevitably influences what we do with it. In our day, we must counter a propensity toward activity ("how to") with a prior examination of the reasons *why* the behaviors are valid in the first place. Theology is the means by which we establish the "why" of our subject, before we go on to establish the "how." Belief undergirds practice, but practice must incarnate belief, so that the result is lived theology. This chapter offers a brief and limited theology of spiritual formation, using three categories: Trinity, Tradition, and Trajectory.[2]

Trinity

Every religion has its corresponding spirituality. As in other religions, Christian spirituality is defined and developed in relation to its concept of God. Distinctive among all world religions is Christianity's concept of God as Trinity: Father, Son, and Holy Spirit. To make this claim is to declare several significant things about Christian spiritual formation.

Relational

First, it means that Christian spiritual formation is *relational*. All three persons of the Trinity are relational. There is no ontological aloofness. There is a proactive desire in the Godhead to be in communion with all that is made. While there is a sacred and essential distinctiveness between the Creator and the creation, there is also an interface between them. There is correspondence, communion, and communication between them.

This is all the more true when it comes to human beings. We are made in the image of God (Gen. 1:26–27). The *imago dei* is our capacity for relationship. We share characteristics with God (e.g., reason, affection, and will), but we also share the desire and the ability to relate to God and to have God relating to us. There is no better place to see this than in the adoption of the word "abba" as our word of address to God in prayer.

But this capacity is further seen in the persons of the Son and the Spirit. If Jesus is the Son of God and we are also beloved sons and daughters, then he is our brother, and we are members of a holy family. If God is Spirit and our essence is that of spirit, then there is a relationship between our being and God's Being. Everything is related and relational.

Incarnational

Second, this concept of trinity means that Christian spiritual formation is *incarnational*. The Word became flesh and dwelt among us, full of grace and truth (John 1:14).[3] This forever eliminates any flesh/spirit dualism, and it also makes impossible any notions of a spiritual life that is only lived in the intangibles and the "heavenlies." The most distinctive feature of Christianity is Jesus. No other religious figure can be equated with him. As both Son of God and Son of Man, he stands unique. As such, he is the paradigm of Christian spirituality. Christlikeness is the aim of Christian spiritual formation.[4] Jesus provides both the objective revelation for our spiritual formation and the means of living an authentic spiritual life (i.e., abiding in him—John 15).

Transformational

Third, it means that Christian spiritual formation is *transformational.* All three persons of the Trinity enter the fallen world with the intent of redeeming and restoring it. As some have said, God's grace accepts us as we are but never leaves us as we are. Life in Christ is new creation (2 Cor. 5:17).[5] For us, this is particularly true as we receive and respond to the Holy Spirit: ministering with the gifts of the Spirit and manifesting the fruit of the Spirit.

In the presence of the Trinity, we exclaim with the saints of the ages, "Holy, Holy, Holy." We connect our spiritual formation to sovereignty, soteriology, and sanctification. We take the Kingdom of God as the picture of how individual and social spiritual life looks.[6] And we engage in the Great Commission (i.e., "making disciples") as our mandate for ministry.[7]

Tradition

Some descriptions of Christian spiritual formation move from Scripture to the present with barely an acknowledgment that anything happened in the intervening twenty centuries. Tradition is the missing link in many theologies of the spiritual life. But it is a problem recognized and addressed in our day, through a return to an historic and classical Christian spirituality, expressed through the renewal of the ancient practices.[8] There is a fresh understanding that Christian spiritual formation is influenced by the great cloud of witnesses and through a solid foundation that spans roughly four thousand years. To recognize the place of tradition in Christian spiritual formation is to make several significant declarations about it.

Ecclesial

First, Christian spiritual formation is *ecclesial.* We reject all notions of privatized spirituality and all expressions of individualistic piety. The Christian spiritual life is "life together"—life in community—life in the Body of Christ. This community is defined and directed by the historic Creeds (Apostles, Nicene, and Athanasian). Furthermore, it is formed by the great manifestations of Church: Roman Catholic, Orthodox, and Protestant. In our day, there is also the contribution of non-denominational churches and parachurch organizations. Within these churches there is further enrichment through the grand streams of the Christian tradition which flow into, among, and through them.[9]

But even as we make our return to an ecclesial spirituality, we do so with the recognition that spiritual formation is not about a perpetuating "churchianity," but rather about developing Christian discipleship.[10] We take membership in the church as the holy starting point for the spiritual life, not its terminus. We understand membership as the beginning of the Christian life, not its end. From the moment of our baptism until our death, we are (as E. Stanley Jones so often put it) "Christians under construction," using all the means of grace to make us increasingly conformable to Christ and to a life of personal and social holiness.[11]

Ecclesial spirituality is not perfect. In fact, it is most often messy, and it pushes against all the tendencies to make the spiritual life quick, easy, neat, and clean.[12] Whatever else it is, spirituality is reality, and the challenges of authentic Christian formation may cause some folks to drop out (preferring the status quo) or to shop around (looking for a church that feeds them). In either case, we forget that ongoing Christian formation involves what we bring (Rom. 12:1) not just what we take.

Worshipful

This leads directly into the second element of Christian spiritual formation that is rooted in tradition: it is *worshipful.* When spiritual formation is understood as "life with God," then God is central, and worship is the central act of the people of God. N. T. Wright puts it this way, "When we begin to glimpse the reality of God, the natural reaction is to worship him."[13] This reaction is rooted in our being created in the image of God, which essentially describes our capacity for relationship with God. It comes to fruition in our new creation, as we live "in Christ" and seek to glorify him in thought, word, and deed. Worship is the highest expression of our creation and new creation. It is impossible to imagine a valid spirituality apart from the worship of God.

Often, this line of thinking moves quickly into the various styles of worship. But prior to that is the theological significance of worship. Worship is the singular testimony that "God is God, and I am not."[14] Worship that is faithfully practiced and conscientiously lived out is the main challenge to egocentrism, consumerism, individualism, and any other sort of "I-Me" spirituality. Worship evokes the two basic responses in the spiritual life: "Help!" and "Thanks!"—both of which reveal our utter dependency upon God and our complete confidence that God will come to our assistance, hasten to help us, and speedily save us.

When our vision is that of a worshipful spirituality, styles are important, but not as important as we have tended to make them in recent years. We all have preferences, but an authentic and vibrant spirituality will not go in search of a "style," it will go in search of God. Therefore, we can worship anytime, anywhere, and with anyone. When that is not the case, we need to step back and see how we have allowed our preferences to become idols. A Christian spiritual formation that can only worship under specified conditions is not true spirituality. A Christian spirituality limited to personal preferences is a severe narrowing of all God has in mind for us.

Missional

Finally, tradition teaches us that Christian spiritual formation is *missional*. We have boatloads of correct language for this (e.g., "the church exists for others"), but it is still one of the main places where the spiritual life ceases to be Christian and reverts to a secularized, pop-spirituality where it's all about me. Whenever we evaluate our spiritual formation (either in personal devotions or corporate worship) by the question, "What did I get out of it?" we know we are skating on thin ice. Instead, Christian spiritual formation is about the production of the fruit of the Spirit: love, joy, peace, patience, kindness, goodness, faithfulness, gentleness, and self-control (Gal. 5:22–23).

Every one of these manifestations includes an exterior quality, as well as an interior one. It is useless to describe ourselves as having the fruit of "love" if we are not actually loving someone. It is pointless to say we have the fruit of joy if we are not actually joyful. The same can be said for the remaining seven aspects of the Spirit-filled life. In fact, we may have inadvertently misled ourselves by calling it the "Spirit-*filled* life" when it is actually the "Spirit-*overflowing* life." The fruit of the Spirit is a singular reality: a quality of life on the inside and a manifestation of life on the outside.

One of the major images used to speak of the spiritual life in the Christian tradition is the image of fire. It is a good image to consider when we are seeking a missional spirituality. Fire *is* hot, but fire also *gives* warmth. Fire consumes, but it also fuels. It does these things simultaneously and without trying to set one dimension over the other. So also, Christian spiritual formation *is* life in Christ, but it simultaneously *gives* life to others.

The fruit of the Spirit is the means for assessing the maturity of our spiritual life, not the gifts of the Spirit. The Corinthian church had all the gifts, but it was one of the most immature congregations Paul had to deal with. That is why he put the thirteenth chapter of First Corinthians between chapters twelve and fourteen—why love (the fruit of the Spirit) must be connected to any of the gifts. The fruit of the Spirit flavors the gifts and makes them winsome and effective instruments for the good of others and the salvation of the world in Jesus' name. Taken together, the gifts and fruit of the Spirit reveal a missional spirituality.

Trajectory

There is much more we could say about Trinity and Tradition—two key elements in a theology of Christian spiritual formation. But we must now ask, Where do these commitments take us? What is the trajectory which they establish for us? From a number of possible responses to these questions, we will look again at three. We will say that Christian spiritual formation establishes the trajectory of identity, vocation, and hope.

Identity

First, Christian spiritual formation provides us with *identity*. We are disciples of Christ. As Dallas Willard rightly notes, this word describes our fundamental, two-fold understanding: we are apprentices, and we are apostles.[15] To be an apprentice means to be a lifelong learner. And that is the fundamental disposition of a disciple: a learner. Jesus is the rabbi, and all the rest of us are pupils in his school—The School of Christian Discipleship. We never graduate, because we are dealing with the Infinite. There is no way we can ever come to the end of that. We are always learning, ever becoming.

Dr. J. C. McPheeters was the second president of Asbury Theological Seminary. He lived to be ninety-one years of age. He preached his last sermon in Estes Chapel when he was eighty-nine. He did not know it would be his last sermon at the seminary, but it was. Not long afterward, "Dr. Mac" suffered a massive stroke that left him unable to speak and eventually took his life. And what do you suppose he preached on at eighty-nine years of age? He preached on the subject, "The New Things God is Teaching Me." As I listened to him, I was deeply moved. I realized I was listening to a true disciple—a lifelong learner. He did not have to look into the rearview mirror of his soul to see what God had done; he was looking through the windshield, gazing at what God was doing in his life in the present moment. This is the disposition of a disciple—someone able to talk about the presence and activity of God in the here and now. We are apprentices.

But we are also apostles; otherwise, our learning becomes nothing more than the accumulation of knowledge applied to ourselves alone. We have received freely—now we are to freely give. To understand that we are apostles means that we see our primary field of service outside the church. We do not live institutionally; we live vocationally. We take our accustomed roles, relationships, and responsibilities and offer them to God. Eugene Peterson captures this well in his translation of Romans 12:1 in *The Message*: "So, here's what I want you to do, God helping you:

Take your everyday, ordinary life—your sleeping, eating, going-to-work, and walk-ing around life—and place it before God as an offering."

Jesus' call to the original apostles provides the insight for how we are to do this. He told them he would teach them to "fish for people" (Mark 1:17). He was talking to fishermen! In other words, he took what they already knew and used it as a bridge into the things they did not know. He continues to say the same thing to us as he calls us to apostolic ministry. What do you know? What do you do? What is an everyday expression of your gifts and graces?

I can imagine Jesus saying to physicians, "Follow me, and I will teach you how to treat diseased souls as well as bodies." He might say to lawyers, "Follow me, and I will show you how to work for justice and mercy among those who do not receive it." He would probably speak to homemakers and say, "Follow me, and I will show you how to care for other people beyond your family circle." He might say to coaches, "Follow me, and I will show you how a winning team in the Kingdom looks." He would surely say to teachers, "Follow me, and I will show you how to communicate knowledge that leads to eternal life." The point is, every one of us already knows a lot, and Jesus wants to use it all. Spiritual formation that creates an apostolic identity leads to a discipleship in places where we already are. It acti-vates the priesthood of all believers.

Our example for this kind of life is found in Jesus himself. He knew who he was, and he lived in relation to God's call upon his life. This is the essence of Christlikeness: living for God as we are and in relation to the work God has called us to do. Along the way, we will develop dimensions of this discipleship we could not have imagined or predicted when we first began. But rather than feeling as though we are being jerked around from one thing to another, we will more nearly feel that a holy "ripple effect" is taking place—widening our life of service, but always in relation to the Center.

Challenge and Transformation

We must not suppose that the theology of spiritual formation we have set forth in this chapter is one that human beings are ready and willing to embrace. Individually, we are persons who have fallen into paying more attention to our egos than to God. We have ordered our lives around ourselves for so long that to attempt to do otherwise will challenge us at the deepest levels we can imagine. We have sinned, and we are sinners. Our embrace of Trinity, Tradition, and Trajectory requires a transforming experience with God in Jesus Christ that delivers us from the false self and guides us into the abundant life of the true self each of us is created to be. This is the basic meaning of repentance.

Institutionally, this theology of spiritual formation will challenge the church at its deepest level as well. We will move beyond a paradigm of ecclesial preservation into one of cultural penetration. We will welcome people as members of the Body of Christ, but we will make it clear that membership is only the start of the lifelong journey God has in mind for us. Our life together from that day forward will be defined and empowered by the two great commandments and by the great commission.

The biblical language we are using here is that of dying and rising—what N. T. Wright calls being "simply Christian."[16] We like the rising part, but too easily forget that the life of God in the human soul does not come to be apart from a death to self (egotism) and all the related things that make us believe we are the masters of our fate and the captains of our souls. Far from being the touchy-feely enterprise which some have caricatured spiritual formation to be, it is instead the most challenging call that any human being can receive and respond to. For leaders it is the travail Paul felt until Christ was formed in the Galatians (4:19), and for the rest of us it is the labor associated with "being born again" (John 3:3).

The Role of the Academy

With this theology in place, we must now respond to the question, What is the role of the academy in all this? That is what this book is all about, and subsequent chapters will deal with key issues in detail. But for now, let us look at some of the non-negotiable elements that help to incarnate the spiritual life within one's educational experience.

Intentional

Spiritual formation in the academy, first and foremost, will be *intentional.* We must not assume that a Christian view of life happens apart from an intentional presentation of it. Spiritual formation tells us that we are living souls, but the soul does not have a built-in compass. The writer of Ecclesiastes spoke of a "sense of eternity" within the human being, but then went on to say that this sense alone does not provide us with the full knowledge of what God has done, and is doing (Eccles. 3:11). Our souls need instruction, guidance, support, and forgiveness. Spiritual formation offers these kinds of things, but they do not happen automatically. The faculty, staff, and student body of our educational institutions must commit themselves to a comprehensive offering of perspectives which will at least provide the invitation for its constituents to choose Christ and live for him.

Interdisciplinary

Second, spiritual formation will be *interdisciplinary.* One of the worst things a school can do is hire someone to teach spiritual formation. As Evelyn Underhill rightly pointed out, the spiritual life thrives wherever it connects with and promotes truth. She wrote that the spiritual life will "develop and use all our capacities and fulfill all our possibilities."[17] This means that every department and curriculum track must consciously determine how it contributes to the formative task. There is indeed a wideness in God's mercy, not just a depth. The spiritual life is more than any narrow definition of "religion" can handle. The spiritual life is abundant life, and every educational aspect enriches it.

Identifiable

Thirdly, spiritual formation in the academy must be *identifiable.* An educational institution must provide specific instruction in spiritual formation. This may sound as though it contradicts the previous point, but I do not believe it does. It simply means that an institutional commitment to spiritual formation will find its way into the curriculum. We would never say, for example, that we believe in the importance of history, but offer no courses in it. We would never say that we believe in the centrality of religion, but offer no courses in it. We would not profess a belief in science with no courses in it. Similarly, if we make the commitment to an intentional and interdisciplinary spiritual formation, we will further express that decision by offering courses in spiritual formation.

Spiritual formation has as much of a theoretical base and practical expression as any other subject matter. It has an identifiable body of normative literature, beginning with the Bible and extending outward into Christian tradition. Spiritual formation can be taught, and it must be if our commitment to it is to go beyond mere lip service. Or to say it another way, we must give a specific place to spiritual formation in the same way we do to the other things we deem to be essential. And if we honor the kind of theology set forth in this chapter, the identifiability of spiritual formation in the institution will be seen ultimately in the fact that we worship God together.

Incarnational

Finally, spiritual formation in the education experience must be *incarnational.* I can go to my files to retrieve what my professors taught me, but I go to my heart to remember their influence upon my life. The Word must continue to become flesh, and in the educational system that largely means in the witness of faculty and staff. Long after our students forget what we told them, they will remember what we showed them.

The NCAA runs advertisements each year that say, "Most of our athletes will be turning pro in something other than sports." The ads go on to show the influence of an entire institution on the shaping of its graduates. The same holds true with respect to spiritual formation. We could adapt the phrase this way: Most Christians will be turning pro in something other than being preachers. In fact, if statistics hold, less than one percent of the Christian population will be clergy. Thus, the greater potential for spiritual formation and the influence of the Gospel on the earth lies outside the Religion Department.

This means that the greater influence will be through the witness of faculty and staff in other subject areas and aspects of campus life. It will be physical scientists who most help students understand that this is our Father's world. It will be the business professors who will teach a generation of leaders how to run organizations where the almighty dollar is not the highest good. It will be the grounds crew leader who instills in student workers the value of hard work. It will be in the educational department where future teachers will discover that a person is only truly educated when the whole person is developed. It will be in the residence hall directors that students will witness radical service to others. In every degree and institutional division professors and staff persons will offer Christ to the students in their care. And in doing so, the entire educational enterprise becomes formative.

This calls for mutual respect between and among subject areas. We who teach must stop acting as if our classes are the only ones that really matter. We must do away with the artificial dichotomy between classical and practical subjects—which has used a Western rationalism to posit the superiority of the classical curriculum. We must ask our students to bring insights from other courses to bear on ours, and we must encourage them to take what they learn from us and connect it with what they are learning from others. If we think of ourselves as a university (whether so named, or not), we will be intent upon creating a "universe"—a singular educational experience where one aspect is not set against another, and where all learning is celebrated as an enhancement of the Christian spiritual life.

A Grand Vision

The vision set forth in this chapter is grand, and that is intentional. It is too large for any one of us to think that we can hold a corner on the market. It is also so large that we know the only way to live into the vision is as a community of learning and faith, where knowledge and vital piety are conjoined. It is a vision so large that when we do recognize achievements, it will be in a way that gives glory to God. But at the same time, it is not a vision so large as to be unattainable. God never calls us to do what we cannot do. If we catch the vision and pray for the grace to fulfill it, we can end the day saying along with the psalmist, "this is the Lord's doing, and it is marvelous in our eyes" (Ps. 118:23).

Chapter 5 Notes

[1] Regent College in Vancouver, Canada is one example. Also, Asbury Theological Seminary has renamed one of its departments to reflect the union: The School of Theology and Formation.

[2] Other valuable theologies of spiritual formation include: Alister McGrath, *Christian Spirituality: An Introduction* (Oxford, U.K.: Blackwell Publishers, 1999); Richard Foster, *Life with God: Reading the Bible for Spiritual Transformation* (New York: HarperOne, 2008), and Eugene Peterson's five-volume series on spiritual theology. The writings of Father Adrian VanKaam and Dr. Susan Muto are also notable from the vantage point of spiritual theology.

[3] I will be forever grateful for the influence of E. Stanley Jones on my life with respect to the Incarnation, through his books *The Way* (New York: Abingdon-Cokesbury Press, 1946); *The Word Became Flesh* (New York: Abingdon Press, 1963), and *In Christ* (Nashville, Tenn.: Abingdon Press, 1980).

[4] This is described in a variety of ways, but often as "having the mind of Christ." Christlikeness is becoming increasingly conformed to the mind, heart, and work of Christ. This is only possible by grace. To go deeper into this idea see Dennis Kinlaw's three books: *The Mind of Christ* (Nappanee, Ind.: Francis Asbury Press, 1998); *We Live as Christ* (Nappanee, Ind.: Francis Asbury Press, 2001); and *Let's Start with Jesus: A New Way of Doing Theology* (Grand Rapids, Mich.: Zondervan, 2005). Eugene Peterson, *The Jesus Way: A Conversation on the Ways that Jesus is the Way* (Grand Rapids, Mich.: Eerdmans, 2007) is another excellent resource in this regard.

[5] For more on this idea see: Richard Foster, *Life With God: Reading the Bible for Spiritual Transformation* (New York: HarperOne, 2008).

[6] E. Stanley Jones, *The Unshakable Kingdom and the Unchanging Person* (Nashville, Tenn.: Abingdon, 1972).

[7] For both a deeper study of this and an excellent resource for a spiritual formation in the church, I commend the Renovare ministry (www.renovare.org).

[8] For more on this see: Alan Hirsch and Deborah Hirsch, *The Forgotten Ways: Reactivating the Missional Church* (Grand Rapids, Mich.: Brazos Press, 2006); Brian McLaren, *Finding Our Way Again: The Return of the Ancient Practices* (Nashville, Tenn.: Thomas Nelson, 2008); and John Michael Talbot, *The Universal Monk: The Way of the New Monastics* (Collegeville, Minn.: Liturgical Press, 2011). This ancient-future vision is finding a particularly powerful expression in "the new monasticism" rising up all over the world.

[9] Richard Foster, *Streams of Living Water: Celebrating the Great Traditions of Christian Faith* (San Francisco, Calif.: HarperSanFrancisco, 1998). Foster presents six major expressions

of the spiritual life: Contemplative (Prayer-filled), Holiness (Virtuous), Evangelical (Word-centered), Charismatic (Spirit-empowered), Social Justice (Compassionate), and Sacramental (Incarnational). These six streams converge to make "the Mississippi of the Spirit"—what Renovaré leaders are calling today "life in Christ."

[10] Dallas Willard has been a pivotal influence for many in our day through his books *The Divine Conspiracy: Rediscovering Our Hidden Life in God* (San Francisco, Calif.: HarperSanFrancisco, 1998) and *The Great Omission: Rediscovering Jesus' Essential Teachings on Discipleship* (San Francisco, Calif.: HarperSanFrancisco, 2006). Others such as Susan Muto and John Ortberg have reawakened their churches to a disciple-oriented spiritual formation, expressed through a vital ministry of the laity.

[11] For my own faith tradition, I have advanced this view in my book *Devotional Life in the Wesleyan Tradition: A Workbook* (Nashville, Tenn.: Upper Room Books, 1995).

[12] See Mark Yaconelli's *Messy Spirituality* (Grand Rapids, Mich.: Zondervan, 2007) and Eugene Peterson's *Practice Resurrection: A Conversation on Growing Up in Christ* (Grand Rapids, Mich.: Eerdmans, 2010).

[13] N. T. Wright, *Simply Christian: Why Christianity Makes Sense* (New York: HarperSanFrancisco, 2006), 143.

[14] In the history of Christian spirituality this idea is often captured in two words: "God Alone." It is the idea of abandonment and surrender. For more on this see Jean Pierre de Caussade, *Abandonment to Divine Providence* (also called *The Sacrament of the Present Moment*) (Garden City, N.Y.: Image Books, 1975); E. Stanley Jones, *Victory Through Surrender* (Nashville, Tenn.: Abingdon Press, 1966); and Robert Mulholland, *The Deeper Journey: The Spirituality of Discovering Your True Self* (Downers Grove, Ill.: IVP Books, 2006).

[15] For more, see Dallas Willard, *The Great Omission: Rediscovering Jesus' Essential Teachings on Discipleship* (San Francisco, Calif.: HarperSanFrancisco, 2006) and also Todd Hunter, *Christianity Beyond Belief: Following Jesus for the Sake of Others* (Downers Grove, Ill.: InterVarsity, 2009).

[16] Wright's *Simply Christian* (see note 13 above) is a valuable way to amplify many of the ideas only briefly mentioned in this chapter. It explores the Christian life from a theological angle, but without falling prey to the complexities that sometimes attend theological interpretation.

[17] Evelyn Underhill, *The Spiritual Life* (New York: Harper & Row, 1937), 22.

THE POWER OF CONTEXT

Spiritual Formation
in the Christian University

Rod Reed

American Christian colleges and universities claim that their students
develop spiritually as well as intellectually, yet little work has been done to explore
how the unique culture of the Christian university affects the processes and
goals of student spiritual formation. Consequently, spiritual formation is often
approached as a process that is dependent solely upon principles and practices
that arise from Scripture, tradition, and theology. This assumption neglects the
influence of the context in which spiritual formation happens. Missiologists commonly understand that the form of various elements of ministry (e.g., preaching,
discipleship, worship, etc.) must be crafted in light of the local culture in which
they are practiced. Likewise, spiritual formation is also a contextual process that
is shaped by the specific communities in which it is practiced. While the essential
goal of spiritual formation in all settings is to become more and more like Christ,
the following characteristics of Christian universities influence the processes and
goals of spiritual formation differently than typical approaches in church-based
college ministries or other forms of higher education, including essentially secular
universities, historically church-related colleges, and Bible colleges, or seminaries:

- **Pervasive Christ-centeredness**—A Christian university is pervasively Christian, as opposed to either the secular or merely church-related university, which implies that spiritual formation is integrally
  connected to its educational mission.

- **Exploratory pedagogy**—A Christian university is primarily an academic organization, as opposed to a church or para-church ministry, which implies that spiritual formation is shaped by the exploratory nature of academic culture.
- **Concern for the whole person**—A Christian university claims to shape the whole person of the student, as opposed to the narrower focus of churches, para-church ministries, or public universities, which implies that spiritual formation includes all aspects of student life.
- **Community**—A Christian university emphasizes the value of community, and is often largely residential, as opposed to essentially secular universities or churches and ministries that only draw students to events for a few hours a week. This difference implies that spiritual formation happens as students live, learn, and serve in community with other people.
- **External engagement**—A Christian university calls students to use their education to make a difference in the world for the kingdom of God. This emphasis implies that spiritual formation happens as students move from being self-focused to others-focused.

Before examining each of these characteristics, it may be helpful to consider briefly how the specific context shapes the process of student spiritual formation. For example, in a typical church, students are encouraged to become like Christ in a way that largely affirms and reinforces the specific theological position of that church. Additionally, their spiritual formation happens in a context that is usually separate from other influential areas of their lives, such as jobs, school, friends, and living arrangements.

A para-church ministry operating near a university campus also strives to help participating students to become like Christ. Contrary to the church, its context is connected closely to one or more of the important components of students' lives (education and/or friends). However, it is very clearly not a part of the university, and so it often encourages students to become like Christ in ways that contradict the ethos of their primary academic and relational environment.[1] The following quote, which appears on the staff recruitment website of The Navigators Collegiate Ministry, indicates how the mission of The Navigators differs from the universities which enroll the students it serves: "Some want to live within the sound of church or chapel bell; I want to run a rescue shop within a yard of hell.—C. T. Studd"[2] While not all para-church ministries articulate their differences with the university so strongly, it is apparent that operating in a culture that does not share a ministry's mission can lead to a focus on strengthening and affirming basic Christian beliefs to help students remain faithful in the face of apathy or antagonism to the Christian life. Both of these types of ministries can be very effective in helping students grow spiritually, and it is clear that their methods and goals reflect the cultural context in which they operate.

The Christian university, however, approaches the task of student spiritual formation differently, largely based upon contextual distinctives. At most Christian universities, the campus is the hub of university life, with a majority of undergraduate students living on or near campus. Spiritual formation, therefore, becomes part of the center of their lives, not something they go elsewhere to receive.

Second, spiritual formation is central to the mission of the university at which they are studying. This means that Christian universities encourage students to become like Christ in ways that are consistent with university culture and mission. They encourage students to grow spiritually through activities involving academics, athletics, relationships, spiritual practices, and vocational exploration, to name a few examples. All of these activities are provided in a way that is consistent with the university's mission and culture.

Third, even in denominational schools that espouse a clearly defined theology, the exploratory nature of higher education implicitly, and often explicitly, encourages students to explore and challenge the parameters of their faith in ways that many churches are not willing to do. Therefore, although the general nature of spiritual formation—becoming like Christ—is constant in all three types of ministries, the differing contexts result in unique processes and goals for student spiritual formation.

In order for contemporary Christian universities to fulfill their commitments to student spiritual formation, it is incumbent upon faculty, staff, and administrators to develop and articulate a theology of spiritual formation that is contextually appropriate and robust enough to stand alongside the philosophies and theologies of intellectual formation that are at the center of the Christian university. This theology must be more than merely an exploration of effective ministry practices to be implemented by campus ministry departments. Likewise, it must be more than an exploration of theories of faith integration and worldview development in the classroom. It must be a theology that includes all aspects of the university in an integral, contextualized way that acknowledges the centrality of spiritual formation as part of the holistic mission of the university. Such a theology incorporates the various factors that characterize the unique culture of the Christian university.

Pervasive Christ-Centeredness

One of the ways in which CCCU schools differ from other church-related colleges, not to mention secular universities, is that they approach education, both curricular and co-curricular, from a pervasively Christ-centered position. CCCU university presidents sing a common tune regarding this characteristic. Huntington University president, Blair Dowden, stated, "Our main thing . . . is our Christ-centeredness."[3] Asbury University president, Sandra Gray, adds, "When the total learning environment fosters the Christian faith and a faith-full way of life . . . higher education finds its highest form."[4] Former Wheaton College president, Duane Litfin, calls this approach the "systemic model" of Christian higher education and quotes former Calvin College president, Anthony Diekema, on its nature: "Christian colleges must give constant attention to institutional mission and its extensive articulation, and then by logical extension that mission must permeate everything we do, giving internal consistency to teaching, scholarship, student life, administration, community relations . . . everything."[5] Such Christian colleges "seek to make Christian thinking systemic throughout the institution, root, branch, and leaf,"[6] most commonly through the integration of faith and learning. As Harold Heie claims definitively, "The integration of knowledge is the most distinctive task of Christian liberal arts education—always was, is now, always will be."[7] This pervasive Christ-centeredness arises from a commitment to philosophically pervasive Christ-centeredness that results in organizationally pervasive Christ-centeredness.

Philosophical Pervasiveness—The Unity of Truth

Philosophically, a commitment to pervasive Christ-centeredness arises from a basic understanding of truth as a unified or interrelated whole. This theme has been explored in many ways, most definitively by Arthur Holmes, who calls this the "theocentric unity of truth" and explains that "by this I mean first that all the truth in various areas of learning is in principle an interrelated whole, and second that the truth about everything relates to God."[8] In his classic text *The Idea of a Christian College*, Holmes asserts that "the truth is a coherent whole by virtue of the common focus (that all of creation is related to Christ) that ties it all into one."[9]

This vision of unity, however, extends beyond cognitive development and the emphasis on worldview to encompass all of a student's life. For example, Martin Marty, in his explanation of vocation as calling from God, states, "Only Christian higher education is committed to what Christians mean by Vocation. They mean lives that find their coherence in Christ, 'in whom everything holds together.'"[10] Nicholas Wolterstorff also encourages Christian universities to push past mere worldview development, and instead to "educate for shalom," challenging students to actively address the needs of the world and help bring about the wholeness of God's kingdom in the world. A philosophical commitment to the unity of truth leads to educational approaches that "provide an opportunity to steward life more effectively by becoming more fully a human person in the image of God, by seeing life whole rather than fragmented."[11] This approach involves the whole university.

Organizational Pervasiveness—Christ-Centeredness throughout the University

Philosophical commitments to pervasive faith integration necessitate organizational structures that reflect institutional priorities. As Richard Hughes states, "A Christian university must nurture Christian commitment at all levels of the institution, and must allow that commitment to shape classroom instruction, the curriculum and the university at large. Apart from this dimension, a university can hardly claim the name 'Christian' at all."[12]

What is often neglected in discussions of Christian commitment, especially in the area of faith integration, is "the university at large." If Christian universities take this level of integration seriously, it means that virtually every staff member and administrator, in addition to teaching faculty, is involved in the enterprise of faith integration. For example, while acknowledging that "integrating faith and learning in the classroom is the distinctive of a Christian college," Steve and Jane Beers also state, "When we take seriously the holistic nature of our institution's educational missions, the student development staff and their programs become a unique and primary tool for integration."[13]

Additionally, this level of pervasiveness calls for partnership and collaboration, not just separate initiatives. Norris Friesen and Wendy Togami declare, "A powerful way to invigorate Christian student learning on college campuses is to promote collaboration among student development and academic affairs in new and creative ways that capitalize on each profession's strengths."[14] Contemporary research affirms the educational and transformative value of influence from many parts of campus. For example, in Todd Hall's study of more than three thousand students at Christian universities, student relationships with staff and administration were the seventh most transformational influence on spiritual formation, with mentoring by faculty occupying the ninth spot (out of nineteen influences rated). What is significant is that these relationships exert more perceived influence than traditional spiritual formation programs such as ministry opportunities or chapel (ranked twelfth and thirteenth, respectively).[15] This research affirms the theoretical commitment to systemic integration that Arthur Holmes addresses.

> The college must therefore cultivate an atmosphere of Christian learning, a level of eager expectancy that is picked up by anyone who is on campus for even a short while. It must sell the idea from the point of student recruitment and admission through freshman orientation into the residence hall program, the curriculum and individual courses. The chapel program must exemplify this attitude rather than the unthinking disjunction that is all too frequent between faith and devotion on the one hand and what goes on in the classroom on the other.[16]

To be truly systemic or integrative, Henry and Agee propose that "faith and learning integration must not be merely institutional rhetoric, armchair recreation, or pedagogical postscript, but the *sine qua non* of Christian higher education."[17]

Contemporary CCCU schools are exerting significant efforts to discover and articulate how such systemic commitments to spiritual formation might look. For example, during the summer of 2010, the CCCU convened a conversation among teams from eleven different member universities. The presidents of these universities brought teams of five to six faculty and administrators to "attempt to define the term spiritual formation in the context of Christ-centered higher education . . . [that will] result in the ability to conduct a broad and systematic assessment of spiritual formation across Council schools."[18]

It is instructive that this process was led by university presidents and included a variety of institutional leaders. It was not merely a conversation among campus ministers because the task of pervasive spiritual formation includes all members of the university. Since one of the main roles that governing boards take at CCCU schools is monitoring faithfulness to institutional mission, specifically as it relates to their Christ-centeredness, it is also significant that the report of this conference is included as one of the resources for trustee boards of member schools on the CCCU's resource library website. Maintaining one's philosophical and organizational commitments to pervasive Christ-centeredness lies at the heart of contemporary Christian higher education.

Exploratory Pedagogy

Another characteristic of most CCCU schools that influences spiritual formation is the liberal arts approach to education and its exploratory pedagogy, as opposed to one characterized by indoctrination. As Darryl Tippens states, "Great liberal arts colleges and professional schools serve their students well by inviting them to join a rich culture of discovery."[19] His use of the word culture is instructive in that it calls the entire university to foster this spirit of discovery and exploration. While some constituents call for Christian universities to affirm unwaveringly the theological tenets of the various churches that support the schools, a liberal arts education always involves exploration, questioning, and wrestling with ideas, both in intellectual and spiritual development. This exploratory approach to faith and learning often differs from that of the local church, and is one contextual characteristic that defines approaches to spiritual formation in the Christian university. Robert Wuthnow challenges Christian universities to see this distinctive as an advantage in its work with students: "Students and faculty often find the academy a more conducive setting in which to engage in frank explorations of religious values than virtually anywhere else. In contrast, the same person may feel uncomfortable in a congregational setting, for example, because certain answers are assumed to be precluded from the outset. . . ."[20] Holmes also speculates that such an exploratory paradigm actually serves to strengthen student faith more than attempts at indoctrination that some desire: "I suspect that a considerable amount of student cynicism and skepticism can be traced to attempts to impose a faith dogmatically rather than . . . assisting students in grappling with issues for themselves in the light of their heritage of Christian faith and thought."[21]

Because this exploratory pedagogy differs from approaches to faith and learning in many churches, it sometimes feels threatening to students and their parents. Mannoia states that "many people wonder if the liberal arts . . . are really consistent with Christian faith at all."[22] Critics of this approach worry that such exploration weakens students' faith or makes real commitment difficult; and it may be that some students struggle with this form of faith, both intellectually and spiritually. However, Holmes reminds us, "The primary purpose of a Christian college is not to insulate and protect students, but to educate them as responsible Christians."[23] Exploratory education of this sort is inherent to the Christian university and necessarily influences the shape of spiritual formation. In so doing, the Christian university declares the scope of its mission in the lives of students.

Concern for the Whole Person: Holistic Student Development

Another distinctive that influences spiritual formation on CCCU campuses is their claim to shape the whole person of the student, and in so doing identify themselves as "formative institutions."[24] These types of schools seek more than just knowledge transfer or career preparation. Likewise, they strive for more than transforming the heart of the student. As longtime Christian college faculty member and administrator Harold Heie stated, "A college cannot be all things to all persons (e.g., a church or a health spa). But a college can and ought to help students learn about all aspects of their whole beings . . . , helping each student learn about and experience development of his/her whole being."[25]

This holistic, transformative approach to education is not just a relic of earlier forms of Christian higher education, destined to be left behind as contemporary Christian universities seek greater credibility in the American higher education establishment. In fact, the opposite is true. Darryl Tippens states, "The faithful university of the twenty-first century will be committed to the formation of the whole person."[26] Such faithful universities often retain this approach in recognition of the inadequacy of dominant models of American higher education. For example, Parker Palmer claims that spiritual hunger permeates American higher education because of "the shallowness of academic culture, its inability to embrace the whole of the human condition, its failure to create community, and its inadequacies in dealing with the deep problems of our time."[27] He proclaims the need for a "gospel epistemology"[28] that is pervasively formational of the whole person, and that prepares that person to connect in holistic ways to the needs of the world. In so doing, he challenges Christian universities to reject the temptation to compartmentalize education, even as they espouse a holistic concern for their students. Calvin College scholar James K. A. Smith also describes this temptation:

> Many Christian schools, colleges, and universities—particularly in the Protestant tradition—have taken on board a picture of the human person that owes more to modernity and the Enlightenment than it does to the holistic, biblical vision of human persons. In particular, Christian education has absorbed a philosophical anthropology that sees human persons as primarily thinking things.[29]

While the temptation for reductionist views of the human person prevails, CCCU schools aspire to "provide something quite different."[30]

These aspirations, and the rhetoric that accompanies them, reflect the conviction that the goal of the Christian university is to help students become a certain type of person. Holmes states, "Education has to do with the making of persons, Christian education with the making of Christian persons."[31] Wolterstorff adds that we cannot avoid asking the questions, "What sort of person is it that we want to educate? What sort of person [is it] that we want to form?"[32] Finally, James K. A. Smith cautions us to consider carefully "how a Christian education shapes us, forms us, molds us to be a certain type of people whose hearts and passions and desires are aimed at the kingdom of God."[33]

Educating the whole person demands a much broader scope of education than mere cognitive development. Christian universities embark on this task because they espouse a vision of wholeness in education. Christian educators strive to shape the whole person because they realize that students are more than minds to be filled or hearts to be warmed. As Heie states, "A person must be viewed holistically, as one who thinks, feels, worships something, plays, relates to others and has a body that needs caring for. Persons are not disembodied intellects."[34] While we agree with this sentiment, our educational institutions often operate very differently. It is easy to compartmentalize the life of the student. With regard to the Great Commandments of Jesus, the literature of Christian higher education focuses mainly on helping students love God with all of their minds. However, as James K. A. Smith states, "Education is not something that traffics primarily in abstract, disembodied ideas; rather, education is a holistic endeavor that involves the whole person, including our bodies, in a process of formation that aims our desires, primes our imagination, and orients us to the world."[35] Such a holistic endeavor addresses both the internal and external worlds of the student. To address the student holistically, Christian universities have developed relational approaches to education.

Community: A Relational Orientation

Literature regarding Christian higher education often uses very individualistic terms to discuss how faculty and staff approach the tasks of teaching and leading, as well as how students develop intellectually and spiritually. This way of speaking about education can lead one to believe that the primary difference between Christian higher education and other forms is how individuals encounter the content of education. However, Albert Meyer claims that Christian universities differ "not only in what is taught but also in how it is taught."[36] These schools intentionally develop relational environments to foster what Holmes calls a "climate of faith and learning . . . [in which] values can be caught from the contagious example of a community at work, in this case a community of enthusiastic and well-equipped scholars."[37]

This climate of faith arises from a commitment by faculty and staff to influence students in various ways. For example, Sharon Parks seeks to counteract the current trend that reduces education to dispassionate objectivity by calling educators to see teaching as the process of developing mentoring communities. She states, "At its best, higher education is distinctive in its capacity to serve as a mentoring environment in the formation of critical adult faith."[38] She goes on to say that "the true professor serves, inevitably, as a spiritual guide [and must avoid] an inappropriate separation of self from truth."[39] The professor does not merely dispense information, but invites students to participate in a community of learning.

This view of the professoriate creates challenges and resistance from some because developing teaching excellence and maintaining professional expertise requires much time and effort, and the scholarly profession necessitates some level of solitude. However, Palmer and Zajonc assert that "Resistance to community undermines faculty growth as well as student learning."[40] Consequently, Christian universities call faculty and staff to develop an approach to teaching that includes the influence of their lives, not just the content of their disciplines. For example, David Gushee provides a framework for faculty influence that he calls "The Professor's Task: Incarnating a Way of Life."[41] In it, he invites faculty to incarnate the following virtues before students:

- Spiritual virtue: authentic piety
- Relational virtue: covenant fidelity
- Intellectual virtue: critical curiosity
- Social virtue: transformative engagement
- Personal virtue: purposeful self-discipline[42]

Embodying such virtues places a different type of expectation on faculty than the fulfillment of typical teaching and research duties. Consequently, it is essential for Christian universities to hire people who are committed to this vision of education. Mannoia states, "Community colleges should not hire like liberal arts colleges. And liberal arts colleges should not hire like universities. The problem is that they all seem to hire like Harvard."[43] Ronald Wells adds, "As all commentators on the church-related college agree, faculty hiring is vital to institutional identity."[44]

The importance of faculty cannot be denied, but the rest of the university staff plays equally important roles in the lives of students, and so care should be exercised in hiring and programming in these areas as well. Hiring of staff is important because the majority of students' time is spent on non-academic activities,[45] and a majority of what they learn is gained outside the classroom.[46] For students to gain a holistic, comprehensive education at CCCU schools it is imperative that curricular and co-curricular departments be equally committed to the institution's mission.

For example, chapel services need to model sound critical thinking in the context of corporate worship. Holmes states, "A college chapel service that renews this vision (of a Christian mind) and keeps things in focus is essential in cultivating a climate of faith and learning."[47] In fact, all programs in campus ministry should model fidelity to the educational task of the university. As one college chaplain stated, "All campus ministry is education—an education that assists students to unite their love for learning with their love for God in the world in which they live."[48] Campus ministry staff members model such an integrative approach to faith and learning by the way they program and lead chapel and other ministry programs.

Similarly, other co-curricular staff must model an integrated life. Because the residence halls are such a "crucial place for dissonance, community and modeling to occur,"[49] it is imperative that staff in these areas operate in conjunction with the university's educational and spiritual goals. Mannoia addresses the importance of such conjunction: "Unless these [areas] are submitted to the overriding goal of promoting cognitive, moral and faith development as well as social development, then they may actually be counterproductive to the aims of the educational institution."[50]

Continuity between the residence halls and the educational mission of the school is also important because of the influence of students upon their peers. Todd Hall's research into spiritual transformation on Christian campuses clearly indicates that peers exert more potentially positive spiritual influence than any other person or program on campus.[51] Consequently, creating an environment that encourages and equips students to exert positive influence on their peers may be as important as ensuring that faculty and staff are committed to this aspect of the university's mission. If Christian colleges and universities wish to match student experience with institutional rhetoric about holistic education, they must intentionally create an environment that fosters influential relationships among faculty, staff, and students.

External Engagement

While Christian universities rightly focus on developing the internal lives of students—intellectually and spiritually—they have also usually challenged those students to recognize their responsibility to the world around them: a fifth distinctive for shaping spiritual formation at CCCU schools. The following excerpts from institutional mission and vision statements of many leading CCCU schools indicate this emphasis:

- Abilene Christian University—"to educate students for Christian service and leadership throughout the world."[52]

- Anderson University—"to educate for a life of faith and service in the church and society."[53]
- Biola University—"equipping men and women in mind and character to impact the world for the Lord Jesus Christ."[54]
- Calvin College—"to be agents of renewal in the academy, church, and society."[55]
- Eastern University—"dedicated to the preparation of undergraduate, theological and graduate students for thoughtful and productive lives of Christian faith, leadership and service."[56]
- Gordon College—"to graduate men and women . . . committed to lives of service, and prepared for leadership worldwide."[57]
- Indiana Wesleyan University—"to prepare each student to become a world changer."[58]
- Messiah College—"to educate men and women toward maturity of intellect, character and Christian faith in preparation for lives of service, leadership and reconciliation in church and society."[59]
- Seattle Pacific University—"to engag[e] the culture and chang[e] the world by graduating people of competence and character, becoming people of wisdom, and modeling grace-filled community."[60]
- Wheaton College—"to help build the church and improve society worldwide."[61]

Much of the external engagement referred to in these statements is seen through the variety of co-curricular service and mission programs that pervade contemporary and historical campuses. Such external engagement seems appropriate given the emphasis on whole-person development, especially as it relates to the Great Commandments of Jesus. A Christ-centered education that does not address the world's needs could not claim to represent him well.

As obvious as this concept may be, many Christian universities struggle with how to encourage external engagement, especially in the curriculum. As these universities have matured and gained credibility in American higher education, the temptation to focus primarily on intellectual development constantly arises, even as rhetoric regarding external engagement continues. Literature on Christian higher education exemplifies this emphasis, as nearly all major works in the field focus on cognitive elements of faith integration and scholarly work.[62] Other voices exist, however, that call the Christian university to consider that external engagement is central to its educational mission, and not merely a relic of a Bible college past, or something relegated to co-curricular departments. Wolterstorff, in particular, has challenged Christian universities to educate for more than worldview development or ethics and values. He notes, "I can now state what I see as the nature and mission of the . . . Christian college. The Christian college is a project of and for the Christian community [and] the Christian community exists not for its own sake but for the sake of all people."[63]

His call for a new approach to education, "Educating for Shalom," mentioned previously, declares that an education centered on Christ must address the deepest needs of the world. "Our traditional models (of education) speak scarcely at all of injustice, scarcely at all of our calling to mercy and justice. I submit that the curriculum of the Christian college must open itself up to humanity's wounds."[64] This approach does not mean that the university should become a church or social service agency, but instead calls Christian universities in their capacity as universities to educate students to meet the needs of the world.

The necessity of such a call to extend the scope of education indicates that many Christian universities struggle with how to appropriately engage the world around them in ways that are consistent with their mission. It also indicates that the nature of Christian higher education is continually being shaped by those who call it to greater faithfulness to Christ—a faithfulness upon which it is built.

Conclusion

Christian colleges and universities offer an approach to education that is qualitatively different from other forms of higher education and ministry to college students. They seek to develop environments that are pervasively Christ-centered so that all facets of the student are addressed in ways that are consistent with the mission of the university. This mission calls students to develop an exploratory sense of discovery, intellectually and spiritually. To help students in this exploratory process, Christian universities have developed relational approaches to education and have hired faculty and staff who are committed to influencing the whole person of the students for the sake of the world. These characteristics differentiate Christian universities from secular universities that divorce faith from learning and rarely emphasize relational influence of faculty and staff. These characteristics also differentiate Christian higher education from Bible colleges and various forms of college ministry that have a more limited scope of student development and employ methods that are more affirming and strengthening rather than exploratory. The context of the Christian university dictates that it differ from other types of educational and ecclesial organizations. In so doing, a unique setting is created that offers much hope for the spiritual formation of students.

Chapter 6 Notes

[1] Ministries, such as InterVarsity Christian Fellowship (accessed May 28, 2009, http://www.intervarsity.org/page/ministry-overview); Navigators (accessed May 28, 2009, http://www.navigators.org/us/ministries/collegiate); and Campus Crusade for Christ (accessed May 28, 2009, http://www.ccci.org/about-us/ministry-profile/index.aspx) have varying approaches, but share common ministry goals of evangelism and discipleship of students on university campuses (typically secular universities). While InterVarsity does speak of redeeming the campus—adapting H. Richard Niebuhr's *Christ and Culture* (San Francisco, Calif.: HarperSanFrancisco, 2001)—it is clear that the organization sees itself as an outside agent seeking to influence an organization in need of change.

[2] EDGE Corps, accessed May 28, 2009, http://www.edgecorps.org/.

[3] G. B. Dowden, "Focus on the 'Main Thing,'" *Huntington University Magazine* 13, no. 3: 2.

[4] S. C. Gray, "The Mission of Asbury College," in *Cornerstones of Spiritual Vitality: Toward an Understanding of Wesleyan Spirituality in Christian Higher Education*, eds. J. S. Kulaga and J. P. Vincent (Wilmore, Ky.: Asbury College, 2009), 7.

[5] Duane Litfin, *Conceiving the Christian College* (Grand Rapids, Mich.: Eerdmans, 2004), 18.

[6] Ibid.

[7] Harold Heie, "Integration and Conversation," in *The University through the Eyes of Faith*, ed. Steve Moore (Indianapolis, Ind.: Light and Life, 1998), 62.

[8] Arthur F. Holmes, "The Closing of the American Mind and the Opening of the Christian Mind: Liberal Learning, Great Texts, and the Christian College," in *Faithful Learning and the Christian Scholarly Vocation*, eds. Douglas V. Henry and Bob R. Agee (Grand Rapids, Mich.: Eerdmans, 2003), 115.

[9] Arthur F. Holmes, *The Idea of a Christian College*, rev. ed. (Grand Rapids, Mich.: Eerdmans, 1987), 17.

[10] Martin E. Marty, "The Church and Christian Higher Education in the New Millennium," in *Faithful Learning and the Christian Scholarly Vocation*, eds. Douglas V. Henry and Bob R. Agee (Grand Rapids, Mich.: Eerdmans, 2003), 60.

[11] Holmes, *The Idea of a Christian College*, 36.

[12] Richard T. Hughes, "Getting It Together: The Role of Cultural Diversity in a Christian University," in *The University through the Eyes of Faith*, ed. Steve Moore (Indianapolis, Ind.: Light and Life, 1998), 134.

[13] Stephen Beers and Jane Beers, "Integration of Faith and Learning," in *The Soul of a Christian University: A Field Guide for Educators*, ed. Stephen T. Beers (Abilene, Tex.: Abilene Christian University Press, 2008), 70.

[14] Norris Friesen and W.S. Togami, "Collaboration: To Labor Together," in *The Soul of a Christian University*, 117.

[15] Todd W. Hall, "The Furnishing the Soul Project: The Spiritual Lives of Students at Christian Colleges in America," presentation, International Forum on Christian Higher Education, February 26, 2010, slides 36–37.

[16] Holmes, *Idea of a Christian College*, 49.

[17] Douglas V. Henry and Bob R. Agee, *Faithful Learning and the Christian Scholarly Vocation*, xii.

[18] Council for Christian Colleges and Universities, *CCCU Report on Spiritual Formation*, accessed October 2, 2011, http://cccu.org/professional_development/resource_library/2011/cccu_report_on_spiritual_formation.

[19] Darryl Tippens, "Scholars and Witnesses: The Christian University Difference," in *The Soul of a Christian University*, 29.

[20] R. Wuthnow, "Struggling to Manifest the Sacred," in *The University through the Eyes of Faith*, ed. Steve Moore (Indianapolis, Ind.: Light and Life, 1998), 150–151.

[21] Holmes, *Idea of a Christian College*, 62.

[22] V. James Mannoia Jr., *Christian Liberal Arts: An Education That Goes Beyond* (Lanham, Md.: Rowman & Littlefield, 2000), 66.

[23] Holme, *Idea of a Christian College*, 85.

[24] James K. A. Smith, *Desiring the Kingdom: Worship, Worldview and Cultural Formation* (Grand Rapids, Mich.: Baker Academic, 2009), 34.

[25] Heie, "Integration and Conversation," 67.

[26] Tippens, "Scholars and Witnesses," 32.

[27] Parker Palmer, "Toward a Spirituality of Higher Education," in *Faithful Learning and the Christian Scholarly Vocation*, 75.

[28] Palmer, "Toward a Spirituality of Higher Education," 81ff.

[29] Smith, *Desiring the Kingdom*, 31.

[30] Mannoia, *Christian Liberal Arts*, 5.

[31] Holmes, *Idea of a Christian College*, 25.

[32] Nicholas Wolterstorff, "Teaching for Justice: On Shaping How Students Are Disposed to Act," in *Educating for Shalom*, eds. Clarence W. Joldersma and Gloria Goris Stronks (Grand Rapids, Mich.: Eerdmans, 2004), 137.

[33] Smith, *Desiring the Kingdom*, 18.

[34] Heie, "Integration and Conversation," 67.

[35] Smith, *Desiring the Kingdom*, 39.

[36] Albert J. Meyer, *Realizing Our Intentions: A Guide for Churches and Colleges with Distinctive Missions* (Abilene, Tex.: Abilene Christian University Press, 2009), 97.

[37] Holmes, *Idea of a Christian College*, 81.

[38] Sharon Daloz Parks, *Big Questions, Worthy Dreams: Mentoring Emerging Adults in Their Search for Meaning, Purpose, and Faith* (San Francisco, Calif.: Jossey-Bass, 2000), 159.

[39] Ibid., 166–167.

[40] Parker J. Palmer and Arthur Zajonc, *The Heart of Higher Education: A Call to Renewal; Transforming the Academy through Collegial Conversations* (San Francisco, Calif.: Jossey-Bass, 2010), 44.

[41] David P. Gushee, "Attract Them by Your Way of Life: The Professor's Task in the University," in *The Future of Christian Higher Education*, eds. David S. Dockery and David P. Gushee (Nashville, Tenn.: Broadman & Holman, 1999), 141.

[42] Ibid.,143–152.

[43] Mannoia, *Christian Liberal Arts*, 166.

[44] Ronald A. Wells, "Back to School," *The Christian Century* (July 26, 2005), 30.

[45] Ernest L. Boyer, *College: The Undergraduate Experience in America* (San Francisco, Calif.: Harper & Row, 1987), 180.

[46] Everett K. Wilson, "The Entering Student: Attributes and Agents of Change," in *College Peer Groups: Problems and Projects for Research*, eds. Theodore M. Newcombe and Everett K. Wilson (Chicago, Ill.: Aldine Publishing, 1966), 88–91.

[47] Holmes, *The Idea of a Christian College*, 84.

[48] Todd E. Brady, "Christian Worldview and Campus Ministry," in *Shaping a Christian Worldview*, eds. David S. Dockery and Gregory Alan Thornbury (Nashville, Tenn.: Broadman & Holman, 2002), 362.

[49] Mannoia, *Christian Liberal Arts*, 155.

[50] Ibid., 155.

[51] Hall, "Furnishing the Soul Project," slide 36.

[52] "Our Mission Statement, Promise and 21st-Century Vision," Abilene Christian University, accessed February 13, 2012, http://www.acu.edu/aboutacu/mission.html.

[53] "AU Mission," Anderson University, accessed February 13, 2012, http://www.anderson.edu/welcome/mission.html.

[54] "Mission, Vision & Values," Biola University, accessed February 13, 2012, http://www.biola.edu/about/mission/.

[55] "Our Mission," Calvin College, accessed February 13, 2012, http://www.calvin.edu/about/mission.html.

[56] "Mission Statement," Eastern University, accessed February 13, 2012, http://www.eastern.edu/welcome/missionstatement.html.

[57] "Mission Statement," Gordon College, accessed February 13, 2012, http://www.gordon.edu/page.cfm?iPageID=385&iCategoryID=31&About&Mission_Statement.

[58] "Mission and Commitments," Indiana Wesleyan University, accessed February 13, 2012, http://www.indwes.edu/About/Mission-and-Commitments/.

[59] "Identity and Mission," Messiah College, accessed February 13, 2012, http://www.messiah.edu/about/.

[60] "Mission & Signatures," Seattle Pacific University, accessed February 13, 2012, http://spu.edu/about-spu/mission-and-signatures.aspx.

[61] "Mission," Wheaton College, accessed February 13, 2012, http://wheaton.edu/About-Wheaton/Mission.

[62] Most of the works that I have cited in this chapter focus on this aspect of education.

[63] Wolterstorff, "Teaching for Justice," 7.

[64] Ibid., 22.

WHO ARE WE
TO FORM STUDENTS?

The Importance of
Remembering Who We Are

Perry L. Glanzer

> *The inattention to all-round formation underlines what is perhaps the most*
> *glaring weakness of contemporary higher education: its inability to cope*
> *adequately either with the "who?" question that the issue of formation raises*
> *or with the related "why?" question.*[1]

—David Ford

Today, most professors in universities lack the knowledge, will, and
confidence to dream of forming human beings. Consequently, they operate with a
very narrow conception of their vocation. They only want to construct engineers,
shape artists, or train accountants. As one professor admitted when discussing the
spiritual development of students, "There are many of my colleagues who would
say, 'Look, we are at a university, and what I do is math; what I do is history. . . .
Moving into this [area of spiritual development] is not my competence.'"[2] As this
quote reveals, part of this reluctance stems from their perceived professional pro-
ficiencies. Professors only feel qualified to engage in a narrow form of vocational
formation.

In contrast, student affairs professionals in the contemporary university operate with an incredibly expansive vision of their vocation. They create positions
entitled student development, discuss the concern to address the holistic needs of

students, and articulate their goal as helping students grow in every facet of their lives.[3] Yet most of this talk about growth and development tends to remain quite abstract and platitudinous, because to discuss the specific ends of development or the ideas we want students to acquire risks excluding and labeling certain ends or ideals as deficient. Thus, the end to which one might commit or the final model into which it is hoped a student grows or develops remains obscure.

The first part of this chapter examines the historical origins of this current situation. Why did the contemporary university end up with this division of labor and these competing vocational understandings? I suggest that one reason for this division involved the abandonment of the university's Christian identity and with it a Christian conception of student formation. Without a Christian conception of student formation, professors at secular research universities gradually neglected holistic student development and student development personnel tried to take up this responsibility but without a clear idea of what a human person is and ought to be. Unfortunately, Christian universities have imitated the habits of the contemporary secular university by inheriting both its structure and its understanding of student development without critically examining and transforming either one according to a theological vision.

The second part of this chapter sets forth a Christian understanding of personhood that can help guide Christian leaders in higher education. Christian colleges and universities should be different because of the theological resources that inform our understanding of the means and ends of human flourishing. At the very least they can operate with a much clearer understanding of the ends of student development and what it means to be fully human.

The Faculty's Abandonment of Student Formation

The first statutes of the University of Paris, commonly considered one of the first universities, stated in 1215 there could be "no student without a master."[4] The master or faculty member was not only to be technically competent but "above reproach in his life and in his morality."[5] Faculty needed to be morally competent, because they not only taught students subject matter, but they also played a formative role in their moral and spiritual lives. Thus, a master "was supposed to practice all the Christian virtues and, above all, those appropriate to his condition (impartiality, goodwill towards his colleagues and his pupils, keenness in work), and conversely, to avoid those sins which directly threatened it (financial rapacity, negligence, vanity)."[6]

In stark contrast, today one finds professors such as Stanley Fish arguing that teachers should not, and cannot, be expected to form the moral character of their students.[7] For Fish, the responsibility of the faculty member is simply "(1) Introduce students to bodies of knowledge and traditions of inquiry they didn't know much about before; and (2) equip those same students with the analytical skills that will enable them to move confidently within those traditions and to engage in independent research should they choose to do so."[8] The notion that the professor should shape the spiritual and moral lives of students distracts from these purposes.

The development of this understanding of the faculty's role is actually quite recent.[9] Even in 1876, Daniel Coit Gilman, the first president of America's first research university, Johns Hopkins University, claimed that the job of the university and its faculty was "to develop character—to make men" and that "it misses its aim if it produced learned pedants, or simple artisans, or cunning sophists, or pretentious practitioners."[10] Research universities such as Johns Hopkins, however, actually changed that focus. While in the old-time American colleges that developed before the Civil War, faculty were expected to supervise and form the moral and spiritual lives of students, in the new research university model that American higher education leaders imported from Europe, the German tradition of freedom for university students (*Lernfreiheit*) took hold.[11] W. H. Cowly summarized the change: "The old college had been an Alma Mater—albeit chiefly concerned with the religious welfare of students—but within its lights it saw the student as a whole person and not as just a mind to be loaded with facts like a tank car with oil. German-trained professors, however, abandoned the holistic conception of the student and of education. In brief, they gave their allegiance to German-inspired impersonalistic intellectualism."[12] As a result, the job of faculty in the new university became primarily to discover and disseminate knowledge.

At first, college administrators saw this transformation as progress, but they later realized its flaws. Around the turn of the twentieth century, Julie Reuben found a surge of nostalgia for the old-style college fill higher education literature: "Commentators missed the unity, moral purpose, and high ideals of the classical college. They perceived the new universities as chaotic and materialistic, and their students as selfish and undisciplined."[13] C. John Sommerville identifies the mistake these administrators made: "When American universities became officially secular, a century ago, the problem of defining the human was not foreseen. Much of a traditional Christian intellectual culture was taken for granted. Mistaking the habits of thinking for rationality itself, those founders thought religion was redundant and could be ignored without loss of substance."[14]

Since administrators realized they could not abandon their commitments to faculty research and certain forms of student freedom, they tried to solve this problem not by asking faculty to engage once again in moral and spiritual forma-tion but by delegating the job to others. They began creating the co-curricular realm, employing deans of men and women to help supervise the moral and spiri-tual formation of students. The idea that faculty should somehow be seen as mas-ters shaping students, however, became a quant relic of the past.

The new division of student personnel work gradually grew inside the uni-versity and in the 1960s it began to gain a theory base. Taken largely from devel-opmental psychology, theorists advised administrators to focus less on shaping students in light of particular moral and religious ideals and more upon the pro-cess of growth and development according to their particular theories of stage development in the realms of intellect, morals, faith, and identity. While this theory base proved helpful at discerning the cognitive and emotional processes many students experienced in these areas, it failed to provide what Christianity had previously supplied: a coherent understanding of personhood.[15] As a result, the theories did not answer questions about what various forms of development had to do with one another and both theories and practice in this area followed a reductionistic impulse. Eventually, students were treated primarily as members of particular classes, races, or genders.

Christian colleges and universities tended to adopt the standard structure of prominent state and private universities, although they incorporated more explicitly Christian development goals. The spiritual and moral formation of stu-dents became the major role of chapel and other parts of the co-curricular realm. Christian education for faculty members primarily involved shaping the minds of students and providing them with a Christian worldview.[16] One could even argue that this division of labor seemed an efficient and effective approach to shaping the body of Christ.

Recovering Who We Are

I open my eyes and don't know where I am or who I am.
Not all that unusual—I've spent half my life not knowing.[17]
—Andre Agassi

Christians in higher education, however, are increasingly raising questions about whether Christian colleges and universities should follow this model. In *Desiring the Kingdom*, James K. A. Smith argues that the old approach encourages profes-sors to focus on the intellectual formation of students' worldview in a way that reinforces a distorted view of human personhood. Thus, he suggests that we need "to re-envision Christian education as a formative rather than just an informative project" by recovering a more Christian understanding of human personhood.[18] Instead of seeing human beings as thinkers or believers, he contends we need to see ourselves as lovers who direct our love toward a vision of the good life.

While Smith's basic understanding of human personhood helpfully corrects some Christian educational models by focusing on the central Christian concern of love, it unfortunately misses a few important aspects that could correct the old model of human personhood. For one thing, Smith fails to place enough emphasis upon God's creational context for understanding human personhood. In this respect, Christian Smith's *What Is a Person?* provides a much more detailed and rich understanding of the various capacities God has endowed upon human persons.[19] Similar to James Smith, Christian Smith identifies the highest human capacity as "interpersonal communion and love." Yet, he also identifies a number of other important higher order and creating capacities—such as aesthetic judgment and enjoyment, forming virtues, moral awareness and judgment, truth seeking, anticipating the future, and identity formation—that remain central to understanding personhood. Regrettably, Christian Smith's work does not provide a specifically Christian insight into the substance and process of shaping a person in all these areas.[20] If we are to delve more deeply into human personhood and the practice of love, we must do so in light of the overall biblical narrative regarding our identity.

Who Are We? Human Personhood in the Context of God's Story

Who are you?
—The Who

The Bible reveals that we need to understand the "Who?" question in relation to the triune God before we ask it about ourselves. In Genesis 1, the story starts by providing insight into God's identity. It begins with the proclamation from Genesis 1:1: "In the beginning God created the heavens and the earth." God is clearly separate from that which is created; he is transcendent. God is also creative and omniscient. Eight times in the first chapter we read that "God said," and each time a new aspect of creation comes into being simply by God's omniscient, commanding word. God is also interested in creating something beyond himself. God cares about having material things such as heavenly planets and earthly creatures come into existence. These stories teach us about God's character.

The importance of understanding God's identity through such narratives and actions appears throughout the Scriptures. When Moses first encounters God in the burning bush and is called to bring the Israelites out of Egypt, he asks who he shall say sent him. God answers "I AM WHO I AM . . . 'The Lord, the God of your fathers—the God of Abraham, the God of Isaac and the God of Jacob—has sent me to you.' This is my name forever, the name by which I am to be remembered from generation to generation" (Exod. 3:14a, 15b NIV). Again, we come to know God by his past actions and it provides the context that informs and motivates our actions. When God gives the Ten Commandments, he prefaces the commands with the identity declaration that reminds the Israelites of his redemptive work: "I am the Lord your God, who brought you out of Egypt, out of the land of slavery" (Exod. 20:2 NIV). Problems come for the Israelites when they forget God or forget God's history and their own identity in light of God's character and actions.

The importance of identity narratives extends to the Gospel stories about Christ and has particular implications for our understanding of love. The Gospels are fundamentally identity documents that reveal the uniqueness of Jesus. For example, the whole book of Mark hinges around answering the question, "Who do you say I am?" and Peter's confession that Jesus is the Christ (Mark 8:29b NIV). Moreover, this Gospel makes clear that we can only fully understood Christ by understanding him as the Crucified Lord who is the Suffering Servant. That is why it is after Christ's crucifixion that the Roman centurion can utter the identity confession about Jesus, "Surely this man was the Son of God" (Mark 15:39b NIV). It is also why we are to love in a Christlike way, by laying down our lives for others.[21]

The Bible makes it clear that we must also understand ourselves in light of God's character and story. Genesis states: "Then God said, 'Let us make man in our image, in our likeness, and let them rule over the fish of the sea and the birds of the air, over the livestock, over all the earth, and over all creatures that move along the ground.' So God created man in his own image, in the image of God he created him; male and female he created them" (Gen. 1:26–27 NIV). What it means to be created in the image or likeness of God has been the subject of much debate over the centuries of Christian thought.[22] J. Richard Middleton points out that the same Hebrew word that we translate as "image" is used to refer to idols. While the essence of idolatry is a rejection of God's kingship, it also involves an attempt to represent God by means of a carved or cast statue. Given that Scripture uses this same word to talk about our being created in the image of God, a faithful biblical interpretation of this phrase would suggest that God means for human beings to be his physical representations here on earth.[23]

If humans are made in God's image, we must acquire God's character or virtue to fulfil our originally created capacities to complete the *Imago Dei* and become fully human. In other words, one can only properly bear the image of God when one imitates the character qualities of the Triune God in whose image we are made (love, holiness, justice, patience).[24] When we acquire God's virtues, we bear God's image. The reason we are primarily lovers is that God made us in his image and God, as 1 John 4:16 simply states, is love.

Later, the apostles pass along the importance of not only understanding Christ's identity but also our identity "in Christ," a phrase used in the epistles repeatedly. In fact, Paul and the other writers consistently seek to help early Christians recognize that they must first understand who they are in Christ before they can realize how to act as Christians. Thus, the first parts of epistles such as Romans, Galatians, Ephesians, Philippians, Colossians, and First and Second Thessalonians do not contain commands but instead discuss the identity and work of Christ and our identity in light of this reality. Only toward the second half of the letters do the writers instruct us how to live in light of that identity. What it means to love, therefore, can only be understood in light of God's story and our identity within it.

Love Needs More than Practice: Complicating Love

Your identity is your most valuable possession. Protect it.
—Elastigirl to her children in *The Incredibles*

In *Desiring the Kingdom*, James Smith contends that since we are primarily lovers and that ninety-five percent of our lives involve habituated action, we must focus upon practicing love. Similar to a good baseball player who continually seeks to develop certain habits of response when batting or fielding, good lovers seek to habituate themselves through practice to create a life that mirrors the vision of the good life they love. While Smith's contention is true to some degree, learning love also requires more than habit and practice. It requires that we consider all aspects of our human personhood, or as Scripture mentions, we must love God with our heart, soul, mind, and strength. In other words, love is complicated.

Dallas Willard provides a more complex description of the biblical model of the human person that can help us understand this point. Willard observes that Scripture describes us as having thought (e.g., mind), feelings, body (e.g., strength), social context/identity, spirit (i.e., heart) and soul. The spirit or heart directs our loves in the way that Smith describes, while the soul "is the aspect of your whole being that correlates, integrates and enlivens everything going on in the various dimensions of the self. It is the life center of the human being."[25]

Love in this mode, as Scripture indicates from the love commands, requires an appreciation of multidimensionality in a variety of ways. This knowledge and the power to love come through the grace of the Triune God. God provides the wisdom, Christ gives us the example and means, and the Holy Spirit empowers us to demonstrate the fruit of the Spirit.

The multidimensionality also must be understood in relation to our personhood. Love requires cognitive insight that one must receive as a gift from God. Thus, Paul prays that the Philippians' love "may abound more and more in knowledge and depth of insight so that you may be able to discern what is best . . ." (Phil. 1:9–10a). The biblical material indicates that we first need to spend time praying and receiving God's gracious gifts of knowledge about our true self and wisdom about how to love before we engage in practices that habituate our love. After all, just as one needs to know the sport, musical instrument, or other endeavor one is doing before one can practice it appropriately, one must understand the nature of God, God's love story, and one's true self in light of that story to engage in the types of practice that prove helpful for the kingdom of God.

Furthermore, consider our social context—what I would label our social identities—and the role of the soul and the spirit. We are completed by being in Christ, but God also made us to have multiple identities, some chosen or created and some bestowed (and some a mysterious combination of both).[26] God made us male and female, sons and daughters. We are given names, nationalities, and family identities (e.g., uncle, aunt). We choose (and are chosen) to be a husband or wife, father or mother, and more. As with God's character, individuals primarily understand their various identities in the form of narratives. In other words, whether it is one's personal name (e.g., John), family name (e.g., Doe), ethnic identity (German-Norwegian, African-American), national identity (e.g., American, Canadian), gender (e.g., male or female), religious identity (e.g., Christian, Jew), professional identity (e.g., doctor, bricklayer, landscaper), family identity (e.g., child, parent, sibling), or another form of identity, all of these aspects of identity have stories attached to them. For example, one of the predominant ways Americans understand what it means to be a citizen concerns not only learning the ideas in the United States Constitution or participating in certain practices (e.g., voting for a president), but also engaging in conversations and disagreements about what those ideas mean in practice. Through learning and creating narratives about these struggles, we understand the core of our identity.[27]

With this understanding, we can understand a key aspect of practicing love related to our soul and spirit. How can the soul integrate our multiple and conflicting selves? How do I balance the tensions inherent among being a good father, husband, professor, American, son, neighbor, uncle, etc.? As Christ made clear, an essential claim of the Christian tradition is that one's identity in relationship to God is one's most important and fundamental identity over and above other identities such as familial or political identities (Matt. 12:46–49; 22:15–22). In fact, one can only properly understand oneself and these other identities in light of one's Christian identity and the Christian story that gives meaning to that identity. As Christ described, we properly order our loves by learning to love God first and not our other identities and their stories (Matt. 22:34–39). Richard Foster states, "Rightly loving God orders all the other loves common to human existence."[28] Christ's ultimate self-sacrificial love for us makes this clear.

With this knowledge and example, the Holy Spirit empowers us to demonstrate this love (Gal. 5:22–23). Love does not come about by knowledge, habit, or hard work alone (although all three can be helpful). It is ultimately, as Christ demonstrated, a gift we must receive, not a possession we can acquire on our own.

God also tells us and demonstrates how to practice this gift. For example, how we practice loving God first involves many of the bodily worship practices—gifts of God's grace that writers such as Dallas Willard, James Smith, Richard Foster, and others have brought to the forefront. My own experience with the practice of Sabbath keeping provides an example. While going through graduate school, I realized that I faced the spectre of intellectual burnout. Part of the reason for my exhaustion lay with the fact that I did not take a break from my writing and studies. I loved my academic identity, self, and success more than God and others. I soon realized that keeping the Sabbath as a day I did not do any academic work demonstrates love and faith in ways similar to the Israelites who did not collect manna on the Sabbath. I discovered and received faith that God can provide in my profession and that my own efforts alone are not what sustain any vocational success I might have. Furthermore, keeping the Sabbath not only expressed my faith in, and love of, God—by trusting in his provision for my professional life, it also refreshed my soul.

Practicing Love in Various Identity Contexts: The Importance of Mentors with Wisdom for Soul Care

If we realize the central importance of the different identity contexts in which love occurs, we must recognize that we need to practice love in different ways. Again, love is quite complicated. For example, love looks different and must be practiced differently depending upon whether we are loving God, our spouses, our children, our enemies, or our neighbors. The differences are similar to the ways the various swings of a golfer, baseball player, and tennis player all require unique types of practice and adjustments.

Moreover, the concept of Christian personhood sketched above also makes clear that while love requires Spirit-received and inspired understanding and practice, it often benefits from something that Christian higher education in particular should be able to offer—wisdom from mentors. In the book *Talent Is Overrated*, Geoff Colvin identifies two things we think are important for excellence—talent and practice—and the one thing he says is actually important: deliberate practice.[29] While it is true we must habituate ourselves to do things right by practicing them repeatedly—a common rule states that excellence requires ten thousand hours of practice—practice itself is never enough. One must engage in *deliberate practice*, which Colvin describes as "activity designed specifically to improve performance, often with a teacher's help; it can be repeated a lot; feedback on results is continuously available; it's highly demanding mentally . . . and it isn't much fun."[30] As this description specifies, one needs a mentor to help guide one's deliberative practice. This proves especially true, because studies reveal that some people even get worse with experience or basic practices. One needs to know how to practice more effectively to get better. As Colvin points out, "anyone who thinks they've outgrown the benefits of a teacher's help should at least question that view. There is a reason why the world's best golfers still go to teachers."[31] Mentors offer this type of wisdom both within particular practices, such as being a golfer, historian, or artist, but also with regard to the means and ends of the good life as a whole.[32]

For Christians, the foremost mentor regarding wisdom for life is the creator of life. The Triune God, who made all creation, obviously knows its workings and our place within it. Not surprisingly, we are instructed to ask God for his spirit of wisdom (such as Solomon, Eph. 1:17, and James 1:5). In addition to wisdom from God, however, Christians also understand that other humans possess wisdom from God to help in these endeavors. As Paul tells us, "Follow me, as I follow Christ." For these people, true wisdom is a gift from God's Spirit and can be contrasted with human or worldly wisdom (1 Cor. 1–2). Worldly wisdom is that found in the novice practioner, the infant, as Paul says, and not the one who has *successfully* practiced something for a long period of time.

The university is supposed to be a place of wisdom. In fact, wisdom is one of the terms most often associated with ancient universities. As David Ford wrote,

"In most pre-modern cultures, wisdom or its analogues had immense, pervasive and comprehensive importance. It was taken for granted as the crown of education, and as what is most to be desired in a parent, a leader, a counselor, a teacher."[33] Today, however, university professors are largely considered sources of technical expertise for professional practices and not societal leaders in the wider arenas of life.[34] In this narrow conception, professors provide knowledge but not wisdom. The idea that they offer any wisdom about how to mix identities and loves (e.g., what it means to be both a Christian and a historian) or the larger meaning of life that combines all of our identities and loves has become passé.[35]

Simplifying a Complicating Love

Why you gotta make things so complicated?
I see the way you're acting like somebody else makes me frustrated
—Avril Lavigne

The Christian university should expect professors to be able to offer wisdom about life in particular ways related to this expansive Christian view of human personhood. This wisdom can be offered through the books students ponder or through the professors themselves. As Richard Foster writes, "In every age, great Christian saints have cultivated their life with God using the writings of Scripture, the theological reflections of others, the capacities of human reason, the cultural resources of the day and the spiritual disciplines. Through their reflections, the great saints witness to the work of the Holy Spirit and, when we study them, guide our spiritual life as well."[36] Thus, even where professors are deficient in this area, they should still be able to point students to other mentors. In particular, I would suggest three things professors or the texts they assign can do.

First, professors should help students discover who they are. Unfortunately, in the past few centuries, the idea developed that one must discover one's self on one's own, perhaps in nature. This odd idea gained particular influence from Jean-Jacques Rousseau's famous book on education, *Emile* (1762/1979), in which he argues that we should allow children to learn about themselves naturally through self-discovery unhindered by human society. In fact, the best kind of education, according to Rousseau, involves protecting children from the corrupting influence of society by taking them away from human culture out to pristine nature. Not surprisingly, Rousseau never raised his own children and had his mistress take those he sired to an orphanage.[37] Spending time in nature may do many things, but students who understand themselves are not cultivated naturally.

119

Students need help and guidance to discover who they are. Edgar Rice Burroughs provides a symbolic example of this reality in the classic story *Tarzan of the Apes*.[38] Tarzan is the son of an English family, Lord and Lady Greystoke. However, due to the death of his parents in the jungle, he grows up in nature among apes and without any knowledge of who he is. Moreover, he does not know how to act like an English gentleman. He acts and lives as an ape, although he retains some element of human reason. While Burroughs optimistically portrays Tarzan as learning to read on his own through books his parents brought to the jungle (a rather dubious piece of fiction), Tarzan still never learns about his true identity by himself in the midst of nature. It takes another human to help him discover that in another kingdom he is Lord Greystoke and possesses a tremendous inheritance. Similarly, the church has to remind us of who we are and the tremendous inheritance we have received in Christ (Col. 1:12–14). Professors can and should help students with this process. Sometimes, I have to remind students what it means to be a student. Sometimes, I need to remind them that they are more than students. Their grades are not the sum total of their worth and identity.

Second, mentors can help provide wisdom about how to live a life of Christian love in their particular field. This kind of wisdom is domain specific, but it involves the combination of two types of identities with their unique practices.[39] A good historian should be able to provide a young historian with wisdom about how to go about that particular practice, interact with sources, and truly love one's subject. A Christian historian should be able to do the same for young Christian historians. In other words, they should be able to provide wisdom about how to combine their Christian identity with their vocational craft. For instance, I often find I need to remind Christian students that the vocation of being a student entails not merely study and the acquisition of knowledge but a form of worship. "The wisdom of loving God for God's sake," David Ford observes, provides "a Christian rationale to inspire and champion the love of truth and knowledge for their own sake—this being perhaps the goal of universities that is most under threat in the twenty-first century."[40] Being a student who loves wisdom makes this vocation more than a temporary stop before one takes a job.

Third, mentors should be able to provide soul care, which in this case I define as the wisdom about how to combine multiple identities so that one can live a life of integrity and meaning, or as "expertise in the conduct and meaning of life."[41] This type of wisdom is the most common understanding of biblical wisdom. How does one balance one's loves in light of one's professional vocation? A professor should incarnate this wisdom and provide it. Unfortunately, few do.

Throughout my four years as an undergraduate at Rice University, I do not recall having a conversation with a professor that related to this kind of soul care or wisdom. As a religion, political science, and history major, I took plenty of classes related to these topics. In addition, I had numerous intellectual conversations with professors about major ideas. Yet beyond my intellectual development, the rest of my formation as a human was left to others. My experience is not unusual. Higher education faculty have largely abandoned the souls of their students as well as the task of soul care. Christian faculty who seek to love God with their whole being and person should be different.

That being said, I even found that as a Christian faculty member at a Christian university I find myself reticent to engage in such attempts. Once when discussing the integration of faith and learning with graduate students the conversation turned to matters of how a professional should balance work, family, and other responsibilities. They had heard that professors as a profession are the most likely to get divorced and expressed concern about how to address this issue. I found myself having to consciously resist shutting down this discussion. Why? I realized I had been intellectually habituated to consider this type of holistic discussion out of bounds. Since that time, I have consciously sought to incorporate discussions about ordering one's loves in all areas of life into my philosophy of education classes.

One of the most effective methods for producing these discussions I have found is to assign what I call "journey" texts. Autobiographical works such as Augustine's *Confessions* or fictional allegories such as John Comenius' *The Labyrinth of the World and the Paradise of the Heart* provide students with examples of individuals wrestling both with how to understand and direct their loves and how to acquire the wisdom for living. For example, while contemplating how, through the Fall, God's world was transformed from a theater of God's wisdom to a labyrinth of deception, Comenius examines various aspects of the world (including academics, marriage, civic life, religious life, and more). In the end, he realizes that only Christ can guide one out of the maze to once again see God's wisdom.

Ultimately, Christian professors should not be content with attempting to undertake the vocational formation of students alone. They can draw upon a rich understanding of the human person and the loves we must develop to set forth a vision of spiritual formation rooted in the Christian tradition. In other words, we can offer answers to the "Who?" question that the issue of formation raises.

Chapter 7 Notes

[1] David F. Ford, *Christian Wisdom: Desiring God and Learning in Love* (New York: Cambridge University Press, 2007), 322.

[2] Alexander W. Astin, Helen S. Astin, and Jennifer A. Lindholm, *Cultivating the Spirit: How College Can Enhance Students' Inner Lives* (San Francisco, Calif.: Jossey-Bass, 2011), 141.

[3] See, for example, Nancy J. Evans et al., *Student Development in College: Theory, Research and Practice*, 2nd ed. (San Francisco, Calif.: Jossey-Bass, 2009).

[4] Jacques Verger, "Teachers," in *A History of the University in Europe*, vol. 1, *Universities in the Middle Ages*, ed. Hilde de Ridder-Symoens (Cambridge, U.K.: Cambridge University Press, 1992), 152.

[5] Ibid., 163.

[6] Ibid.

[7] Stanley Fish, *Save the World on Your Own Time* (New York: Oxford University Press, 2008), 14.

[8] Ibid., 18.

[9] For a more expansive explanation, see Perry L. Glanzer and Todd C. Ream, *Christianity and Moral Identity in Higher Education* (New York: Palgrave Macmillan, 2009), 31–56.

[10] Daniel Coit Gilman, "Inaugural Address of Daniel Coit Gilman as First President of The Johns Hopkins University," Johns Hopkins University, accessed March 11, 2009, http://www/jhu.edu/125th/links/gilman.html.

[11] George M. Marsden, *The Soul of the American University: From Protestant Establishment to Established Nonbelief* (New York: Oxford University Press, 1994), 153–55.

[12] W. H. Cowley, "Some History and a Venture in Prophecy," in *Trends in Student Personnel Work: A Collection of Papers Read at a Conference Sponsored by the University of Minnesota to Celebrate a Quarter Century of Student Personnel Work and to Honor Professor Donald G. Paterson*, ed. E. G. Williamson (Minneapolis, Minn.: University of Minnesota Press, 1949), 19.

[13] Julie Reuben, *The Making of the Modern University: Intellectual Transformation and the Marginalization of Morality* (Chicago: University of Chicago Press, 1996), 230.

[14] C. John Sommerville, *The Decline of the Secular University* (New York: Oxford University Press, 2006), 24.

[15] Glanzer, *Christianity and Moral Identity in Higher Education*, 56–73.

[16] See, for example, Arthur Holmes, *The Idea of a Christian College*, rev. ed. (Grand Rapids, Mich.: Eerdmans, 1987).

[17] Andre Agassi, *Open* (New York: Vintage, 2010), 3.

[18] James K. A. Smith, *Desiring the Kingdom: Worship, Worldview and Cultural Formation* (Grand Rapids, Mich.: Baker Academic, 2009), 18.

[19] Christian Smith, *What Is a Person? Rethinking Humanity, Social Life and the Moral Good from the Person Up* (Chicago: University of Chicago Press, 2009).

[20] For a similar comma see James K. A. Smith, "The Return to the Person in Contemporary Theory," *Christian Scholar's Review* 40, no. 1 (2010): 77–92.

[21] Richard Hays, *The Moral Vision of the New Testament: Community, Cross, New Creation, A Contemporary Introduction to New Testament Ethics* (San Francisco, Calif.: Harper Collins, 1996).

[22] See, for example, J. Richard Middleton, *The Liberating Image: The Imago Dei in Genesis 1* (Grand Rapids, Mich.: Brazos Press, 2005); or Stanley Grenz, *The Social God and the Relational Self: A Trinitarian Theology of the Imago Dei* (Louisville, Ky.: Westminster John Knox Press, 2001).

[23] Middleton, *The Liberating Image.*

[24] For an essay that expands the role of the Trinity in student formation, see Wyndy Corbin Reuschling, "Being and Becoming: The Trinity and Our Formation," in Jeannine K. Brown, Carla M. Dahl, and Wyndy Corbin Reuschling, *Becoming Whole and Holy: An Integrative Conversation about Christian Formation* (Grand Rapids, Mich.: Baker Academic, 2011), 109–24.

[25] Dallas Willard, *Renovation of the Heart: Putting on the Character of Christ* (Colorado Springs, Colo.: Nav Press, 2002), 199.

[26] Smith, *What Is a Person,* 54. Smith labels identity formation as one of the important capacities of a person (p. 54). I would add that identity is not merely formed by a person; it is also bestowed by others.

[27] See Perry L. Glanzer and Todd C. Ream, "Whose Story? Which Identity? Fostering Christian Identity at Christian Colleges and Universities," *Christian Scholar's Review* 35, no. 1 (Fall 2005): 13–27.

[28] Richard J. Foster and Gayle D. Beebe, *Longing for God: Seven Paths of Christian Devotion* (Downers Grove, Ill.: IVP Books, 2009), 19.

[29] Geoff Colvin, *Talent Is Overrated: What Really Separates World Class Performers from Everyone Else* (New York, N.Y.: Portfolio Trade, 2008).

[30] Ibid., 66.

[31] Ibid., 67.

[32] Paul B. Baltes and Ursula M. Staudinger, "Wisdom: A Metaheuristic (Pragmatic) to Orchestrate Mind and Virtue toward Excellence," *American Psychologist* 55, no. 1 (January 2000): 122–36.

[33] Ford, *Christian Wisdom,* 1.

[34] Sommerville, *The Decline of the Secular University.*

[35] Anthony T. Kronman, *Education's End: Why Our Colleges and Universities Have Given Up on the Meaning of Life* (New Haven, Conn: Yale University Press, 2007).

[36] Foster and Beebe, *Longing for God,* 15.

[37] Paul Johnson, *Intellectuals: From Marx and Tolstoy to Sartre and Chomsky* (New York: Harper & Row, 1988), 21–23.

[38] Edgar Rice Burroughs, *Tarzan of the Apes* (New York: Book of the Month Club, 1995).

[39] For more about the domain specific nature of wisdom, see Robert J. Sternberg, ed., *Wisdom: Its Nature, Origins and Development* (New York: Cambridge University Press, 1990).

[40] Ford, *Christian Wisdom,* 349.

[41] Baltes and Staudinger, "Wisdom," 124.

INVITATION TO AN ACADEMIC JOURNEY OF SPIRITUAL FORMATION

Robert Mulholland

The conjunction of "academic" and "spiritual" is an oxymoron in many contexts, often even in Christian institutions. Of course, spirituality can be studied as an academic discipline in which the history, beliefs, and practices of one, several, or all human spiritualities can be organized, objectively analyzed, and presented in a coherent manner. The primary purpose of such an enterprise, however, is knowledge *about* the subject, not experience *of* the subject.

Generally a professor's or a student's spiritual life is benignly tolerated in academia as long as it remains a private matter and does not intrude into one's academic relationships or into the classroom. Problems arise whenever a professor or student begins to proselytize or seeks to indoctrinate others into their particular spirituality. In such a setting, professors who happen to be practicing Christians[1] have a serious problem. On the one hand, are they to keep their academic discipline, their teaching, and their faculty activities in a separate compartment unaffected by their life in Christ? On the other hand, is it possible to integrate their life in Christ with their academic discipline in a way that has integrity for both? How are they to be a means of God's transforming grace to their faculty and administrative colleagues without proselytizing and to their students without indoctrination?

These kinds of questions may be framing the problem in a manner that precludes or at least makes it more difficult to integrate the academic and the spiritual. The primary issue for the academy is knowledge. In this information age, knowledge consists mainly in amassing, synthesizing, and mastering a body of objective information in order to enhance the effectiveness of one's performance in life and/or improve the life of the world. In such a setting, scholars tend to perceive spirituality as another field of information. Various religious traditions are seen as sub-fields of information distinguished from one another, both by the content of the information as well as the adherents' commitment to that information as the guiding principle of their lives.

Knowledge and Vital Piety

It was John Wesley's life-long pursuit to "unite those two so long disjoined, knowledge and vital piety." If this disjunction was pertinent in Wesley's day, how much more so today. This raises two questions: Is such a union possible and, is it necessary? The latter is the primary issue,[2] and its answer depends upon one's understanding of the Christian life.

When the Christian life is understood as a set of propositions to which one gives assent, a structure of dogma which one espouses, a collection of beliefs to which one adheres, or a body of theological tenets which one embraces, then the Christian life is defined by those propositions, dogmas, beliefs, and tenets. In other words, the Christian life is characterized by belief in and adherence to a certain body of information. When this body of information encounters alternative bodies of information, conjoining the two is often difficult, if not impossible, since the Christian body of information is always posited as the norm by which all others are judged. In this case, conjunction means the adjustment of the other body of information to that of the Christian, which is more coercion and control than conjunction.

There is an alternative. When the Christian life is understood as a genuine, vital, love relationship[3] with God in Christ, a dynamic life in Christ (Col. 3:3), then the Christian life is an active, vibrant, growing and deepening bonding with God in which the believer is being nurtured toward wholeness in the image of Christ for the sake of the world. Propositions can be developed to try to capture something of the reality of this relationship, dogmas created to attempt to frame something of this truth, beliefs articulated which point to this reality, theologies developed to endeavor to picture something of this vitality. These are informational constructs, however, which can only point in the direction of the reality but not contain or control it. Consequently, when those living in this reality encounter genres of information, the information can be engaged creatively as a means to encounter God since God is revealed in all things. Such bodies of information form a context in which to experience God's grace in the world shaped by that information. In this way there can, indeed, be a conjunction of knowledge and vital piety.

For the practicing Christian, such conjunction is not only necessary but an essential dimension of life in Christ. Later we will discuss the nature of the Christian life as a process of being conformed to the image of Christ for the sake of the world.[4] The final part of this definition is crucial. All too often, the Christian life is seen as a privatized, individual relationship with God. Concern for the world is often secondary at best, or totally disregarded at worst. This allows professors and students in the academic setting to compartmentalize their faith on the one hand, and their engagement with the disciplines of the academy and the interaction of these disciplines with the world on the other hand. Such compartmentalization is antithetical to the Christian life.

The Christian life is lived in creative and transformative engagement with the world. As "citizens" of God's kingdom in a non-kingdom world or, in the imagery of John's vision, citizens of New Jerusalem in a Fallen Babylon world, we are to incarnate kingdom perspectives, values, and behaviors in our daily engagement with the world. In the academic setting, this entails framing one's discipline within the larger reality of these kingdom perspectives, values, and behaviors. If one believes all truth is God's truth, then the quest for truth in any discipline always takes place within the reality of God's presence and purpose. The issue becomes crucial at the point where the truths of an academic discipline impinge upon the life and activities of the world. Are these truths employed in ways that incarnate kingdom perspectives, values, and behaviors? Or are they employed so as to support and enhance non-kingdom beliefs, structures, and actions?

This raises an interesting question: What is the nature of a spiritual-academic or an academic-spiritual community? Where should the priority lie? There is a significant danger here. One temptation is to presume the foundation is an academic community into which spiritual dimensions are introduced. The other temptation is to presume the foundation is a spiritual community to which academic dimensions are added. Either approach results in a bifurcation of the academic and spiritual. An example is mixing oil and water. No matter how thoroughly they are blended, sooner or later they separate into their individual identities, with the oil always taking its place on top. As we noted earlier, such bifurcation is antithetical to the Christian life.

There is an apparent tension between the academic and the spiritual, between knowledge and vital piety. To resolve the tension by giving priority to one, however, denigrates one at the expense of the other. Perhaps Jesus provides a healthier resolution when he says we are to love God with all our soul and all our mind (Matt. 22:37). Could we not simply substitute "soul" for "spiritual" and "mind" for "academic"? Perhaps, but that is not where Jesus begins. He begins by exhorting us to love God with all our heart. In the Jewish tradition, "heart" was the seat of being.[5] "Heart," then, points to the deeper reality within which both "soul" and "mind" exist, suggesting a deeper center from which to hold soul and mind, or spiritual and academic, in a dynamic tension.

To love God with all one's heart is to have one's being grounded in a love relationship with God. This love, however, is not having warm feelings toward God or even an affection for God. *Agape* love is a radically other-referenced way of being in relationship with another. The essence of this love from God's side is revealed in the cross[6]; from our side it is seen in Jesus' call to lose one's self for his sake (Matt. 10:39). When our hearts are ruled by selfish desires, self-referenced motives, self-protective behaviors, self-promoting activities, our souls become compromised and our minds imprisoned by egoism, vanity, willfulness, passion, aggressiveness, jealousy, and greed.[7] In Jesus' words, we may gain the whole world, but lose our souls (Matt. 16:26). However, when our hearts are ruled by an ever-deepening love relationship with God, our souls are nurtured to their intended wholeness in the image of Christ,[8] and our minds become the mind of Christ (1 Cor. 2:16).

The meaning of "soul" is complex. The Genesis account of creation says, "God breathed into his face the breath of life and Adam became a living soul" (Gen. 2:7).[9] Obviously the soul is the consequence of God's breath of life. It is the life of God within a person. The many references which link heart and soul,[10] especially those which refer to loving God, serving God, seeking God, or keeping God's word with "heart and soul,"[11] indicate that one's relationship with God is to involve both heart and soul. The soul, however, sins (Mic. 6:7), clings to the dust (Ps. 119:25),[12] needs to repent (1 Kings 8:48, 2 Chron. 6:38), is capable of being revived (Ps. 17:9, 23:3), but can also be lost (Matt. 16:26). The soul, too, thirsts for God (Ps. 42:2, 63:1, 84:2, 143:6). It would seem that soul reflects the nature of the heart's relationship with God.

We now have a revised perspective on spirituality. Every human is a spiritual being, living life in some state of relationship with God. Either God is the desire of their heart, or self-referenced desire is the god of their heart. The soul of every person, consequently, is in a process of development into either a more Christlike or a more non-Christlike being. This process becomes incarnate in the ways a person interacts with the world. Consequently, everything in life is a spiritual matter: every relationship, every situation, every circumstance, every action, every perceptual framework embraced, every value espoused, every behavior endorsed is the arena in which Christlikeness or non-Christlikeness is manifested. Paul seems to be pointing to this when he says, "Whatever you should do, work from the soul as to the Lord and not to men" (Col. 3:23).[13] One can engage life either from a God-referenced orientation or from a non-God-referenced orientation. *Both are spiritual orientations!* Consequently, there can be no dichotomy between spiritual and academic. The academy is simply one arena in which a person's spirituality is lived out.

If knowledge and vital piety are to be united, Christian faculty must learn to live into the world out of a heart ever more deeply rooted in the love of God (Eph. 3:17)—to live in a centeredness in God. Care must be taken lest "center" comes to be defined, as noted above, by a set of propositions to which one gives assent, a structure of dogma which one espouses, a collection of beliefs to which one adheres, or a body of theological tenets which one embraces. All these may point to the center, but are not themselves the center. The center is a deepening, growing, maturing love relationship with the living God at the core of one's being; or, in the words of the mothers and fathers of the Christian spiritual tradition, "mystical union" with God.

Ever since the Enlightenment with its deification of human reason, the mind has been presumed to be the center of human life. Descartes' "I think, therefore I am," expresses it succinctly. The reality of mystical experience, a norm for the Christian spiritual tradition until the Enlightenment, was largely rejected. Consequently, the mystics came to be seen as eccentrics on the fringes of Christianity. Mystical experience became highly suspect, especially in the academic realm, and Christian experience became primarily cognitive rather than affective. Jesus and the New Testament writers, however, make it clear that mystical experience is at the heart of the Christian life: "Abide in me as I abide in you" (John 15:4ff.); "The Spirit of truth . . . will be in you" (John 14:17); "You will know that I am in my Father, and you in me, and I in you" (John 14:20); "We [Jesus and the Father] will come to them and make our home with them" (John 14:23); "I pray . . . that you may be strengthened with power through his Spirit in your inner being, and that Christ may dwell in your hearts through faith . . . that you may be filled with all the fullness of God" (Eph. 3:16–19); "Your life is hid with Christ in God" (Col. 3:3). While one may theologize about these passages, Jesus and Paul are not theologizing; they are speaking of the mystery of God indwelling the believer and the believer indwelling God. Thomas Kelly puts it this way:

> Deep within us all there is an amazing inner sanctuary of the soul, a holy place, a Divine Center, a speaking Voice, to which we may continuously

return. . . . It is a Light Within which illumines the face of God and casts new shadows and new glories upon the face of men. . . . It is the Shekinah of the soul, the Presence in the midst. Here is the Slumbering Christ, stirring to be awakened, to become the soul we clothe in earthly form and action. And He is within us all.[14]

One must be careful not to equate mystical experience with a world-denying retreat into a privatized realm of subjective personal experience, especially in the academic setting. True mystical experience thrusts one into the world as a transformative means of God's presence and purpose. Again, Thomas Kelly: "We are torn loose from earthly attachments and ambitions—*contemptus mundi*. And we are quickened to a divine but painful concern for the world—*amor mundi*. He plucks the world out of our hearts, loosening the chains of attachment. And He hurls the world into our hearts, where we and He together carry it in infinitely tender love."[15] Thomas Merton expresses the same understanding of the role of mystical union with God: "The purpose of our life is to bring all our strivings and desires into the sanctuary of the inner self and place them all under the command of an inner and God-inspired consciousness."[16]

The Spiritual Formation of Faculty

How, then, do we come to live into the world out of a deep centeredness in God? Through an intentional and disciplined process of spiritual formation. It should be obvious by now that the task of a practicing Christian in the academy, or anywhere else for that matter, is to engage in a spiritual journey into God for the sake of the world. There are two inseparable issues here: the nature of this spiritual journey and its nurture.

The Nature of the Journey

The nature of the journey is a process of being conformed to the image of Christ for the sake of the world.[17] We are created to be Christlike. Paul indicates this in numerous ways. In describing Jesus, Paul says, "In him all the fullness of God was pleased to dwell" (Col. 1:19). In Ephesians 3:19, he prays, "that you may be filled with all the fullness of God." Also in Ephesians, Paul writes, "we are to grow up in every way into him who is the head, into Christ" (4:15). Two verses earlier he defined maturity as "the measure of the stature of the fullness of Christ" (4:13).

Peter has the same idea in 2 Peter 1:3–4:

His divine power has given us everything needed for life and godliness, through the knowledge of him who called us to his own glory and goodness. Thus he has given us, through these things, his precious and very great promises, so that through them, having escaped from the destructiveness that is in the world because of selfish desires, you may *become partakers of the divine nature.*

Where did Paul and Peter get this idea? Probably from Jesus. Look at Jesus' prayer for believers in John 17:20–23. After praying for the eleven disciples still with him, Jesus prays:

> I ask not only on behalf of these, but also on behalf of those who will believe in me through their word, that they may all be one. As you, Father, are in me and I am in you, may they also be in us, so that the world may believe that you have sent me. The glory that you have given me I have given them, so that they may be one, as we are one, I in them and you in me, that they may become completely one, so that the world may know that you have sent me and have loved them even as you have loved me.

Jesus prays that believers would be in the same relationship of loving union with God that he is.[18] He then frames this relationship in a deeper reality when he continues, "The glory that you have given me I have given them, so that they may be one, as we are one." What is the glory God gave Jesus? It was God's very nature: "The Word became flesh and dwelt among us, and we have seen his glory, glory as of the only begotten of the Father" (John 1:14). Jesus is indicating that he has made it possible for us to be restored to the image of God for which we were created (Gen. 1:27),[19] and what enables this is being one with God. Note that the purpose of this restoration to unity with God is "so that the world may believe/know that you have sent me." The union with God for which Jesus prays is to manifest itself in the way believers engage their world, characterized by process, conformity to Christ, and a missional orientation.

Process

A process is inherent here since the issue is a relationship, a love relationship. A relationship is a living, dynamic reality, not a static state. A relationship is either growing and deepening or it is weakening and dying. A love relationship is also freely engaged by both parties. The beloved is always free to say, "No," to the relationship; otherwise it is not a love relationship but a coerced relationship. God fervently nurtures a love relationship from his side; we must actively and daily commit ourselves to nurturing the relationship from our side.

Conformity to Christ

Nurturing any relationship necessitates change. In the case of our relationship with God, since we are not Christlike, it is obvious that what we are presently must give way to what we are to be—persons in the image of God. James Finley expresses it well:

> Merton leads us along the journey to God in which the self that begins the journey is not the self that arrives. The self that begins is the self that we thought ourselves to be. It is this self that dies along the way until in the end "no one" is left. This "no one" is our true self. . . . It is the self in God, the self bigger than death yet born of death. It is the self the Father forever loves.[20]

The crux is that we cannot conform ourselves to the image of Christ. This is God's work, not ours.[21] This is why Paul speaks repeatedly of "being saved," "being transformed," "being renewed"; and "be conformed," "be transformed," "be strengthened," "be filled," "be renewed."[22] Thus an essential part of the process is yielding ourselves to God, allowing him to regenerate us in his image.

As we noted above, we are created to be in the image of Christ. This is the image of our wholeness, the fulfillment of our being. This is not something that is "added on" from the outside by following a list of "do's and don'ts." Rather, it is engendered from within by the transforming work of God in us through the Holy Spirit. This means that where God will nurture our relationship with him most insistently is at the points of our unlikeness to Christ.

For the Sake of the World

Finally, the ultimate purpose of the journey is our missional orientation—that we may be in the world persons in whom God's transforming presence touches that world and those in it. We are to be those in whom God's resurrection power touches the deadness of the world, God's light illumines the darkness of the world, God's healing ministers to the woundedness of the world, God's wholeness meets the brokenness of the world, God's liberating power delivers people from the destructive and dehumanizing bondages of the world.

The Nurture of a Spiritual Journey

The nurture of one's spiritual journey is, at heart, the nurture of one's relationship with God. Since this is a love relationship, it is a dynamic, living, growing reality. The primary step in this relationship has already been taken by God: "We love because he first loved us" (1 John 4:19). The cruciform love of God manifested in the cross reveals that God maintains the love relationship from his side.[23] This is the ultimate meaning of grace as the unearned, undeserved, unwarranted love of God for us, even in our rejection of him and our usurpation of his place in our lives. God's love is neither punitive, nor retributive, nor vengeful; it is God's giving of himself to his human creature so as to make it possible for that person to be restored in a love relationship with God. Even before we awaken to such love, its light already shines in the darkness of our alienation from God, and the darkness has not overcome it.[24] As the mothers and fathers of the Christian spiritual tradition remind us, God indwells every person.[25]

Awakening

The first step, then, in the nurture of our spiritual journey is to awaken to the indwelling presence of God. Is not this what God urges when he says, "Seek me, and you will find me if you seek me with all your heart" (Jer. 29:13, cf. Deut. 4:29)? When we remember that "heart," in the Jewish context, is a referent to one's inner being, God is urging us to seek him where he is, in our inmost being. How, then, do we do this? We must, as God says, "Be still and know that I am God" (Ps. 46:10). The Hebrew term for "be still" (*harpū*) means to sink down, to let drop, to relax, to let go.[26] We must learn to still our mind, let go of our feelings, quiet the inner noise that constantly reverberates within us, and sink down into our inner being, into our heart. We come with no agenda, no wants, no needs. We come simply to "be" in God's presence. The Psalmist has a beautiful image for this: "I have set and silenced my soul like a weaned child upon its mother" (131:2). The weaned child, in contrast to the unweaned, is without agenda. It simply rests the whole of its being upon the mother and lets the mother be whatever she desires to be. Thomas Kelly states it well, "Eternity is at our hearts, pressing upon our time-worn lives, warming us with intimations of an astounding destiny, calling us home unto Itself. Yielding to these persuasions, gladly committing ourselves in body and soul, utterly and completely, to the Light Within, is the beginning of true life."[27] The primary and essential discipline of the spiritual journey, then, is to devote time each day to attentiveness to the indwelling presence of God, as well as finding moments throughout the day to recollect one's self in the Presence.

Beware! This is not quietism nor escapism nor a privatized, world-denying "navel gazing." As Isaiah discovered, awakening to the presence of the living God is a very dangerous experience (Isa. 6:1–6). Awakening to God is, at the same time, to be awakened to one's false self—that insidious, deeply entrenched structure of perspectives, values, and behaviors which have formed us as a pervasively self-referenced being rather than a radically God-referenced being.[28] It is to be awakened to our unlikeness to the image of Christ for which we were created and to which God is seeking to restore us.

Another means by which God awakens us to the condition of our being is Scripture. The Word has become text in Scripture, to provide a means of transforming encounter with God, so that the Word might become flesh in us for the world. We need a disciplined time daily to immerse ourselves in Scripture. Such immersion is not an exercise in information gathering, nor class preparation, nor sharpening up our theology—all of which have their place, but not here. The purpose of this immersion is to meet the living Word and to be shaped by the Word into God's image.[29]

Abandonment

Awakening to God and to our true state of being leads to the second step in the spiritual journey—abandonment. It is the triune process of confrontation, crucifixion, and consecration. The confrontation that comes with awakening to the non-Christlike dynamics of our being calls us to crucifixion: in Jesus' words, to deny our self and to take up our cross (Matt. 16:24). The denial Jesus calls for is not merely divesting ourselves of certain non-Christlike perspectives, values, and behaviors. It is the abandonment of the self-referenced being shaped by them and expressed through them. Again, in Jesus' words, it is "losing oneself for his sake" (Matt. 16:25). The depth of this abandonment is highlighted by Jesus' demand to "take up your cross." At this point in the Gospels, there has been no mention of Jesus' crucifixion.[30] However, the image would not have been lost on the disciples. In their Roman-dominated world, the cross was the symbol of utter dehumanization and marginalization, the loss of one's very being. Consequently, to deny one's self and take up one's cross both say the same thing. This is what Paul is affirming when he says, "I have been crucified with Christ, it is no longer I who live but Christ who lives in me" (Gal. 2:19–20). The "I" Paul mentions here is his false self, his "life in the flesh," which he has counted as "loss" in Philippians 3:7–8.

One means of crucifixion is to keep Jesus' question to Peter at the center as God confronts us with the non-Christlike aspects of our lives: "Do you love me more than these?" (John 21:15). The "these" is not the real focus, but the love. Whenever we love anything more than we love Jesus, that which we love, we love for self-referenced motives. The question takes us to the nature of the "self" that loves "these." Will we deny that self for his sake?

The confrontation that leads to crucifixion of the false self must be followed by consecration to God in Christ. The "life hid with Christ in God" (Col. 3:3) strips off the old self and clothes itself with the new self being renewed according to the image of its creator (Col. 3:9–10). This new Christ-referenced self must allow God to nurture Christ-referenced perspectives, values, and behaviors and to incarnate them in its life in the world.

Being in God for the World

The third step in the nurture of the spiritual journey is becoming a person whose life is "for the sake of others." Jesus' command to love God and our neighbor are not two separate things. Our relationship with God and our relationship with others are two dimensions of a single reality. The way we relate to others incarnates the way we relate to God. Jesus makes this unmistakably clear in his parable of the sheep and the goats (Matt. 25:31–46): "In as much as you did it for one of the least of these you did it for me . . . in as much as you did it not for one of the least of these you did it not for me."

John certainly realized this:

Whoever says, "I am in the light," while hating another person, is still in the darkness (1 John 2:9). We know that we have passed from death to life because we love one another. Whoever does not love abides in death. All who hate another are murderers, and you know that murderers do not have eternal life abiding in them (1 John 3:14–15). Beloved, let us love one another, because love is from God; everyone who loves is born of God and knows God. Whoever does not love does not know God, for God is love (1 John 4:7–8). No one has ever seen God; if we love one another, God lives in us, and his love is perfected in us (1 John 4:12). Those who say, "I love God," and hate others, are liars; for those who do not love others whom they have seen, cannot love God whom they have not seen. The commandment we have from him is this: those who love God must love others also (1 John 4:20–21).

The consequence of the spiritual journey is being in God for the world. Many are in the world for God, such as those of whom Jesus speaks in Matthew 7:22–23: "On that day many will say to me, 'Lord, Lord, did we not prophesy in your name, and cast out demons in your name, and do many deeds of power in your name?' Then I will declare to them, 'I never knew you; go away from me, you evildoers.'" To be in the world for God allows us to set the agenda, determine the schedule, and establish the parameters of the ministry. To be in God for the world is to live into the world out of a deep centeredness in our love relationship with God. To repeat Merton's words, "But the purpose of our life is to bring *all* our strivings and desires into the sanctuary of the inner self and place them all under the command of an inner and God-inspired consciousness."[31]

This places the role of a practicing Christian in the academy in a different frame of reference. Every practicing Christian is to live into her or his world out of this growing and deepening centeredness in God. The academy is simply one arena in which this is incarnated. Every professor brings to the academy a unique giftedness from God as well as training and experience in his or her field of study. These attributes, placed "under the command of an inner and God-inspired consciousness," serve as the means by which a professor manifests Christlikeness and integrates knowledge and vital piety. The primary responsibility of such a faculty member is to model for both peers and students how a life hid with Christ in God plays itself out in the academy. When such modeling awakens—in either students or peers—a hunger for such a life, then mentoring becomes the task.

An academic journey of spiritual formation, then, is a process of being conformed to the image of Christ for the world which a professor or student incarnates in his or her life in the academy.

Chapter 8 Notes

[1] "Practicing Christian" will be used in this chapter to denote one who has a vital, dynamic, and ever deepening love relationship with God, in Christ, animated by the Holy Spirit. Such a person is, in St. Paul's words, "growing up in every way into him who is the head, into Christ" (Ephesians 4:15), toward the goal of Christian maturity: "the measure of the stature of the fullness of Christ" (Ephesians 4:13).

[2] If it is not necessary, then the question of its possibility is moot.

[3] "Love relationship" here and throughout denotes an abandonment of one's self-referenced way of being in response to God's cruciform love, i.e. God's radical other-referenced-ness revealed in the cross. Cf. *supra* 4–5.

[4] *Infra*. 8.

[5] "...in its abstract meanings, 'heart' became the richest biblical term for the totality of man's inner or immaterial nature." (TWOT 1071a).

[6] Romans 5:8—"God demonstrates his own love for us in that *while we were still sinners* [italics added] Christ died for us."

[7] This catalog is adapted from Thomas Merton, *Contemplation in a World of Action* (Notre Dame, Ind.: University of Notre Dame Press, 1998), 114.

[8] "Once his image is formed in the soul, the person of Christ in return forms the soul and transforms it into his own type: 'It is no longer I that live, but Christ who lives in me.' In the end the soul appears really Christified." Paul Evdokimov, *The Struggle with God*, trans. Sister Gertrude, S. P., (Glen Rock, N.J.: Paulist Press, 1966), 165; "The soul, image and mirror of God, becomes the dwelling of God." Ibid., 216.

[9] In the Hebrew, God blew (*yippach*) and Adam became a soul (*nefesh*). *Yippach* means to blow or breathe (BDB 6228), *nefesh* is that which breathes (BDB 6251.1).

[10] Deuteronomy 4:29, 6:5, 10:12, 11:13, 18; 13:3, 26:16, 30:2, 6, 10.

[11] Loving: Deuteronomy 6:5, 13:3, 30:6; Serving: Deuteronomy 10:12, 11:13, Joshua 22:5, 1 Kings 2:4; Keeping: Deuteronomy 11:18, 26:16, 30:2, 30:10, 2 Kings 23:3, 2 Chronicles 34:31; Seeking: 2 Chronicles 15:12, Psalm 119:20, Lamentations 3:25.

[12] "Dust" denotes what is earthly, contrary to God, even death (Psalm 22:15, Isaiah 26:19, Daniel 12:2).

[13] Colossians 3:23.

[14] Thomas Kelly, *A Testament of Devotion* (San Francisco, Calif.: HarperCollins, 1992), 3.

[15] Ibid., 19–20.

[16] Thomas Merton, *The Inner Experience: Notes on Contemplation* (San Francisco, Calif.: HarperCollins, 2003), 92.

[17] For a more complete development of this theme, cf. M. Robert Mulholland Jr., *Invitation to a Journey: A Roadmap for Spiritual Formation* (Downers Grove, Ill.: InterVarsity Press, 1993), 15–44.

[18] "... that they all may be one. In exactly the same way you Father are in me and I am in you, may they also be in us ..." (John 17:21).

[19] Paul has this understanding: "For all have sinned and fallen short of the glory of God." (Romans 3:23), the clear implication being that we are created to be in the image of God.

[20] James Finley, *Merton's Palace of Nowhere: A Search for God through Awareness of the True Self* (Notre Dame, Ind.: Ave Maria Press, 1978), 21–22.

[21] Ephesians. 2:10, Philippians 2:13.

[22] 1 Corinthians 1:18, 15:2; 2 Corinthians 2:15, 3:18, 4:16; Colossians 3:10; Romans 8:29, 12:2; Ephesians 3:16, 3:19, 4:23.

[23] For deeper discussions on this cf. Michael J. Gorman, *Cruciformity: Paul's Narrative Spirituality of the Cross* (Grand Rapids, Mich.: Eerdmans, 2001); Richard Bauckham, *God Crucified: Monotheism and Christology in the New Testament* (Grand Rapids, Mich.: Eerdmans, 1999); Jürgen Moltmann, *The Crucified God: The Cross of Christ as the Foundation and Criticism of Christian Theology*, trans. R. A. Wilson and John Bowden (New York: Harper & Row, 1974). The cross is the ultimate definition of *agape* love—the total, non-self reflective giving of one's self for the wellbeing of another.

[24] John 1:5. In the Greek, the "shining" is a present and ongoing activity which the darkness has not (aorist) and, by implication, cannot overcome.

[25] "... our being somehow communicates directly with the Being of God, Who is 'in us.' If we enter into ourselves, find our true self, and then pass 'beyond' the inner 'I,' we sail forth into the immense darkness in which we confront the 'I AM' of the Almighty." Merton acknowledges, "there is an infinite metaphysical gulf between the being of God and the being of the soul, between the 'I' of the Almighty and our own inner 'I.' Yet, paradoxically our inmost 'I' exists in God and God dwells in it." Merton, *Inner Experience*, 11–12.

[26] TWOT 2198.

[27] Kelly, *Testament of Devotion*, 3

[28] For a full development consult M. Robert Mulholland, *The Deeper Journey: The Spirituality of Discovering Your True Self* (Downers Grove, Ill.: InterVarsity Press, 2006) or Albert Haase, *Coming Home to Your True Self* (Downers Grove, Ill.: InterVarsity Press, 2008).

[29] For the informational-transformational role of Scripture see, M. Robert Mulholland Jr., *Shaped by the Word: The Role of Scripture in Spiritual Formation* (Nashville, Tenn.: Upper Room Books, 1985, 2000). For the discipline of *Lectio Divina* as means of formation, see M. Robert Mulholland and Marjorie J. Thompson, *The Way of Scripture* (Nashville, Tenn.: Upper Room Books, 2010).

[30] The first mention is Matthew 20:19. In fact, this is the only of the passion predictions in the Gospels that mentions crucifixion. All the rest simply say Jesus will be killed (Matthew 16:21, 17:22–23; Mark 8:31, 9:31, 10:33–34; Luke 9:22, 18:33)

[31] Merton, *Inner Experience*, 91.

Implementation, Praxis, and Models

"ON THE LOOKOUT FOR WHAT WOULD BE REVEALED"

Faculty and Spiritual Formation

Keith Anderson

"Port William repaid watching. I was always on the lookout for what would be revealed."[1] So Wendell Berry introduces his stories about what he saw from his perch in the barbershop in the fictional small town in Kentucky. It is also a picture of centuries of Christian spirituality that started with Jesus' words, "He who has eyes to see, let him see."[2] Spirituality is learning to pay attention to the presence of God in everything. Our teachers of the past have always taught us to watch and to see.

As a college student in the late sixties, I too learned to watch: faculty, staff, other students, administrators, Founder's Week speakers, residence life staff, local pastors, and artists who came to our Christian college campus. Those were the golden years for faculty involvement in spiritual formation, some would say. In those days, campus ministry was not a profession—my campus pastor was a literature professor who led chapels—and spiritual formation was something Catholics did, not evangelicals in the Midwest. But those years were formative and transformative for me. I have often reflected on how that happened without highly developed programs for spiritual formation. It happened because of faculty. "Doc" Dalton was one of those professors who loved students, his academic discipline of history, and more than anything else, teaching.

- He taught me to look out "for what would be revealed" in the study of the human story.

- He taught me to critique what others said was most important and true, thus teaching me to critique the very profession he loved most.
- And, he taught me to see there is no line of demarcation between the sacred and the secular, between the disciplines of academics and the spiritual practices of those who follow and love Jesus.

As a seminary student I was privileged to be mentored by a homiletics professor, then himself a preacher of excellence, a skilled teacher, and an honest and authentic student of the human condition. We met weekly and he introduced me to the life of Harry Emerson Fosdick, a liberal preacher of the 1920s who, among other notable things, experienced a nervous breakdown in his early professional life. It was a failure of the human spirit that, he would say, led him to an authentic encounter with the gospel because he desperately needed what he preached to others. His was a search for an authentic faith that could bring coherence to a broken and fractured spirit. My professor shocked me one day when he told me that prayer was something one should practice out of need and not simply something one should do out of habit. "If it brings coherence to life, then it will emerge out of your need; if not you should wait until you do." We spent three years talking about what that might mean for me and for my ministry.

The Importance of Academic Pursuits and Attention to Spirituality

The days of faculty in the 1960s sound anachronistic and dated, almost sentimental. Today faculty feel they must be engaged in greater academic rigor, more intellectual pursuits, publishing, accreditation, cultural diversity, and academic governance. Christian universities have found greater credibility in the guild of the academy than their earlier colleagues, and faculty must take their place at the table of scholarship in new ways.

My own foray into academe as a profession came with a fortuitous contract—half time in the classroom and half time as campus pastor. I taught biblical studies and theology, and tried to balance my academic load with preaching in weekly chapels, leading small groups, and pastoring a small campus community in the prairies of South Dakota. I was proud when our faculty elected me as faculty chair—my introduction to academic administration that later led to a new post as academic dean and now as the president of the Seattle School of Theology and Psychology. I started out in academic life with vibrant living mentors who somehow embodied something of the living integration of faith, academic disciplines, and life. I now take my turn as a leader who longs for faculty to engage the spirituality of students.

Looking back on my work over the years, I did not intend to spend so much time in the academy. As a first-year college student I was a member of the "major of the month" club and moved quickly from Speech to English to Business to History as my academic abilities were revealed for their weaknesses. Then it happened, and I can remember the moment for it shines as a vivid memory from yesterday and not from forty-three years ago. Dr. Garth Rosell stood in a class teaching us about an early American figure named Tituba, a woman in Massachusetts during what we now know as the Salem witch trials. She was a seventeenth-century slave accused of practicing witchcraft in Salem by two women, Betty Pariss and Abigail Williams. As Dr. Rosell taught, the lights came on and an uncontrollable joy was revealed to me that day: These people and their stories are relevant to people in 1968! Since that moment, I have never tired of learning the stories of others—through my continuing study of history or in conversation with the students whom I have known over my years as professor and campus pastor.

I am convinced that education requires attention to spirituality. In the world of educational thought we live in a kingdom with two competing monarchs, one of reason and one of faith. The reign of reason is demanded today by an academic system that is held tightly in the grips of rationalism, objective and technical thinking, and what some describe as the life of the mind. In Christian education there is another competitor for the throne, namely faith, or what we might call the life of the spirit. We are faced constantly with these familiar dichotomies: faith and reason, belief and intellect, trusting and thinking, heart and mind.

The Contributions of Clement

In an early church document, Clement of Alexandria speaks of education, learning, and the role of the teacher. Clement's treatise takes a harmonizing turn, for he would have us walk freely between the competing polarities of academics and spiritual teaching. For him, faith is aided by intellectual understanding. There is no dualism of reason *versus* faith, belief *versus* intellect, or heart *versus* mind. He understands that students walk freely and interactively between their roles as academics and their lives as people of faith.

Throughout his writings Clement speaks of Christ—the Word—as Educator and Heavenly Guide. For him, "Christ" and "education" are used almost synonymously: "Let us call him, then by one title: Educator of little ones, an Educator who does not simply follow behind, but who leads the way, for his aim is to improve the

143

soul, not just to instruct it; to guide to a life of virtue, not merely to one of knowledge."[3] Clement affirms a dialectical relationship between faith and reason, noting that habits, deeds, and passions are but one:

> For, be it noted, there are these three things in man: habits, deeds, and passions. Of these, habits come under the influence of the word of persuasion, the guide to godliness. This is the word that underlies and supports, like the keel of a ship, the whole structure of the faith. Under its spell, we surrender, even cheerfully, our old ideas, become young again to gain salvation, and sing in the inspired words of the psalm: "How good is God to Israel, to those who are upright of heart. As for deeds, they are affected by the word of counsel, and passions are healed by that of consolation."
>
> These three words, however, are but one: the self-same Word who forcibly draws men [and women] from their natural, worldly way of life and educates them to the only true salvation: faith in God.[4]

His understanding of the person calls us from the seduction of the multi-versity to a uni-versity. Such a noble *vocatio* is in short supply in the world of academe today. In too many places, academic life is a bastion of competitive individualism. In the secular university and the Christian college alike, the task of higher education seems to focus on dissecting the world of the student into discrete and disparate pieces. We are good at this task. We are less effective when it comes to an integration or "re-membering" of these now-separated parts. Over the years, many students have come to my office to discuss the issues raised in the vacuum of the classroom. These students seem to know intuitively that there is an ecological connection between the material in the classroom and their lives of faith, but are not sure that their professors have noticed the connections. Clement's vision is that faith and intellectual reasoning are inter-connected, which supports an argument for the generative work in the spirituality of education.

Clement caught on early to the truth that we take as axiomatic today, namely that "all truth is God's truth." He states, "Now, if there is, as the Scripture says, but 'one teacher, in heaven,' then, surely, all who are on earth can with good reason be called disciples. The plain truth is that which is perfect belongs to the Lord, who is ever teaching, while the role of child and little one belongs to us, who are ever learning. . . ."[5] Clement makes an important contribution to our pedagogy as educators in the distinction he draws between teaching and education. Teaching, in Clement's view, has to do with concrete instruction, with education, with wisdom. What is the task of the teacher? He says, "his [and her] aim is to improve the soul, not just to instruct; to guide to a life of virtue, not merely to one of knowledge. . . . As Teacher, he explains and reveals through instruction, but as Educator he [or she] is practical."[6] Later he adds, "There can be no doubt that we also call the most excellent and perfect possessions in life by names derived from the word 'child,' that is, education and culture. We define education as a sound training from childhood in the path of virtue."[7]

And so it begins. The debate rages between spirituality and scholarship: faculty as spiritual guides or faculty as scholars, Christian universities as centers for education or centers for spiritual training. It is fair to say that, in general, academics do not believe spirituality is a necessary part of academic life. In the major study, "Spirituality in Higher Education: National Study of College Students Search for Meaning and Purpose," Alexander and Helen Astin observe that only three out of ten agree that "colleges should be concerned with facilitating students' spiritual development."[8] Our work with colleges of the CCCU, however, brings a different conclusion. After more than thirty spiritual formation program assessments at CCCU schools across denominational and geographical lines, we find a common commitment from Christian faculty to the spiritual mission of their school. The issues in play relate more to time and role rather than mission. So it causes us to ask in this chapter, What is the role Christian college faculty play in the spiritual development of their students? Is this an added burden to over-busy faculty? As serious academics, how can faculty engage in the spiritual life of a school when they are already focused on an academic discipline?

Five Essential Paradigms

What I offer in the remaining pages of this chapter is a reflection on how faculty members can play in the street—in the intersections between academics and spirituality. It is a call for the next generation of educators who are rigorously academic and bold people of faith. I propose the following five paradigms as essential for educators tasked with the academic and spiritual integration of their students:

1. Educators who understand the spiritual nature of teaching and learning
2. Educators who remain committed to the journey of transformation, including their own
3. Educators who think and see the "whole" picture
4. Educators who love God through the very discipline they practice
5. Educators who practice the humility to be apprenticed

1. Educators who understand the spiritual nature of teaching and learning

T. S. Eliot said that education is about the deepest questions of life and the world.[9] Questions such as, What is man (humankind) and what is man (humankind) for? These are questions of the human spirit, of community, of the search to understand and engage the sacred, and of the soul. Catholic educator Thomas Groome said, "surely all education should engage the deep heart's core of people—teachers and students—and change them in life-giving ways. At its best, education invites toward new horizons, to life-long growth, to reach beyond ourselves; in sum, it fosters the human desire for the Transcendent."[10] He added:

> That education is a spiritual affair is not a new notion. Indeed, this is the better understanding that has endured throughout the history of Western civilization. Some 2,500 years ago, Plato described the function of the teacher as 'to turn the soul' of students toward the true, the good, and the beautiful. Augustine, writing circa 400 C.E., said that the teacher's function is to engage 'the teacher within' each person, and he meant the divine presence at the core of people—their very soul.[11]

All of education is inherently sacred, which means it is inherently integrated. Parker Palmer speaks of the disintegration of academe:

> One of the greatest sins in education is reductionism, the destruction of that precious otherness by cramming everything into categories that we find comfortable, ignoring data, ignoring writers, ignoring voices, ignoring information, ignoring simple facts that don't fit into our shoebox, because we don't have a respect for otherness. We have a fear of otherness that comes from having flattened the terrain and desacralized it. A people who know the sacred know otherness, and we don't know that anymore. We have flattened our landscape. My image of this objectivist landscape in higher education is that it is so flat, so lacking in variety, so utterly banal that anything that pops up and takes us by surprise is instantly defined as a threat. . . . The sacred landscape has hills and valleys, mountains and streams, forests and deserts, and is a place where surprise is our constant companion and surprise is an intellectual virtue beyond all telling. . . . [12]

2. Educators who remain committed to the journey of transformation, including their own

Students today hunger for authentic ways of knowing, including ways of knowing God. Most of us are hungry to know God in the grit of life. One of my colleagues has said often, "You can't pass on what you yourself have never experienced." What if that is true? What if I cannot pass on to others what it means to know God in all of life, including my own profession or discipline? It means that I will spend my life as a "detective of divinity"[13] as Barbara Brown Taylor has said—one who is on the lookout for what may be revealed, including my own transformation.

We would do well to remember the developmental context in which our students live. If your life is spent as a professor, then the work of spiritual formation starts with your realization that your students are people in process, not people in hardened cement. A man I consider a mentor, Dr. James Houston, said to me once that the role of Christian higher education is the development of human persons—not the development of the individual, as American as that might be, but the development of *persons* in relationship with others.

Students desire to hear professors tell stories from their own journey of transformation: stories of family or singleness, of success and failure, of joy and sorrow, and to know them in the authenticity of their own pilgrimage. The shock of being introduced to a brilliant young pastor whose nervous breakdown opened the journey to the gospel was beyond the pale of my own experience as a young seminarian. But the failure, the finitude, and the human flaws of this young pastor would provide a place of comfort and hope for me in my own times of darkness, failure, and finitude. Of course, there are boundaries to be built but we are better at boundaries in education than we are at vulnerability. How do professors make their own stories accessible to their students? The answer is far less important than the question.

I work now in a building that was built as a fish processing plant in the early 1900s in Seattle. It was then called "Railroad Avenue" because the tracks sat right out the back door of the Chlopeck Fishing Company, and Elliott Bay washed up underneath the tracks and almost to the back door of the building. Across the street is now a high-end hotel, The Edgewater, a place where the Beatles once stayed as they fished from their windows in the salty waters of Puget Sound. For a while that building was also a manufacturing plant for the Skyway Luggage Company. When we took over the building, the floors were blackened and beat up by over one hundred years of life and living. A wise decision was made: they sandblasted the original floors and left them in place—flawed, knicked, marred, imperfect, and beautiful. The imperfections reflect the journey of each student and teacher in that place of learning. In theology we speak of the *Imago Dei*—the image of God in each person—created, fallen, redeemed, and given a calling. Perhaps the greatest role we can play as teachers is to understand the classroom as a table for hospitality, curiosity, and respect. In the way we approach the sacred task of teaching, we can be those who merely listen as a pedagogical gimmick or for the sake of the learner. We all know the former: you listen only enough to move the class to your own conclusion. The latter is a way of listening that allows students the freedom to discover their own conclusions. Such listening gives life through the teacher-learner's curiosity, respect, and hospitality. Gabriel Moran writes that ultimately, "to teach is to show someone how to live and to die."[14]

3. Educators who think and see the whole picture

In the academy, perhaps the most damaging dynamic is that of compartmentalization. As the academic departments and disciplines remain separated and compartmentalized from each other, the education of their students becomes an exercise in taking their world apart rather than in synthesis and analysis. In his book *We Scholars: Changing the Culture of the University*, David Damrosch assesses the state of scholarship in the academy and concludes that specialization and the individualistic bent of graduate education shapes us into an isomorphic style of teaching and working. He calls us, instead, to a collaborative community which is more personally reflective and attentive to style, concluding, "A university department is not so much of a joint stock corporation after all, but more like a record label, whose performers do an occasional concert together to promote their own individual albums."[15]

The monastic worldview is helpful to me as I think about education in this present era. Monks believe in bringing together the powerful spheres of life: prayer and learning, spirituality and education, piety and work. It is the integration that some call an integration of liturgy, learning, and living. These are necessary intersections in the lives of students. Integration of faith and learning is a profound way of saying that biblical faith is an integral part to all of life. It was Charles Wesley whose pre-Civil War hymn "Sanctified Knowledge" includes the line, "O to unite the two so long disjoined, knowledge and vital piety."

My vision for education is that we set the table for conversations in the middle of the street—where intersections abound rather than in the places of the cul de sacs of compartmentalized, esoteric knowledge. I suppose we feel compelled to that only if we have a theology that is truly incarnational, which brings together spirit and body, mind and heart, the physical and the spiritual. Could it be that we prefer the Gnosticism of the early centuries which separated the world into polarities of opposites and confined knowing to certain esoteric information available only to those initiated in a special form of education?

In *Christ Plays in Ten Thousand Places,* Eugene Peterson makes the case graphically to see the world whole:

> The end of all Christian belief and obedience, witness and teaching, marriage and family, leisure and work life, preaching and pastoral work is the living of everything we know about God: life, life, and more life. If we don't know where we are going, any road will get us there. But if we have a destination—in this case a life lived to the glory of God—there is a well-marked way, the Jesus-revealed Way. Spiritual theology is the attention that we give to the details of living life in this way. It is a protest against theology depersonalized into information about God; it is a protest against theology functionalized into a program of strategic planning for God.[16]

One of my graduate school professors taught me that the most political thing a teacher does is to create the syllabus. In the syllabus, you decide what questions will be asked. You determine which voices will be heard and which will be excluded. You decide the parameters for the group experiences of learning. That is what we think happens. Thankfully, after twenty-seven years of teaching, I know that the learner also brings her own questions, creates his own space for wondering, and the Holy Spirit intervenes to bring additional insights, questions, information, formation, and transformation. I do not take my role as the teacher as one who imparts something to receptors who simply receive. Something more is going on than what I bring to the classroom.

There must always be humility as we enter the sacred space of the classroom. There is more at work in the mystery of teaching and learning than any of us can know. It is hubris of the worst kind to assume that what happens in your classroom is in a purely causal way related to what you do in the classroom. We would do well to see the classroom experience in the way our ancient human family saw the fire— as a gathering place for stories and teaching the next generation. Stories were told; questions were asked. It was a time for laughter and for gravitas. They were on the lookout for what would be revealed.

The best teachers I ever had somehow knew themselves to be teachers in that same way. They did not see themselves as pastors or student development professionals but as pilgrims on a journey with wisdom. I did not have language for it then, but I do now thanks to Parker Palmer, who says that good teachers know about the grace of great things.[17] Was Doc Dalton less of a historian because he taught boldly what had been revealed to him? I give witness and say no. The great cloud of witnesses I will honor always are those who stood in the place between and refused the compromise of choosing one over the other. It takes courage to stand between—it feels like a sellout to the guild; but wisdom learning takes place in the trembling space between—between sacred and secular, spirit and body, academics and faith. Garth Rosell, Dwight Jessup, Roy Dalton, G. W. Carlson, Dan Erwin, Thomas Groome, Mary Boys, Eugene Peterson, Henri Nouwen, Brennan Manning, and Sharon Daloz Parks—these are just some who taught me to see the world as a whole.

4. Educators who love God through the very discipline they practice

It is not enough for Christian faculty to love their discipline. To acknowledge God as maker of heaven and earth is to see the teaching task as sacramental, a way to see through to the deep thing within. I honor the ones who love God precisely by the love of the discipline they practice. I have been generously treated to faculty who live and love in that way.

Even though he has spent the majority of his academic life as a dean and university president, Dave Brandt is still moved by the mystery of God's transforming love in the world of physics. Be careful when you are with him because even now, forty years later, his eyes glow and his heart pounds as he talks about laws of the universe. What a gift he must have been as a young physicist who dared to believe that physics matters! And what a gift is every professor whose love for their discipline is captured by their students. God transforms the world through physics; I believe that. God transforms the world through the arts; I know that. God's transforming love is found in the academic work that can become commonplace on every campus—literature, history, sociology, the natural sciences, the social sciences, anthropology, business, and everything in between. Palmer states:

> We say that knowing begins in our intrigue about some subject, but that intrigue is the result of the subject's actions upon us: geologists are people who hear rocks speak, historians are people who hear the voices of the long dead, writers are people who hear the music of words. The things of the world call to us, and we are drawn to them—each of us to different things, as each is drawn to different friends.[18]

How does a professor love God through his or her discipline? By remaining an excellent scholar, committed to the study of the discipline, committed to serious work on serious matters, but with the bold faith to see and name where God is revealed.

The difference for Christian faculty is what Arthur Holmes immortalized so clearly long ago: "All truth is God's truth wherever it is found." But he was not the first to say it. In 1942 Jacques Maritain made the same case from his reading of earlier history and philosophy:

> Education ought to teach us how to be in love always and what to be in love with. The great things of history have been done by the great lovers, by the saints and men of science and artists; and the problem of civilization is to give every man a chance of being a saint, a man of science, or an artist. But this problem cannot be attempted, much less solved, unless men desire to be saints, men of science, and artists, and if they are to desire that continuously and consciously, they must be taught what it means to be these things.[19]

5. Educators who practice the humility to be apprenticed

Much is made of the faculty member's role as guide, mentor, teacher, and professor, but Jesus reverses the emphasis and insists on an imitative, submissive practice of trusting apprenticeship. "Follow me," he said, and seemed to mean it not only in a physical sense, but in a comprehensive sense—"do what you see me do in the way that you see me do it." The spiritual leadership of Jesus does not concentrate on leading as much as on following. Parker Palmer reflects on the daily work of the teacher:

> Each time I walk into a classroom, I can choose the place within myself from which my teaching will come, just as I can choose the place within my students toward which my teaching will be aimed. I need not teach from a fearful place: I can teach from curiosity or hope or empathy or honesty, places that are as real within me as my fears.[20]

James Houston calls this kind of listening "recursion," a listening that is deep and responsive.[21] He once told me that one of the most important things Jesus did was listen to people in such a way that they discovered the image of God within themselves.

Conclusion

Great teachers are discovered by the community rather than self-proclaimed. I have taught with many of those folks—people recognized by others for their giftedness as teachers. And I have known more than a few who were not, but were rather self-proclaimed educators. The greatest threat to faculty is to fly solo—to believe that you are uniquely qualified and therefore uniquely and singularly a gift to your campus. Cowell College in California aspires to a motto that says, "The pursuit of truth in the company of friends."

What if Christian faculty give to students the very things they teach? Hospitality, curiosity, and respect for the other? And what if faculty found the way to do the same with each other? One of the painful observations I make is that many Christian faculty are lonely, isolated people who feel marginalized in their own departments or campuses. The scholar, alone in research and study, is a myth we must explode. We are called by the very nature of learning into community with one another—faculty and students. We are called to the disciplines of hospitality, curiosity, and respect.

Chapter 9 Notes

[1] Wendell Berry, *Jayber Crow: The Life Story of Jayber Crow, Barber, Of the Port William Membership, As Written by Himself* (Washington, D.C.: Counterpoint, 2000).

[2] Cf. Matthew 13:15–17; Mark 8:18.

[3] Clement of Alexandria, *Christ the Educator*, trans. by Simon P. Wood, C.P., vol. 23, *The Fathers of the Church: A New Translation* (Washington, D.C: The Catholic University of America Press, 1954).

[4] Ibid., (I:1, p.3).

[5] Ibid., (I:17, p. 18).

[6] Ibid., (I:2, p. 4).

[7] Ibid., (I:16, p. 17).

[8] Higher Education Research Institute, "Strong Majority of College and University Faculty Identify Themselves as Spiritual," news release, February 26, 2006, http://spirituality.ucla.edu/docs/news/faculty_report_release.pdf.

[9] T. S. Eliot, "The Aims of Education," in *To Criticize a Critic* (New York: Farrar, Straus & Giroux, 1965), 75–76, quotes in Steve Garber, *The Fabric of Faithfulness: Weaving Together Belief & Behavior During the University Years* (Downers Grove, Ill: InterVarsity Press, 1996), 82.

[10] Thomas Groome, "Spirituality to Education and Education to Spirituality," www.relgiouseducation.net/reach/thomas_groome.htm [Accessed 28 April 2002].

[11] Ibid.

[12] Parker Palmer, "The Grace of Great Things: Recovering the Sacred in Knowing, Teaching, and Learning," (keynote address, Spirituality in Education Conference, The Naropa Institute, May 1997), accessed April 29, 2002, http://csf.colorado.edu/sine/trans.html. An

adaption of Palmer's address is available at http://www.couragerenewal.org/parker/writings/grace-great-things.

[13] Barbara Brown Taylor, *The Preaching Life* (Cambridge, Mass.: Cowley Publications, 1993), 15.

[14] Maria Harris and Gabriel Moran, *Reshaping Religious Education: Conversations on Contemporary Practice* (Louisville, Ky.: Westminster John Knox Press, 1998), 32.

[15] David Damrosch, *We Scholars: Changing the Culture of the University* (Cambridge, Mass.: Harvard University Press, 1995).

[16] Eugene Peterson, *Christ Plays in Ten Thousand Places* (Grand Rapids, Mich.: Eerdmans, 2005), 1.

[17] Parker Palmer, *The Courage to Teach* (San Francisco, Calif: Jossey-Bass, 1998), 107.

[18] Ibid., 105.

[19] Jacques Maritain, *Education at the Crossroads* (New Haven, Conn.: Yale University Press, 1943), 23–24.

[20] Palmer, *Courage to Teach*, 57.

[21] James Houston, The Eastbourne Conference on Discipleship, Eastbourne, England, 1999.

CONVERSATION CREATES CULTURE
Student Development and Spiritual Formation in the Christian University

Susan Reese

It was a summer ritual. I was one of several college students who would gather at the local B&G Milky Way for a chocolate chip banana malt and conversations about summer jobs and life. While working as a summer representative for my Christian college, I attended Christian camps, serving as a counselor, worship leader, recreation director or whatever else was needed to ensure a quality camp experience. This summer job confronted me with questions of who God was, who I was, and what God had for my future. I recall a significant "B&G" conversation during which I stated, "I just don't know what God has for my life." Fortunately, a mentor of mine was present and after asking a few questions and listening with a sincere heart, my mentor's response was, "Never underestimate the high call of God on your life." His response sounded impressive but left me feeling a bit lost. But, because of who he was and what his life meant to my peers and me, I trusted his words. This mentor did not drive my question of vocation to a conclusion nor mislead me with some superficially optimistic response. He simply received my question as a holy listener and encouraged me to listen for the call of God. He also reminded me of Ephesians 4:15–16: "Instead, speaking the truth in love, we will in all things grow up into him who is the Head, that is, Christ. From him the whole body, joined and held together by every supporting ligament, grows and builds itself up in love, as each part does its work."

The promise of this passage meant two things to me. First, my mentor was willing to speak the truth in love by teaching me to wait on the Lord for who I was becoming and what the Lord would require of me. Second, this passage reminded me that life in Christ is a process and I would eventually fulfill my role in the body of Christ. The mentor I write of was a student development professional who knew my story and was willing to notice me and what God was doing in my life. I left the conversation having enjoyed a tasty malt and reassured that my life trajectory would be revealed in time.

The Role of the Student Development Professional

Student development professionals have a unique calling and daily opportunities to notice and enter into the conversations of students in their midst. Student development staffs have been referred to as the heart of the early warning system and the safety nets that assist students through academic, social, emotional, and physical difficulties.[1] The student development staff is the support system that encourages students to take responsibility, take risks, and learn about themselves in relationship to God and to those different from themselves. Typically, student development professionals are the institutional agents expected to deal with students' out-of-class lives.[2] It is my observation that the expectation of student development professionals to be engaged in the spiritual life of students has greatly increased over the past twenty years. Unfortunately, the administrative workload has not been reduced or job descriptions redesigned in order for the professionals to give additional time and attention to the spiritual life of students. Nonetheless, student development professionals' engagement in the spiritual lives of students has permeated higher education.

From the beginning, American colleges have given attention to more than the mind: "The early American college did not doubt its responsibility to educate the whole person—body, mind, and spirit; head, hearts and hands. Classroom, chapel, dormitory, playing field—all these areas of college life were thought of as connected."[3] Later on, individuals such as Thomas Arkle Clark, appointed dean of men at the University of Illinois in 1901, and Evelyn Wright Allen, appointed dean of women at Stanford in 1910, were pioneers in the emerging profession then known as student personnel work. For these two groundbreaking professionals, there was no coherent institutional philosophy or purpose to guide their work. Clark said, "I had no specific duties, no specific authority, no precedence either to guide me or to handicap me. . . . My only charge was that of the action of the Board of Trustees which said I was to interest myself in the individual student."[4] Thus the professionals were left to decide for themselves how to handle the student service functions of their time. They, along with many others, helped shape the events that led to the publication of *The Student Personnel Point of View*. This pioneering document is credited with giving the profession its soul.[5]

The Student Personnel Point of View document defined the essential nature of the student personnel profession. This statement of 1937, and the 1949 revision, imposed on colleges and universities an obligation to consider each student as a whole person and to conceive of education as including attention to physical, social, emotional, and spiritual development, as well as intellectual development.[6] The principles of the profession have withstood the test of time and have guided the profession through many cultural and societal changes. Komives, Woodard, and Associates, in *Student Services: A Handbook for the Profession*, stated:

> When implemented, this belief is a powerful tonic for the academic mission of an institution. It is why no institution would organize the collegiate experience so that only the cognitive development of students received attention. Just as it is important for there to be activities that develop the intellect, so too must there be activities to help students mature in other areas of their lives as means to promote intellectual development.[7]

Certainly, a defined role of the student development professional is difficult to describe. However, common themes have evolved with regard to the purpose of the student development professional and, more importantly, an urgency to define the role for the future. Again, *Student Services* is instructive: "Specifically, student affairs staff need to identify generational trends that will affect traditional-age students, set new priorities indicated by changing demographics, and help students prepare for a complex world."[8] Student development professionals are expected to lead their campuses in understanding the changing needs of students and are typically held accountable for articulating and responding to students' out-of-class needs, in collaboration with faculty and others. These professional staff should be able to appreciate, design, and implement the ways in which out-of-class environments and events influence student learning, as well as the institutional mission.

Consider the role of the student development professionals on your campus. Do their job descriptions address the development of the whole person? Do they allow space for conversations regarding spiritual formation? Katherine Houghton's dissertation entitled *Application of Christian Faith Development Theories by the Chief Student Affairs Officers of the Christian College Coalition*[9] revealed that the CCCU deans/directors of residence life and the directors of leadership development/student activities surveyed were intentionally fostering the spiritual development of younger college students, therefore supporting the mission, goals, and purposes of the institutions. Respondents to Houghton's survey firmly agreed that the students who were active in spiritual formation programs tended to be growing and mature Christians. Conversations regarding spiritual formation were happening in the dining hall, student leadership training, judicial processes, co-curricular activities, and so on. As student development professionals, it is important to start these conversations and ask of students "What's the story?"

A life-long mentor of mine served on the board of trustee's student development committee of the university in which I served as director of admissions. In meeting this trustee it would not take long for him to ask, "What's the story?" It also would not take long before one would tell him their story! This trustee knew how to ask soul-searching questions which would shape the conversation around paying attention to God in the midst of the conversation. As a trustee, he reminded the student development committee that if we focused on relationships the rest of the work would take care of itself. He blessed us with the insight to live our jobs as ministry to one another and to the students.

In *Big Questions, Worthy Dreams*, Sharon Park Daloz writes of being present to students as they embrace the shipwrecks or the dark nights of their lives. She contends that we experience life and growth through encounters with one another and through a community of mentoring. Student development professionals have the wherewithal to create conversations which create a culture of spiritual formation through encounters with one another and through establishing a community of mentoring. Often these conversations happen in a place along the way to another place. As Marie Loewen writes in *Conversations*, "People will walk into our lives for a time, find something here that draws them closer to God, and then continue on with the trajectory of their own journey towards God altered in some way."[10] Student development professionals are the "place along the way" for the students who are navigating their way through the landscape of learning. Student development professionals find themselves in conversations where God-given hopes and dreams are shared, as well as the sufferings of this earthly life. These conversations invite us as companions on the spiritual journey that students seek out to make sense of life and to listen to the movement of the Spirit. We will need to invite each other to "be still" in this place along the way—to enter into the spiritual journey more deeply, to accept the gift of seeing the old in a new way.

The Spiritual Life of the Student Development Professional

"May I have a moment?" What happens in your heart, soul, and mind when someone asks this question? An invitation to embrace the moment? A sense of anxiety? A deep sigh? A sense of irritation? Perhaps when you are asked this question you can conjure up a compassionate look and a courteous verbal response while your physical being and soul drops within you. My vocational journey has led me to teaching in a seminary. I am concerned and at times deeply grieved by the overall state of the souls of Christian leaders. Perhaps we have bumped into our fears, arrogance, and pride long enough to realize that the good works of ministry can lead us to a chaotic way of living.

In *Strengthening the Soul of Your Leadership,* Ruth Haley Barton invites us to consider the rhythm of life, the state of our souls, and our understanding of God. Barton's life story depicts the busyness of ministry, the demands of everyday life, the ongoing commitment to fix others or assume they can be fixed, and the unexamined inner dynamics of the life of a leader. How might you answer this question? "What would it be like to find God in the context of my leadership rather than miss God in the context of my leadership?"[11] Barton acknowledges that many have found success in ministry but may have missed finding God in the context of leadership. She compares the life themes in the story of Moses alongside her own journey and helps us identify with the life-long struggles and the joys of rediscovering God, ourselves, and our calling. She writes, "Moses . . . got a glimpse of the dark thing that had been lurking under the surface of his consciousness and was starting to surface so powerfully. That one glimpse of the destructive power of his raw and unrefined leadership was so frightening to Moses that he fled into solitude."[12] Moses may have thought he was fleeing from his responsibilities and his identity. The unique twist in his story is that his entry into solitude was the beginning of the transforming work of his soul. It was in this time of solitude that he gained spiritual awareness, family, and friendship. Jethro became the God-given mentor needed for this season of Moses' life. He was the best guide for Moses' journey due to his life experience. Barton's book reminds me that many who are seeking God in the crucible of life and ministry are attempting to live it alone. Barton emphasized that those who came alongside Moses helped shape his calling and the realization of his ministry. Who is coming alongside you? Who is the person(s) who invites you to the conversation of your soul?

Barton invites us to a new normal: "In a culture of spiritual transformation it becomes normative to take time for breathing, for prayer, for quiet at the beginning of important meetings and at important junctures during any meeting. It becomes normal for staff people to have a solitude day each month . . . to take vacation time and to be completely unplugged . . . to take Sabbath."[13] A new way of experiencing culture and conversations sets before us the art of spiritual formation rather than the tasks of ministry. It reveals ways of *being* in community and allowing our *doing* to flow out of our being. These words—our doing flows from our being—invite us to move from isolation in leadership to implementing best practices of living within a leadership community which engages conversations about spiritual formation and transformation. This type of community invites participants to weave spiritual practices into everyday life and receive the gifts of pause . . . breathe . . . read . . . reflect . . . listen . . . respond.

The Ministry of Student Development

In *Student Affairs Reconsidered,* David Guthrie reminds those in student development that the work is purposeful. He suggests that a Christian perspective of student learning requires moving away from rote fulfillment of the typical functions of the profession. Instead, he favors investigating more integrated approaches to organizing and executing student learning initiatives and procedures while not ignoring particular tasks that still must occur. The question on the table is how does one accomplish the administrative demands and relational components of the student development positions? Guthrie writes, "The efforts of student affairs staff in a Christian college must occur within the framework of wisdom-focused student learning that is shaped by a Christian view of reality."[14] Here lies the tension in the context of higher education.

There is minimal time, space, or conversation focusing on the connection of the whole person which is a crucial element in spiritual formation and wisdom-focused student learning. College students are in the crucible of knowing God even when they are unable to give words to this journey. The research conducted in higher education acknowledges that college students are on a spiritual quest or journey that is not yet completed. Students are seeking mentors and conversations to decipher their beliefs. Our role is to enter that conversation and ask, "What is God already doing here?" In *The Slow Fade,* the writers suggest younger adults are not coming to us for answers; rather they are seeking a person(s) who will allow their questions to be voiced and their story to be told.[15] We cannot force answers on the spiritual journey of another, but through good questions we can help them discover their own story more fully.

In the ministry of student development, I offer insights from the discipline of spiritual direction. I suggest a way of noticing what God is doing in the lives of students. Francis Nemeck and Theresa Coombs, in *The Way of Spiritual Direction,*[16] have studied the spiritual journeys of believers and I will adapt their insights to the ministry of student development. A student's spiritual passion is expanded and his or her faith challenged by observing and struggling through various stages of the journey: suffering, moral development, intellectual development, vocational/ career transitions, Christian worldview and responsibility, life crisis, challenges, and revelation. Nemeck and Coombs describe these struggles or crises as "thresholds." A threshold can be passed through and back again. Thresholds are usually times of transition when students are ready for change; when they move from one stage of spiritual formation to another; when their worldview shifts and they move into a new stage of faith; and when they mark the beginning of a new stage of being. The passage through a threshold will typically have three phases:

1   There will be a season of *restlessness* characterized by an inner disquiet or anxiousness. Students will process this inner disquiet or anxiousness in ways reflecting their personalities and behaviors. Be mindful of the life stories and the current contexts of the students. What are they learning in the context of their life?

2   There will be a time of *transition*. This is a time when students reevaluate their identities and their surroundings. They will decide what they believe, who will influence their life choices as they come to a better understanding of who they are, and what they have to contribute to this world.

3   These phases will be followed by a time of *stabilization*. During this time, students exhibit contentedness with letting go of the past and accepting current challenges. They are willing to shed past ways of living life and false identities, and gain a new compassion to embrace the future.

Thresholds do not have a timeframe. We cannot impose spiritual formation on anyone. I can find myself in a conversation with a college student today that actually started twenty years ago when she was learning to pay attention to God's voice and word for her life. We can design learning environments and be present in the moment for the time when a student desires truth, is open to new outcomes, and is willing to wait and wade through the process of discernment, and enter fully into a life of prayer.

My own research[17] indicates that student development professionals actually do create culture through conversations by intentionally integrating spiritual formation conversations and practices into small groups and student leadership development experiences. These experiences offer space for listening in community with others. In a noisy world we must allow students space for conversations that help them hear the voice of God in the quiet as well as in the chaos.

Another research finding is that student development professionals perceived the programs and conversations to be more meaningful and effective when spiritual formation practices were integrated into student development programs. My assumption is that the spiritual formation practices were more intentional than an opening prayer. The spiritual formation practices were based on noticing God's story in the midst of our story. Student development professionals also noticed that how they relied on the way God moved in their own personal stories had significant influence on who they ministered to and how they paid attention to the lives of their students. The personal and professional interest of staff was identified as the strongest positive effect on spiritual development/formation programming. The student development professionals noted lastly that the students who were active in the student development programs emphasizing spiritual development were growing and maturing as Christians.

What does this mean for the profession, for the ministry of student development? As professionals, we must commit ourselves to the study of the spiritual life of the student. What do our students need to understand who God is, who they are, and what God has designed them to do? James Fowler emphasized that faith is not a separate component of an individual's life but is intricately related to the whole person.[18] We are being invited daily to pay attention to the movement of God within the lives of students, whether through encouraging their God-given dreams or redirecting the behavior. We can create a culture where conversations and prayers shape students' understanding of calling and vocation. We can consider whether or not our prior practices and conversations foster spiritual development. We can acknowledge the difficulty in knowing how to measure an institutional impact on a student's spiritual development without the end result of an academic grade, an honor, or a transcript notation. We can create rituals which will allow us to recognize and celebrate a transformed life in Christ through the power of story and conversation.

A Tribute to the Professionals in Student Development

I conclude this chapter with a tribute to Tracy Riddle who served as a student development professional for twenty-one years. As campus pastor, Paul Rohde read

Psalm 139 at Tracy's bedside the day she died from cancer. He was taken with how fully and freely she had lived it. In her memory, he offered this paraphrase at the memorial service in the Chapel of Reconciliation on the campus of Augustana College, July 26, 2011:

Psalm 139: As Told by a Dean of Students

How wonderful are your works, O God!
How vast is the sum of them!
If you, in fact, know every word before it passes my lips,
You are indeed a creative and colorful God.

Where shall I flee from your presence?

If I go to the mosh pit, you are there.
And if I ascend to the top of Stavig or Granskou to chase students off the roof, you are there.

If I call the privileged to service, you are there.
And if I stand with the broken and downtrodden, you are there.

If I am awakened at 1 a.m., you are there.
And if I get back to bed at 4 a.m., you are there, too.

If I go to Guatemala or Chile, you are there, and if the international students have a bake sale on my yard, you are there.

If I stir enthusiasm into yet another Covenant Award committee for how blessed we are to serve students who live our values, you are there.
And if I grant mercy [or receive mercy] for yet another time we fail our values, you are there.

If I celebrate student triumphs, you are there.
And if I sit with disappointment one more time, you are there.

You have called me to this work, O God, so every student and colleague may know that they are fearfully and wonderfully made. You bless me with compassion and delight in the promise that from your womb, O Mother God, you have made us sisters and brothers. You knit our stories in intricate and astonishing ways.

How vast is the sum of your gifts, O God. I come to the end—I am still with you.

Chapter 10 Notes

[1] George D. Kuh, John H. Schuh, and Elizabeth J. Whitt, and Associates, *Involving Colleges: Successful Approaches to Fostering Student Learning and Development Outside the Classroom* (San Francisco, Calif.: Jossey-Bass Inc, 1991), 259.

[2] Susan Komives, Dudley B. Woodard, and Associates, *Student Services: A Handbook for the Profession* (San Francisco, Calif.: Jossey-Bass Inc, 1996).

[3] Ernest L. Boyer. *College: The Undergraduate Experiences in America* (New York: Harper and Row, 1987), 177.

[4] J. Fley, "Student Personnel Pioneers: Those Who Developed Our Profession," *NASPA Journal* 7 (1979): 23–39.

[5] Komives, Woodard, and Associates, *Student Services*.

[6] Nancy J. Evans, Deanna S. Forney, and Florence Guido-DiBrito, *Student Development: Theory, Research and Practice* (San Francisco, Calif.: Jossey-Bass, 1998).

[7] Komives, Woodard, and Associates, *Student Services*, 28.

[8] Ibid., 547.

[9] Katherine J. Houghton, "Application of Christian Faith Development Theories by the Chief Student Affairs Officers of the Christian College Coalition" (Ann Arbor, Mich.: University Microfilms International, 1994).

[10] Marie Loewen, "A Place Along the Way," *Conversations* 5, no. 1 (Spring 2007).

[11] Ruth Haley Barton, *Strengthening the Soul of Your Leadership: Seeking God in the Crucible of Ministry* (Downers Grove, Ill.: InterVarsity Press, 2008), 25.

[12] Ibid., 39.

[13] Ibid., 132.

[14] David S. Guthrie, *Student Affairs Reconsidered: A Christian View of the Profession and Its Context* (Lanham, Md.: University Press of America, 1997), 70.

[15] Reggie Joiner, Chuck Bomar, and Abbie Smith, *The Slow Fade: Why You Matter in the Story of the Twentysomethings* (Colorado Springs, Colo.: David C. Cook, 2010).

[16] Francis Kelly Nemeck and Theresa Coombs, *The Way of Spiritual Direction* (Wilmington, Del.: Liturgical Press, 1985).

[17] Susan Reese, "Student Affairs Practitioners Implementation of Spiritual Development Programs in the CCCU" (Ed.D. diss., University of South Dakota, 2001).

[18] J. W. Fowler, *Becoming Adult, Becoming Christian: Adult Development and Faith Development* (San Francisco, Calif.: Jossey-Bass, 2000).

STRENGTHENING A CHRISTIAN COLLEGE AS A FAITH MENTORING ENVIRONMENT THROUGH *KNOWING—BEING—DOING*

Bob Yoder

At Goshen College (GC), a Christ-centered liberal arts college, we have embarked upon a two-year study of our faith-mentoring environment. The first year's results, the subject of our discussion here, focus on the role of GC faculty in faith mentoring. The second year's study, which is being conducted during the 2011–2012 academic school year, focuses on the role of GC administration and staff in faith mentoring.

In this chapter we will first look closely at the results of the survey and its study on the role of GC's teaching faculty as faith mentors. Then we will reflect upon the framework GC faculty created, *Knowing—Being—Doing*, for strengthening the campus as a faith mentoring environment. This framework invites the following reflective questions:

- What do we need to *know* to be helpful in student faith development?
- How should we *be* as faith mentors?
- What can we *do* to nurture the faith of students? Where is the disconnect?

The following statistics briefly summarize the study's findings on the role of faculty members as faith mentors.

- Sixty percent of student respondents at GC wished that they had more opportunities to hear about their professors' faith journeys, Christian perspectives, and spiritual practices; eighteen percent did not and twenty-one percent were unsure.
- Fifty-one percent of GC students wished that they had more opportunities to discuss matters of faith with their professors, either in or outside of the classroom; twenty-three percent did not and twenty-six percent were unsure.
- When asked, "Do you view your teaching faculty as 'faith mentors'?" only twenty-two percent answered "yes;" forty-three percent said "no" and thirty-five percent indicated "I'm not sure."
- No members of the teaching faculty disagreed with the statement, "I believe that Goshen College teaching faculty should serve as 'faith mentors' to our college students." Seventy-three percent either "strongly agreed" or "agreed" while twenty-seven percent remained "neutral."
- Ninety-five percent of teaching faculty indicated that they had opportunities to share with students, in or outside of the classroom, aspects of their faith journey, Christian perspectives, and spiritual practices.

These findings reveal a disconnect. The GC teaching faculty—caring people with spiritual depth—indicate they have had opportunities to relate with students on matters of faith, yet the majority of students want more. Is this a case where students should be content with what they have been offered, or a situation where many students are missing out, even though some receive individualized attention? If the latter, then how can a Christian college assure itself of reaching all its students in ways they yearn for in matters of faith and spirituality? At the same time, when the teaching faculty were invited to respond to the following statement, "Goshen College has oriented and prepared me well to be a faith mentor in and out of the classroom," only twenty-two percent "strongly agreed" or "agreed." Twenty-nine percent "disagreed" or "strongly disagreed," and forty-nine percent responded "neutral."

Though the initial hope of this research study was to equip teaching faculty as faith mentors, thereby placing significant emphasis on the individual relationships between professors and students, it has evolved to encompass a more holistic investigation of the college context as a faith mentoring environment. In this wider perspective, professors serving as faith mentors is one significant factor among other factors, such as extracurricular activities, international study and service, and informal conversations with other students.

The Faith Mentoring Environment and Faith Mentors: Phase One of Goshen College's Study

Sharon Daloz Parks, in her book *Big Questions, Worthy Dreams: Mentoring Young Adults in Their Search for Meaning, Purpose, and Faith*, outlines the "gifts of a mentor" and "features of a mentoring environment." She states, "Mentoring, in its classic sense, is an intentional, mutually demanding, and meaningful relationship between two individuals, a young adult and an older, wiser figure who assists the younger person in learning the ways of life."[1] Daloz Parks notes that in her research, "students indicated that often their most valued learning occurred with a teacher and a small group of students."[2] She describes the "gifts of a mentor" in that they:

- recognize promise and vulnerability
- support students as guides, leading them to resources
- challenge students, at times with "tough love"
- inspire students to go beyond "mere cynicism"
- dialogue with students in mutually beneficial ways[3]

She articulates the following "features of a mentoring environment":

- serve as a network of belonging
- extend hospitality to the "big questions" of life
- foster a genuine hospitality to "otherness"
- initiate such habits of the mind in our students to hold diversity and complexity, and to wrestle with moral ambiguity, in ways that develop deeper wells of meaning and purpose, and a larger and stronger faith
- nurture students in pursuit of their "worthy dreams"
- provide images of hope, truth, transformation
- engage in practices that pause and reflect, and share with one another[4]

Through the survey, GC students were invited to indicate the degree to which they encountered Daloz Parks's "gifts of a mentor" in their teaching faculty. Table 11.1 shows that overall many students do not receive regular attention from faculty through these gifts.

Table 11.1. Student Experience of Teaching Faculty as Faith Mentors (Percentages*)

	Often	Fairly Often	Some-times	Rarely	Never
To what degree, either in or out of the classroom, have Teaching Faculty . . .					
Recognized and pointed out your promise and vulnerability?	1	17	39	24	19
Supported you by serving as an advocate, a guide to resources, a source of comfort and healing?	5	24	43	21	8
Challenged you to live into your potential, and at times, made you feel like it is "tough love"?	6	16	36	27	15
Inspired you in ways that lead to the possibility of meaningful commitment and hope on the other side of the critical thinking process, and in some ways, serve as an "antidote to mere cynicism"?	4	22	41	25	8
Dialogued with you in ways that you understand the professors and feel that they are learning from you?	8	20	37	27	8

*Percentages in tables may not add up to 100% because of rounding.

Similarly, teaching faculty were invited to respond to the degree to which they carried out these gifts. The results in Table 11.2 suggest that teaching faculty perceived that they were more effective as mentors than what students experienced. However, the comparison between student responses in Table 11.1 and teaching faculty responses in Table 11.2 is not a direct comparison. Teaching faculty respondents may very well be offering these "gifts of a mentor" to some students, but it is also evident that not all students are recipients of these gifts to the same degree.

Table 11.2. Teaching Faculty as Faith Mentors, Self-rating (Percentages)

	Often	Fairly Often	Some-times	Rarely	Never
To what degree, either in or out of the classroom, do you . . .					
Recognize in and point out to individual students their promise and vulnerability?	5	26	49	16	2
Support individual students by serving as their advocate, a guide to resources, and a source of comfort and healing?	8	25	60	8	0
Challenge individual students to live into their potential, at times practicing a kind of "tough love"?	8	23	55	15	0

	Often	Fairly Often	Some-times	Rarely	Never
Inspire in individual students the possibility of meaningful commitment and hope on the other side of the critical thinking process, and in some ways, serve as an "antidote to mere cynicism"?	5	33	45	15	3
Dialogue with individual students in a way that you know they understand you and that you seek to learn from them?	15	38	45	2	0

Another set of questions explored how well Goshen College serves as a mentoring environment. Table 11.3 reveals that many students regularly experience these seven features.

Table 11.3. Student Experience of Goshen College as a Mentoring Environment (Percentages)

	Often	Fairly Often	Some-times	Rarely	Never
To what degree has your Goshen College experience enabled you to . . .					
Experience a sense of belonging here?	26	38	26	7	3
Articulate your "big questions" of life, meaning, and faith?	15	32	37	14	2
Interact with and learn from people who are different than you?	24	43	26	6	0
Hold together diversity and complexity, and wrestle with moral ambiguity in ways that lead to deeper wells of meaning and purpose, and to a larger and stronger faith?	14	38	37	10	1
Develop your "worthy dreams" that help you imagine how you want your life to be as an adult?	18	35	38	7	2
Gain images of hope, truth, transformation, positive images of self and of the other, and images of interrelatedness?	15	35	38	11	1
Take time to pause and reflect, to share with others, and to experience a common and connected life with the Goshen College community?	14	33	35	17	1

Similarly, teaching faculty responses portrayed in Table 11.4 also suggest that they believe students benefit from these seven features of a mentoring environment.

Table 11.4. Teaching Faculty Perception of GC as a Mentoring Environment (Percents)

	Often	Fairly Often	Some-times	Rarely	Never
To what degree has your Goshen College experience enabled you to . . .					
Serve as a network of belonging that constitutes a spacious home for the potential and vulnerability of the young adult imagination in practical, tangible terms?	3	41	51	3	3
Actively extend hospitality to students'"big questions" of life, meaning, and faith?	8	43	43	8	0
Foster a genuine hospitality to "otherness," where students are encouraged to interact with and learn from students outside their own "tribe" (e.g. "them" vs. "us")?	4	45	38	13	0
Initiate such habits of the mind in our students to hold diversity and complexity, and to wrestle with moral ambiguity in ways that develop deeper wells of meaning and purpose, and a larger and stronger faith?	8	50	38	5	0
Nurture in our students those "worthy dreams" that help them imagine and articulate their self as an adult in the world, and to vocationally pursue those dreams that are consistent, authentic, and congruent with who they are becoming?	25	38	38	0	0
Provide for our students images of hope, truth, transformation, positive images of self and of the other, and images of interrelatedness?	15	46	33	5	0
Engage in practices that allow us to pause and reflect, to share with one another, and to confirm a common and connected life to each other?	5	44	41	10	0

In general, teaching faculty perception of how well Goshen College is serving as a mentoring environment is similar to student experience. This series of questions along with the previous focus on the gifts of a mentor again affirms the notion that students benefit from their collective experiences, and not solely from individual mentorship. It also conveys that their college education mentors them in ways beyond the academic realm of student experience.

Though Goshen College offers much as a mentoring environment, greater improvement is needed and called for by students regarding faith mentorship by teaching faculty. Again, most teaching faculty responding to the survey are willing to share their faith with students, but it is also clear that what they are doing is not sufficiently meeting student expectations. However, teaching faculty raised several matters in the survey regarding faith mentorship at Goshen College. When asked, "What are your hesitations about this role [faith mentor]?" the following key issues surfaced:

- The term needs clarity.
- They are not sure what Goshen College expects of them in this regard.
- They are not sure if it is actually part of their teaching role.
- Do not want to impose their faith and beliefs onto students.
- Students might not see them in this way.
- Do not believe they are qualified to speak to such matters.

Through follow-up individual interviews with fourteen teaching faculty, the following themes were also raised regarding their questions and concerns about faith mentorship:

- Goshen College seems to possess no clear, explicit expectations of teaching faculty. There is no real orientation, training, or equipping done by the academic affairs office.
- Faculty possess their own insecurities. Some are not comfortable verbally sharing or do not feel qualified to address matters of faith.
- Some faculty believe that some students would not want faith mentorship either because they perceive students who attend Goshen College are there more for an academic education and therefore compartmentalize their faith from their education, or the theological differences between them and certain students is too great.
- Some faculty noted that they do not feel comfortable sharing their own theological and faith convictions with other teaching faculty for fear of judgment by their peers.

Through surveys and interviews, it is also clear that members of the teaching faculty who attended a secular college as an undergraduate, or who have been trained or previously taught at a secular institution, are the most disadvantaged by the lack of explicit expectations for GC faculty regarding faith mentorship. Twenty-two percent of faculty "strongly agreed" or "agreed" that "Goshen College has oriented and prepared me well to be a faith mentor in and out of the classroom," but twenty-nine percent "disagreed" or "strongly disagreed," and forty-nine percent were "neutral." However, thirty percent of those who attended a Christian college only as an undergraduate "strongly agreed" or "agreed," while eighteen percent "disagreed." No one "strongly disagreed" and fifty-two percent were "neutral." But for those who attended only a secular college as an undergraduate no one "strongly agreed" or "agreed" with this statement, whereas fifty-seven percent "disagreed" or "strongly disagreed," and the rest were "neutral." And for those who attended both Christian and secular colleges, seventeen percent "strongly agreed" or "agreed," while fifty percent "disagreed" or "strongly disagreed," and the rest were "neutral."

Perhaps this data supports an idea that Goshen College operates with more of an implicit faith than an explicit one when it comes to faculty-student interactions around matters of faith. And those teaching faculty who have not benefited from some sort of faith modeling/mentorship as undergraduates remain unclear about how GC expects them to engage faith issues with students. Goshen College, a Christ-centered institution, would better serve its students by equipping their teaching faculty in the area of faith mentorship.

Furthermore, seventy-one percent of students indicated that they "never" or "rarely" sought spiritual guidance from teaching faculty. However, fifty-two percent "strongly agree" or "agree" that teaching faculty are interested in students' spiritual lives. To strengthen Goshen College as a faith-mentoring environment in which teaching faculty and all employees have a formative role in student faith development, the *Knowing—Being—Doing* framework is offered.

Knowing: What Do We Need to *Know* to Be Helpful in Student Faith Development?

Five members of the teaching faculty were consulted as a focus group several times in November of 2011 to further reflect on and discuss the findings of the first phase of this study. The *Knowing—Being—Doing* framework developed from these conversations. They agreed that the following content would be helpful to *know* in order to be more effective faith mentors:

- Define faith mentorship for the GC context.
- Become familiar with pastoral care issues of college students.
- Learn about faith development of emerging/young adults at GC.

Specifically, they agreed that the "gifts of a mentor" and "features of a mentoring environment" described by Daloz Parks is beneficial information. Her work begins to explicitly define faith mentorship for our context—what has been only implicit at GC to this point.

Some of the most important pastoral care challenges of college students originate before they arrive at college. Considering the family context, the divorce rate has dramatically increased over the years, along with blended families and single-parent households. Some college students have parents who suffer from a mental or physical illness, or who are deceased. Some will have experienced some form of abuse. Parents may have been underemployed or unemployed.

Media, in all its forms, plays a significant role in the lives of young people. Before coming to college, the average young person is exposed to eight hours and thirty-three minutes of media content per day, which far exceeds the two hours and seventeen minutes of time hanging out with parents, the one hour and twenty-five minutes of physical activity, and the one hour of pursuing hobbies or other activities.[5] The average older teenager listens to two hours and twenty-four minutes of music a day, and will have listened to almost as much music from seventh through twelfth grades as time spent in the classroom from kindergarten through high school.[6]

Other pastoral care concerns include the rise of suicide, the third leading cause of death among young people (the suicide rate among adolescents has nearly tripled since 1970); depression; eating disorders and other self-injurious behaviors; and substance abuse of alcohol, marijuana, and other drugs. Some of these challenges are less visible than others, and so it is important for all college personnel to be aware of the hidden faces behind the lives of the students we encounter. Collectively, all of these realities impact the lives of young people who attend our college.

To better understand young adult development, Daloz Parks is again helpful. She suggests that the key task of the young adult era lies in the "experience of the birth of critical awareness and the dissolution and recomposition of the meaning of self, other, world, and 'God.'"[7] A younger adult deserves the respect and trust due another adult when they "shift from just 'being a life' to 'knowing [they] have a life.'"[8] In that moment there is an undeniably different form of consciousness and with it comes the acceptance of new responsibilities. Jeffrey Arnett, in *Emerging Adulthood: The Winding Road from the Late Teens through the Twenties*, describes five features of "emerging adulthood" as the age of identity exploration, instability, self-focus, feeling in-between, and possibilities. He points out that some of the traditional adult markers, such as median age of marriage, parenthood, and those attending college, have increased over the past century. He observes: "the spread of college education has been an important influence in creating a distinct period of emerging adulthood in American society."[9] Christian Smith suggests that several macro social changes have contributed to this new stage of American life, including growth of higher education, delay of marriage, changes in American and global economy, and parents extending financial support for material needs well into the students' twenties and early thirties.[10]

To better understand faith development of GC's traditional-aged college students relative to a national sample, several survey questions were included from the National Study of Youth and Religion (NSYR) led by Christian Smith. NSYR is designed to enhance the understanding of the religious lives of American youth from adolescence into young adulthood. Numerous books have been published utilizing this research, including *Soul Searching: The Religious and Spiritual Lives of American Teenagers* and *Souls in Transition: The Religious and Spiritual Lives of Emerging Adults*. The following survey questions were asked of GC students:

- If you attended a church prior to your attendance at Goshen College, how frequently did you attend?[11]
- How important is your religious faith in shaping your daily life?[12]
- How important is your faith when facing major life decisions?[13]
- How interested are you in learning more about your religion?[14]

Overall, Figures 11.1, 11.2, 11.3, and 11.4 illustrate that GC students seem to be more active in their faith than the national sample, which is not surprising since GC is a Christian, denominational college where a high majority of students indicate they are Christian. Smith claims that "adolescent religious and spiritual understanding and concern seem to be generally very weak. Most U.S. teens have a difficult to impossible time explaining what they believe, what it means, and what the implications of their beliefs are for their lives." He concludes by suggesting that "parents and faith communities should not be shy about teaching teens.... it seems to us that religious educators need to work much harder on articulation." Though GC students may or may not be better versed in describing their faith beliefs than the national high school sample, the fact remains that students need teachers and faith mentors to help them articulate their forming beliefs, convictions, and faith practices.

Figure 11.1 Church Attendance (Percentages)

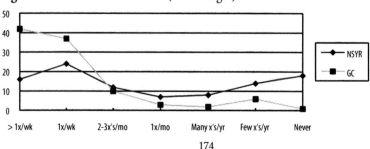

Figure 11.2 Importance of Faith Shaping Daily Life (Percentages)

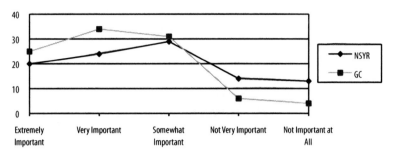

Figure 11.3 Importance of Faith When Facing Major Life Decisions (Percentages)

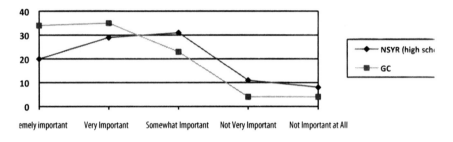

Figure 11.4 Degree of Interest in Learning About Religion (Percentages)

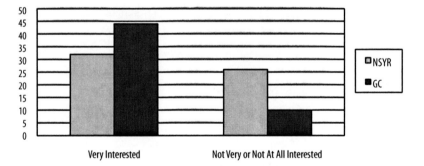

In addition, student responses to two questions outlined in Table 11.5 offer further insight as to how seriously GC students say their faith matters to them. Three out of four "strongly agree" or "agree" that their faith plays a role in their future vocational pursuits, and two out of three "strongly agree" or "agree" that in choosing Goshen College it was important that it was a Christian school. Again, these findings can inform teaching faculty on some level how much faith matters to our students. This perhaps offers further explanation for the motive and desire that students have in wanting to know more about the faith of our teaching faculty, and why they wish to engage faith more with their teaching faculty in and out of the classroom.

Table 11.5 Importance of Faith for Future Vocation; Importance that GC Is Christian (Percentages)

	Strongly Agree	Agree	Neutral	Dis-agree	Strongly Disagree
My faith is important to me and plays a shaping role as I consider my future vocational pursuits.	40	35	16	5	4
When I chose to attend Goshen College, it was important to me that it is a Christian college.	35	31	19	9	7

Being: How Should We *Be* as Faith Mentors?

The five teaching faculty members acknowledged that *being* may be the most difficult aspect of the proposed framework to achieve. They feel much is expected of them with seemingly little time to accomplish all that needs to be done. The thought of elevating their role as faith mentors to the long list of to-do's might be daunting for some faculty. How then should GC personnel be, both individually and collectively, in order to serve authentically and honestly as positive faith mentors?

Eighty-three percent of teaching faculty "strongly agree" or "agree" that "In my application and hiring process, it was clear to me that there is a direct link between faith and teaching at Goshen College." However, this study has demonstrated that students want more interactions with teaching faculty regarding their faith journeys, spiritual practices, perspectives, and to have more opportunities to discuss matters of faith in and out of the classroom. To better understand the complexity and challenge regarding teaching faculty as faith mentors, individual follow-up interviews were conducted with fourteen teaching faculty members. They were asked, "How well has Goshen College prepared teaching faculty to serve as faith mentors and in what ways can we better do so?" A number of their responses appear below:

- "I don't feel like a whole lot has been done."
- "I don't think we have enough opportunities to really share with one another as faculty . . . ."

- "I don't feel like I received any direction in how I run my classes in terms of bringing up spiritual components."
- "I don't think Goshen College as an institution has helped me, especially when I hear some of my colleagues who are adamantly opposed to praying in class."
- "I feel Goshen College prepares us to do something, but it's fuzzy."
- "I'm trying to make the university the way I want it to be and the kind of professor that I would like to have and I don't even know what page my colleagues are on. Nobody talks about it."
- " . . . I think right now it's pretty open and unspecified . . . . I think the best thing that could happen is if we made space for people to do that . . . if we made the time to talk about faith."
- "I've not received any explicit training in Mennonite pedagogy or Mennonite belief so when I work with faith I have to kind of take it wherever it is."
- "Probably not very well."
- "I remember being asked some of those questions when I applied and I'm sure if I sought them out with more force I could probably find contexts and people to talk about those things with, but it hasn't been obvious for me about where I would go to do that . . . it doesn't feel like there's been a whole lot of infrastructure."

These interviews further demonstrate that teaching faculty do not feel adequately equipped to serve as the kind of faith mentors students may seek. However, it also became clear that these faculty care deeply about their students and live out their own vocational calling at GC because of their faith. In other words, the teaching faculty are not apathetic towards student faith development, but they do not always know what students want or what the administration expects of them regarding faith mentorship.

These findings suggest it would be helpful if GC administrators would increase efforts to orient and equip the teaching faculty to better serve as the kind of faith mentors that students yearn for and that fit with the mission of the college. Some ideas include workshops, book discussion groups, half-day and full-day retreats, smaller groups of employees who meet for support, taking time in faculty meetings to simply share how we approach faith mentorship with students, and nurturing our own individual and collective prayer practices. Many of these ideas, however, come with a cost of both finances and time. Perhaps this is why it is so easy to overlook this aspect of the *Knowing—Being—Doing* framework. However, for students to want to seek out faculty as spiritual resources, we also need to let them see and know how we faithfully strive to follow after Jesus in our lives.

Doing: What Can We *Do* to Nurture the Faith of Students?

What can be done on a Christian campus by teaching faculty that strengthens the faith development of our students? Which ones will be most effective? The ideas are limitless, but the mission of Goshen College states:

> Goshen College is a liberal arts college dedicated to the development of informed, articulate, sensitive, responsible Christians. As a ministry of the Mennonite Church, we seek to integrate Christian values with educational, social and professional life. As a community of faith and learning, we strive to foster personal, intellectual, spiritual and social growth in every person. We view education as a moral activity that produces servant-leaders for the church and the world. At Goshen College we intend to create a community of faith and learning built on five core values: Christ-centeredness, passionate learning, servant leadership, compassionate peacemaking and global citizenship.[15]

Whatever "best practices" are done need to support the mission of the college.

To better examine if practices are linked directly to academic student learning outcomes, this study included survey questions for both students and teaching faculty stemming from key findings of the Spirituality in Higher Education project at UCLA led by Alexander Astin, Helen Astin, and Jennifer Lindholm. This seven-year project began in 2003 and examined how students change during the college years and the role that college plays in facilitating the development of their spiritual and religious qualities. They analyzed extensive data collected from 14,527 students attending 136 colleges and universities nationwide, undertook personal interviews with individual students, held focus groups, and also surveyed and interviewed faculty.

Overall they concluded that "spiritual growth enhances other college outcomes, such as academic performance, psychological well-being, leadership development, and satisfaction with college."[16] Their data suggests that this growth is not merely due to student maturation, but because of some significant experiences during the college years, including study abroad, interdisciplinary studies, and service learning. Goshen College's motto is "culture for service" and students are required to participate in our Study-Service Term in which students journey to another country to learn about a different culture from the inside out—its language, its customs, its history and, most importantly, its people. Approximately half the time is spent studying and the other half in a service assignment.

Teaching faculty responded to survey statements which arose out of certain "best practices" identified in the Spirituality in Higher Education project. Overall, the results in Table 11.6 demonstrate that GC teaching faculty members seldom utilize these practices in their course content. Since a significant percentage of GC students wish to engage in discussions about faith with their professors, increasing the use of these seven practices could be a helpful start.

Table 11.6 Teaching Faculty Ideas from Spirituality in Higher Education Project (Percentages)

	Often	Fairly Often	Some-times	Rarely	Never
I regularly incorporate elements of faith learning outcomes into my course syllabi.	7	10	32	46	5
I regularly address faith implications of my courses in my classes.	7	24	54	15	0
I regularly provide opportunities through assignments or part of the class period for students to reflect upon faith implications related to the contents of the course in my classes.	2	17	37	44	0
I utilize reflective, meditative, and contemplative practices such as journaling, reflection papers, prayers, or silence in my classes.	7	17	29	37	10
I assign students to participate in group activities that are designed to serve others, such as community service, leadership training, and participation in student clubs and groups.	0	15	34	24	27
I encourage and involve students in class discussion about matters of meaning and purpose in life.	10	29	44	15	2
I engage and involve students in class discussion about matters of faith and spirituality.	2	20	37	37	5

In addition, other ideas were collected from teaching faculty during the interviews regarding what they were already doing in and out of the classroom to support student faith development. The following represent some "in the classroom" ideas:

- have students write a spirituality paper linked directly to some aspect of the course content; open the class with prayer or other brief devotional
- invite an outside guest speaker to talk about his or her profession (e.g. hospital chaplain in a nursing course)
- explore some particular church practice with course content (e.g. tithing)
- have students pick a passage from the Bible relevant to course content and write about it (e.g. passage about money in business class)
- engage pop culture items through the lens of faith, ethics, and morality related to course content
- create a class of respectful community conversation
- use contemplative practices (e.g. fifteen minutes of silence and then write about it in English class)
- have students complete journal reflections
- practice yoga and link to the idea of one's body as a "temple"
- follow a character in a novel that has religious themes
- explicitly state how this course might shape or interact with their faith
- utilize real-life examples of people as faith exemplars relevant to course content
- share personally from the professor's life in ways that link to course content
- assign several articles to read on spirituality and course subject matter

The following are some "out of the classroom" ways faculty engage faith with students:

- facilitate a small group of students studying a book on faith
- appropriately engage them about faith during one-on-one academic advising sessions
- serve as an advisor for student clubs and activities
- informally talk with students about church life
- attend chapel services
- model faith
- serve as a listening ear
- pray for students prior to class
- host special banquets for students that link faith and vocation

- teach a college-age Sunday school class at church
- talk with students who come to their church
- post a personal faith pilgrimage biography on the course website for students to read

One other area examined in this study that bears hope and encouragement is in regards to four of GC's eighteen Student Learning Outcomes:

- The Christian story: The biblical basis and theological exploration of Christian faith
- Identity: One's self in relationship to multiple communities
- Faith in Action: Reflect on the relationship between personal faith and life choices that support God's justice, reconciliation, and peace
- Ethical reasoning: Living and serving with integrity in a variety of communities

Teaching faculty were invited to respond to the following statements:

"I help students, in or out of the classroom . . .

1. Gain knowledge of the Christian story through the biblical basis and theological exploration of Christian faith.
2. Gain a sense of identity as one's self in relationship to multiple communities.
3. Reflect on the relationship between personal faith and life choices that support God's justice, reconciliation, and peace.
4. Consider what it means to live and serve with integrity in a variety of communities.

Students were invited to respond to the following:

"Since coming to Goshen College, . . .

1. I have gained knowledge of the Christian story through the biblical basis and theological exploration of Christian faith.
2. I have gained a sense of my identity as one who is relationship to multiple communities.
3. I have reflected on the relationship between personal faith and life choices that support God's justice, reconciliation, and peace.
4. I have considered what it means to live and serve with integrity in a variety of communities.

The results in Figures 11.5, 11.6, 11.7, and 11.8 demonstrate that even though teaching faculty did not always view their individual roles as contributing to student learning in these specific areas, it is evident that students indicate they are indeed learning these out of their collective college experience.

Figure 11.5 Gaining Knowledge of the Christian Story, Student and Faculty Response (Percents)

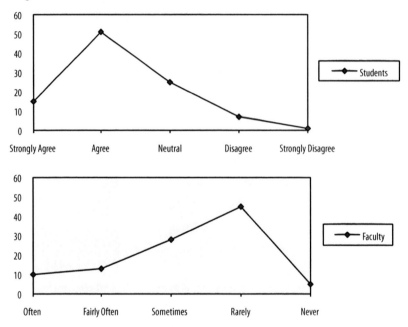

Figure 11.6 Gaining Sense of Identity in Relationship to Multiple Communities (Percents)

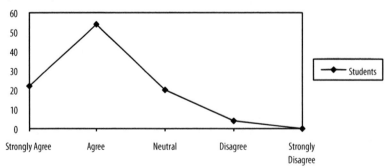

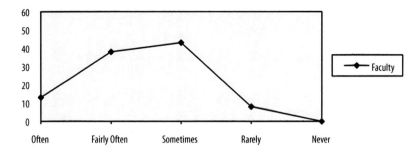

Figure 11.7 Considering What It Means to Live and Serve with Integrity (Percents)

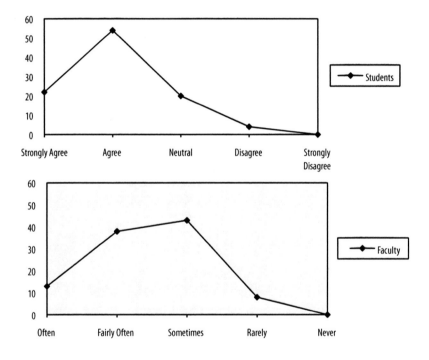

Figure 11.8 Relationship between Personal Faith and Life Choices that Support God's Justice, Reconciliation, and Peace (Percents)

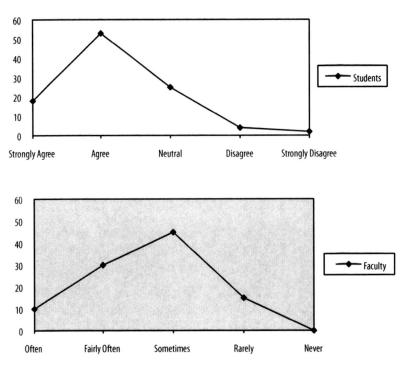

Conclusion

This study revealed some opportunities for growth at Goshen College, but it also surfaced many aspects of how the collective college experience is positively shaping the faith of our students. More individualized mentoring may be ideal for some students, but is perhaps difficult to accomplish due to the constraints of time and faculty-to-student ratio. Yet there are ways that GC can strengthen itself as a faith-mentoring environment. Faith mentors possess gifts that can be offered to students, and the use of the *Knowing—Being—Doing* framework will better aid Goshen College as a faith-mentoring environment to deepen the faith of its students.

Chapter 11 Notes

[1] Sharon Daloz Parks, *Big Questions, Worthy Dreams: Mentoring Young Adults in Their Search for Meaning, Purpose, and Faith* (San Francisco, Calif.: Jossey-Bass, 2000), 127.

[2] Ibid.

[3] Ibid., 127–133.

[4] Ibid., 135–157.

[5] Walt Mueller, *Youth Culture 101* (Grand Rapids, Mich.: Zondervan, 2007), 80.

[6] Ibid., 88.

[7] Daloz Parks, *Big Questions, Worthy Dreams*, 5.

[8] Ibid., 6.

[9] Jeffrey Jensen Arnett, *Emerging Adulthood: The Winding Road from the Late Teens through the Twenties* (New York: Oxford University Press, 2004), 121.

[10] Christian Smith, *Souls in Transition: The Religious and Spiritual Lives of Emerging Adults*, with Patricia Snell (New York: Oxford University Press, 2009), 5–6.

[11] Christian Smith, *Soul Searching: The Religious and Spiritual Lives of American Teenagers*, with Melissa Lundquist Denton (New York: Oxford University Press, 2005), 37.

[12] Smith, *Souls in Transition*, 112.

[13] Smith, *Soul Searching*, 40.

[14] Smith, *Souls in Transition*, 114.

[15] "Goshen College Mission," Goshen College, accessed December 23, 2011, http://www.goshen.edu/aboutgc/mission.

[16] Alexander W. Astin, Helen Astin, and Jennifer Lindholm, *Cultivating the Spirit: How College Can Enhance Students' Inner Lives* (San Francisco, Calif.: Jossey-Bass, 2011), 10.

SOUL PROJECTS

Class-Related Spiritual Practices in Higher Education[1]

James C. Wilhoit, David P. Setran,
Daniel T. Haase, and Linda Rozema

My "spiritual adventure" truly was that which it is entitled. I was given the opportunity to explore several spiritual disciplines which, in a three-week period, allowed me to taste a lifestyle of serious reflection that applied many of the concepts and formation techniques we had been learning in class.

—Jeff, student

In recent years, scholars have urged those working in Christian higher education to attend more purposefully to student spiritual and character formation. Anchored by the belief that college is a formative time for the development of values, commitments, identity, and life purpose, these calls have taken many different forms. One consistent theme, however, has been the need to expand character formation beyond ethical training and moral decision-making.[2] While such tools are necessary, these scholars note, there is also a pressing need for the development of righteous virtues, affections, commitments, and patterns of living rooted in a right understanding of God and self. As Arthur Holmes points out, shaping student character involves not only the intellectual tasks of moral and ethical analysis but also the growth of conscience, virtue, worthy desires, and personal responsibility. "College," he contends, "is for character."[3]

The development of collegiate character and spiritual sensitivity, however, has become more challenging in recent years. Sociologist Tim Clydesdale, for example, speaks of how freshmen tend to do very little reflection on personal and spiritual issues, choosing instead to place their identities in a "lockbox" while they focus on managing relationships, money, and personal gratification.[4] As Sharon Parks notes, young adults are "increasingly distracted by the lures of an entertained, consumerist, and anxious society, making their way as best they can, enjoying what life has to offer, and keeping up."[5] Such distractedness has only been heightened through recent cultural changes. Technological innovations—particularly texting and internet-capable cell phones—create contexts for students to be in multiple places at any one time. The fact that such devices are ultraportable means that student multitasking can now occur almost anywhere, including the college classroom. Since students are always wired in, they probably lack the solitude and silence that can encourage the development of spiritual depth. Students live in a culture, as William Deresiewicz argues, where there is little opportunity for introspection, deep reading, and the solitary encounter with God that refreshes the ability to live well in community.[6]

The common denominator characterizing many of these cultural trends is a failure to preserve focus and attention. Increasingly, students seem to lack the ability (or the desire) to be fully present in any one context, preferring virtual dispersion to embodied connections with God, people, and texts. The move toward multiple majors and growing relational superficiality (i.e., my five hundred Facebook friends) demonstrate a lack of commitment and a nearly obsessive desire to keep options and possibilities open at all costs.[7] Along with other critics who have addressed these themes, we believe that such realities possess negative academic and spiritual consequences. As Cornelius Plantinga suggests, students at Christian colleges cannot expect, in such a world, to form knowledge, skills, and virtues without guidance. Instead, he argues, they must struggle and labor in "attempting to open spaces at the depths where the Spirit of God may descend and dwell."[8] We desire the formation of deep students, and depth requires a degree of attentiveness and reflection that is diminishing on college campuses.

How can professors encourage spiritual attentiveness and transformation within the academic setting of a college classroom? What assignments foster spiritual focus and growth into Christlikeness? What helpful practices from the historic Christian tradition can be included in syllabi and course experiences? As professors committed to educationally based spiritual formation, we are concerned with how to best encourage student spiritual growth. This article is the culmination of conversations, as well as trial and error in our classrooms, in an attempt to answer these questions.

In our work with students, we have discovered that growth toward Christ-likeness is most likely to occur when we create assignments that allow students to practically engage in classroom-related spiritual activities. This growth, born out of sensitivity to the role of the Holy Spirit in teaching, helps to train in righteousness those students who are in our care. The scope of this article is to explore the role and function within the university classroom of what we have termed "soul projects": class assignments designed to foster spiritual attentiveness. Our experience is rooted in the context of an evangelical liberal arts institution offering both graduate and undergraduate degrees.

It is our understanding that intentionality and clearly articulated expectations are crucial for encouraging spiritual growth in the lives of students. When these are properly implemented through an explicit curriculum that includes partnership with the Holy Spirit, students meet with Jesus in intimate and transformational ways. Truth is fostered and the students begin to cultivate an open heart and the longing to seek goodness. They are thus able to echo Augustine: "I desire to know God and the soul . . . let me know myself, let me know Thee."[9]

We are not seeking to be exhaustive in this summary. Rather, the intent is for readers to consider the educational contexts in which they find themselves and how they might glean from the techniques and typology that are described here. It is our hope that this will encourage others to explore intentional and explicit ways to help students grow spiritually within academic settings. The following questions have guided our conversations and experiments and serve as an outline for what follows:

- What perspectives from the fields of philosophy, education, sociology, psychology, and business provide a foundation for classroom-related spiritual activities?
- What are "soul projects" and how do they relate to spiritual development?
- What are the major categories of soul projects that encourage student spiritual growth?
- What are some best practices when using soul projects?
- How does one evaluate and assess such experiences?

We are convinced that when students are given a clear vision, with instruction that inspires them to engage in classroom-related spiritual activities, they can enter into the academic life in a spiritually transformative manner. In collegiate settings where creating space for the Holy Spirit seems more challenging than ever, soul projects have the potential to create contexts in which students are directed to pay attention to their subjects, to their peers, to their souls, and, ultimately, to Christ and his call upon their lives.

Defining and Describing Soul Projects

The soul projects were a way for me to take what we were learning in class and make it an authentic spiritual experience. Without them, it would have been much more difficult to apply the course material.
—Stephanie, student

Soul projects, as described here, build upon the more foundational concept of spiritual practices. Philosopher Alasdair MacIntyre famously defines a "practice" as "any coherent and complex form of socially established cooperative human activity through which goods internal to that form of activity are realized in the course of trying to achieve those standards of excellence which are appropriate to, and partially definitive of, that form of activity, with the result that human powers to achieve excellence, and human conception of the ends and goods involved, are systematically extended."[10]

Christian spiritual practices fit MacIntyre's definition because, in the words of Craig Dykstra, they are forms of activity "through which powerful internal goods are realized and through the pursuit of which our capacities as human beings to do and to be and to conceive of what God is calling us to become are systematically extended."[11] Kathleen Cahalan affirms that distinctively *Christian* practices constitute one of three key approaches to practical theology, emphasizing their importance in the personal affirmation and continuation of identity within the Christian community.[12] They are "things Christian people do together over time to address fundamental human needs in response to and in the light of God's active presence for the life of the world."[13] Such practices express the distinctive way of Christian living, in contrast with often destructive messages from the culture. Practices embody the faith.

Soul projects, as we use the phrase, involve a variety of adaptations of Christian practices to higher education contexts, sometimes within the classroom, but at least as often assigned and described in that context but carried out in solitude or occasionally in a small group setting with others.[14] These projects can provide opportunities for students to link course content to the emerging affections of their souls, to their growing vocational and life commitments, and to the larger purposes of God. Parker Palmer argues that teaching is in part marked by its capacity to "create a space in which obedience to truth is practiced."[15] Among many other things, spiritual practices provide a place for the Holy Spirit to work as students 1) respond to God and communicate with him about course content, 2) speak to God about the personal spiritual implications of course material, 3) personally commit to certain causes, truths, or patterns of living, 4) speak to God about the recognition of personal and corporate sin and brokenness, 5) worship God in response to new revelations about his character and global work, and 6) speak and listen to others to provide wisdom and accountability for emerging commitments.

Engaging in spiritual practices—reflecting, listening, speaking, acting, praying, worshipping, confessing, forgiving, committing—involves recognition of the truth that spiritual formation and knowledge acquisition are linked in powerful ways. As Dykstra contends, "It is not because we know that we trust or because we trust that we know. Rather we know in trust, in love, in gratitude, in adoration. The attitudes and the knowing come together; they are parts of one another."[16] Practices, in short, can be an important means of helping to set one's heart with regard to the content of Christian higher education.

Higher Educational Context

These "soul projects" gave me an opportunity to spend time with God that I otherwise probably would not have made time for. They were a blessing and helpful in making me more able to rest in God's peace in the busyness of life.
—Vanessa, student

In considering student participation in spiritual practices, historical inertia often works against proposals that involve the academic sphere. As many scholars have previously argued, the growth of the university model in the late nineteenth and early twentieth centuries generated a growing divide between the tasks deemed appropriate for collegiate curricular and co-curricular activities. Many faculty members, driven by visions of specialization and the positivist ideal of the separation of facts and values, began to view spiritual and character formation as outside the realm of scholarly pursuits, more appropriate to the context of campus life than the collegiate classroom. In an era characterized by division of labor, it was quite natural for faculty members to embrace their roles as pure scholars while leaving religious and character influence to co-curricular campus ministries. In addition, as the student development profession emerged in the early 1900s to assume responsibility for the personal lives of undergraduates, such divisions became structured and institutionalized in increasingly entrenched forms.[17]

This historical legacy is still with us, and the Christian college is certainly not immune to its effects. The tendency to link academic study with the formal curriculum and personal spiritual or character growth with the co-curriculum can be pervasive. Faculty view themselves as objective disseminators of factual information, scientifically communicating data dispassionately so as to retain an appropriate scholarly distance. Value-laden Christian practices and soul formation are thought to take place in other settings, such as chapel, discipleship small groups, dormitory discussions, and specialized programs implemented by student development professionals. As Christians, faculty often desire to play a role in student spiritual growth as well. Yet they often believe that such influence should be placed in co-curricular settings or in one-on-one mentoring conversations.

Specialization has obvious advantages, but such divisions can generate troubling long-term ramifications. Students can begin to see their lives compartmentalized into academic (factual) and personal (value-laden) domains, thereby missing out on the potent interpenetration of these dimensions of the Christian life. They can begin to read the Bible in a dualistic fashion, studying it analytically for classes, and then examining it reflectively for heart transformation in their dorm small groups, never imagining that the two might be intertwined. They can be developing a Christian worldview in their classes while attempting to develop a Christian spirituality outside of class. In other words, while faith and learning may be integrated at high levels, there is often a disconnect between faith, learning, and the spiritual life generated by this public/private split. Such a fissure, we believe, can generate long-term adult tendencies to divorce spiritual formation from public and academic experience. Nicolas Wolterstorff comments:

> It used to be said that the goal is to impart to the student a Christian 'world and life view. . . .' But this formulation is inadequate, for it puts too much emphasis on a 'view,' that is, on what we have called cognition. To be identified with the people of God and to share in its work does indeed require that one have a system of belief. But it requires more than that. It requires the Christian way of life. Christian education is education aimed at training for the Christian way of life, not just education aimed at inculcating the Christian world and life view.[18]

The result of this gap is often a failure to capitalize on the potential fullness of Christian knowing in a collegiate institution.[19] Scripture is clear that full knowledge is dependent not only upon cognitive understanding and assent but also upon a response of obedience to and experience with revealed truth. John 8:31–32 speaks to this reality by proclaiming Jesus' words that, "If you hold to [abide in, indwell] my teaching, you are really my disciples. Then you will know the truth, and the truth will set you free" (NIV). The failure to indwell the truth of the Christian worldview, therefore, produces not only a dearth of responsible action but also a diminishing of biblical knowing. While such personal knowledge clearly happens incidentally or through the efforts of self-motivated students, faculty members would do well to reflect upon more purposeful and generalizable means of achieving these important aims.

Foundational Perspectives

One of the most rewarding and helpful assignments has been the journey paper. It helped me name certain sin patterns and chapters in my life that I hadn't worked through before. When we name things, some of the power it has on us is broken, and I really experienced that through the journey project/paper.
—Camie, student

A number of theorists provide helpful frameworks for bridging this divide between the classroom and spiritual formation. For example, John Dewey comments upon the interactive and cumulative nature of experiences, both of which are critical for spiritual and character formation. First, he notes that experiences always involve an interaction between external/environmental factors and inner desires, feelings, and commitments. When a teacher is concerned only with external content, this interaction still occurs but takes place in a haphazard fashion. Attentiveness to the purposeful interaction between the inner life of the student and external content/environment is the most effective means, Dewey argues, by which a teacher can establish a context for a truly educative and formational experience.[20]

Second, Dewey contends that learning is never isolated but rather cumulative in nature. Elements from each educational experience live on in future experiences, expanding or constricting the ways in which growth and learning occur in subsequent experiences. What lives on in this experiential continuum is not so much the experience itself but rather the attitudes, purposes, desires, and commitments formed in the midst of learning. Such "collateral learning," as Dewey terms it, is critical because it shapes responses to future experiences, and gradually develops—and increasingly solidifies—a posture towards life in general.[21] At a minimum, this means that one of the best ways to help students prepare for the future is by incorporating experience into the present, promoting the gradual internalization of spiritual postures that will continue in the future. Collegians often speak in terms of future goals, noting that they desire to be spiritually deep someday in their adult lives.

However, Dewey's notion of the continuum would imply that the most effective means of securing future spiritual depth is through engaging purposefully in spiritually formative activities in the midst of present experiences. If students do not engage the spiritual life in relation to their academic work—which surely constitutes a significant amount of time during college—they will develop attitudes and dispositions that view spirituality as a secondary theme appropriate only for private life and leisure. However, if learning is enacted, reflected upon, prayed out, and spoken to others, it begins shaping tendencies so that desires, habits, and long-term commitments are progressively developed. Educators must be deliberate, not only about the transmission and assimilation of content, but also about the lasting attitudes and desires that are generated through the learning process—the cumulative affective dimensions that have long-term consequences for spiritual formation.

Similarly, Wolterstorff argues that cognitive learning (the acquisition of information) and ability learning (the acquisition of skills) are rarely sufficient to develop within students the cognitive skill and inclination tendencies needed to live out their education. Tendencies, he contends, are rooted in emerging desires, wishes, commitments, and values, factors that shape one's proclivity to commit to particular truths and ways of living. While much education enables students to "know that" something is true and to have the "ability to" perform certain tasks, only when they also develop an "affection for" and a "commitment to" something will they be prepared to organize their lives around these realities.[22] Tendencies are obviously formed in many ways. Classroom environments, teacher modeling, powerful communication techniques, reward structures, and socialization within the campus community all play significant roles in shaping student commitments, values, and desires. However, we contend that spiritual tendencies can also be positively shaped by student engagement with various Christian practices purposefully connected to course subject matter.

The formation of identity is another important theoretical construct that underscores the potential importance of soul projects. In much of Western civilization, this aspect of adolescent development is understood to extend into and beyond the college years, the collegiate classroom serving as a crucial locus for identity forma-tion.[23] Students often enter college with "identity foreclosure," a "borrowed" identity from one or more authority figures (often parents or teachers), or more commonly with "identity diffusion" marked by lack of commitment or crisis of identity, seen in checking out rather than recognizing the point of a search. When provided the opportunity to reflect upon, experience, or wrestle with the ideas they are learning, however, students can either enter a stage of moratorium marked by a prolonged crisis of identity, or they may reach identity achievement by owning and internaliz-ing truths, and making commitments. Clearly, identity status can motivate a student towards spiritual formation, and soul projects may help produce a shift in iden-tity. As Sharon Parks and others have pointed out, college-age students are moving from dependence upon external authority to a posture of "inner" and ultimately "inter-dependence."[24] As they move along these lines, it is critical that teachers allow students space to develop their own voices in conversation with the teacher, fellow students, and the Holy Spirit. Spiritual practices provide a context in which such ownership can take place under the careful guidance of a teacher-mentor.

Ultimately, judicious incorporation of spiritual practices points to a powerful means of integrating a mentoring component into classroom activities. As many recent authors have established, mentoring is, at its core, a process of helping others pay attention to the already-present work of God in their lives and in the world around them. The college class provides a fruitful context for such attentive-ness, encouraging students to see God's work through subject content, and to see and nurture receptivity to the work of the Holy Spirit in their own souls as they interact with this material.

In addition, a salient opportunity for spiritual formation comes in helping students pay attention to how the *processes* of education are influencing their spir-itual lives. The academic process can promote within students postures of pride, despair, self-reliance, perfectionism, sloth, and "work hard, play hard" rhythms. It can foster particular patterns of reading that will influence students' interac-tion with Scripture and patterns of prioritizing certain values over others. Because these activities consume so much time and energy, students need to reflect con-sciously on the spiritually formative power of these processes. Spiritual practices open up helpful opportunities for students to take these largely unconscious activ-ities and make them a subject of careful reflection.[25]

Since identity development of this kind is quite unique to the person, spiri-tual practices provide a variety of ways of connecting persons with God in all of their God-given individuality. One area of variation is personal intelligence. The attempt to summarize intelligence in a summary score (IQ) or even a set of sub-scale scores, reflecting primarily linguistic, logical, or mathematical intelligence, is now questioned. While IQ tests are pragmatically valuable in predicting school performance, it is argued by some that they fall short of reflecting a global estimate of intelligence. This is in part because intelligence is not considered to be as global as was once thought. Howard Gardner identified multiple realms of intelligence,[26] many of them fairly removed from general educational intelligence. These spiritual practices respect this insight about intelligence and help teachers move beyond the characteristic domains of education, to focus on less conventional areas of understanding and intelligence.

For example, soul projects have the potential for resonance with musical intelligence (communicating and making meaning through sound), bodily-kinesthetic intelligence (such as dance), naturalist intelligence (an experience with God in the natural environment) and so on. Similarly, inborn temperament characteristics,[27] such as activity level, sociability, and emotionality, highlight the individuality that soul projects can address due to their diversity. Highly sociable learners are probably attracted by spiritual practices that might not appeal to those who are less sociable. Yet the instructor should resist the temptation to match student preferences and characteristics to various types of soul projects—students need to be pushed, at least occasionally, to do tasks that are outside their zones of comfort. The latter is more likely to produce disequilibrium, and thus have great potential for transformative impact.[28]

Many students face an inner tension between the reality of the current situation and their vision of the future. Peter Senge calls this "creative tension"[29] because, while the gap between the current reality and the vision may be discouraging, it can also energize creative and productive behavior. However, when motivated by a desire to decrease the dissonance between the two, students often lower their vision rather than raise the present reality. Soul projects offer the potential for a generative shift from the normal outward orientation to an inward reflection that can precipitate change. The dissonance between real and ideal is given needed attention by creating a space for welcoming the numinous presence of the divine during moments of reflection. Such liminality, where creativity and transcendent experience are honored, can produce not only insight but deep, personal meaning for students.

Learning Outcomes

Soul projects may precipitate deeper learning that challenges standard ways of thinking. For example, Chris Argyris pioneered the concept of "double loop learning,"[30] which contrasts typical problem solving involving the identification and correction of erroneous thought with solving problems by detecting and changing systemic malfunction. Single-loop learning is present when goals, values, paradigms, and significant practices are taken for granted. In the personal and academic realms, students with a single-loop approach focus on what techniques and procedures will make them more effective. Double-loop learning, in contrast, involves stepping back and questioning the intellectual frame and disposition one brings to spiritual practices. So the person frustrated with his or her prayer life might try in a single-loop approach to simply change prayer practices. A person with a cultivated double-loop orientation is willing to ask the reflective questions: What am I expecting from prayer? What is triggering my dissatisfaction? Argyris recommends that standard solutions (single-loop learning) may need to give way to systemic change (double-loop learning), and that shifts the attention from the *content* of thinking to the *way* people think. When soul projects are placed in the context of a course they can become vehicles for deep double-loop learning.

Soul projects represent a systemic change in the classroom, as students become more reflective and more actively involved. One-way communication, complemented with occasional discussions, gives way at least occasionally to intra-personal analysis and experience, which can be communicated to the instructor and other students. Spiritual experience and insight thus can be student initiated, and the framework for systemic interaction shifts as the instructor (probably temporarily) becomes an observer-participant of the Spirit's movement among individuals and within the class as a whole. Thus traditional systems of education, functioning within existing boundaries, norms, objectives, and procedures, may be challenged and alternative frameworks considered.

While spiritual development is affirmed as a goal of soul projects, this is not defined exclusively in terms of tangible outcomes that can be precisely measured. This is in part because any such outcome may be accomplished with the wrong motivation and apart from a genuine relationship with the divine, and thus can be a substitute—or worse yet, a fabrication—of the connecting with divinity that is desired. Fixed outcomes are also questionable because the presence of God is often marked by surprising and unpredictable results. To ask only that instructor-made objectives be accomplished is to limit God to the teacher's plans and imagination. Soul projects are as likely to involve experiments in listening as they are performance of activities.[31]

It should also be noted that the idea of development is itself suspect. Indeed, spirituality considered as development suggests a movement from the lesser to the greater, from the undeveloped to the more developed, an idea quite different from some biblical passages that indicate the greatest is the least, the first shall be last, children can teach adults, the sinner in the temple is closer to God than the righteous Pharisee, and the like. Perhaps alongside a general concept of growth should be an equally emphasized notion of journey: travel that has phases of movement from one place to another, and not necessarily from one level to another.

In contrast with the concept of hierarchical development, soul projects have the potential to generalize a process of transformative learning in collegiate education. By fostering disequilibrium with a student's current perspective and practice of spirituality, there is motivation to achieve equilibration through cognitive restructuring, Jean Piaget[32] suggests. James Loder elaborates the process of disequilibration and broadens the application to non-cognitive domains. He articulates an "epistemology of convictional experience"[33] through a five-phase "transforming moment" that constitutes a "grammar" of the work of the human spirit. These phases include conflict, scanning, insight, release, and interpretation/verification.

The soul project is most likely to be introduced as a task to achieve, producing disequilibrium and conflict, particularly if the task is unfamiliar to students. Scanning the environment by examining the ideas of fellow students or one's own thoughts and feelings may bring an intuitive spiritual event, often in the form of insight and new understanding. As the process moves towards equilibration, emotional release may be experienced, and the probability of reporting the event verbally, in writing, or through other means (e.g. art) is high. This sort of spiritual transformation, whether major or minor, is an important aspect of soul projects.

While soul projects are associated with spiritual transformation, transformation is always God-initiated. It is difficult to reconcile the priority of divine initiative and the importance of human practices in such experiences. Rabbi Shlomo Carlebach is quoted as stating, "Full experiences of God can never be planned or achieved. They are spontaneous moments of grace, almost accidental." When the rabbi was asked why followers of God must work hard at spiritual practices if they are mere accidents, Carlebach responded, "To be as accident-prone as possible."[34]

A Typology of Soul Projects with Selected Examples

The Love of God project was my favorite. To intentionally set aside time to spend with the Lord in quiet, even for a class assignment, was such a blessing.

—Laura, student

We chose the "typology" as a means to frame the various kinds of soul projects we have created and discovered through our work. A typological framework is based upon examples that illustrate the major differences between ideal types. Unlike the taxonomy, a typology does not imply the listing is exhaustive—additional categories are indeed likely, particularly as soul projects become better known and understood. Also in contrast with the taxonomy, typologies do not have mutually exclusive categories—the types are more likely to overlap to some extent.[35] The classic work *Christ and Culture* by H. Richard Niebuhr is a prime example of a typology, and the most recent edition of that work includes an added chapter outlining the typological method, as well as important limitations of this approach.[36] What a typology clearly underscores is that there are multiple approaches to soul projects, even though some kinds could legitimately be located in more than one category. We encourage the use of soul projects that may fit more than one of the categories provided, as doing so may increase the probability that a given project will resonate spiritually with a variety of students.

We have identified a number of class projects that support spiritual and integrative outcomes in higher education. These projects are not intended simply as supplemental to more traditional assignments. We see them as necessary to achieve the spiritual transformation desired in Christian education. The assignments are classified below in broad categories based on the learning strategies they employ. While these categories reflect the same broad strategies, the actual soul projects may have a very different look and feel depending on whether it is a group or individual project and the specific activities and intellectual skills emphasized in its implementation.

Following each of the brief definitions are one or more actual examples of projects we have used in our classes. The descriptions are distinctively worded to maintain the language of the original author to the degree possible, while explanations have been added to provide necessary context.

Reflective Exercises

These structured experiences are designed to encourage students to reflect on the spiritual significance of the course material and to promote the development of wisdom through integrating academic material into the student's values and belief structures. These projects are very personal, often reflective, and thus require an ability to self-evaluate.

Small Group Conversation. All of you participated in a field learning project this semester. Meet in a small group three times (at least one hour) to reflect on your experience. Build reflection around the following questions: What is going on? Why is it going on? What ought to be going on? What will I/we do?

> *Product (individual):* Submit a two-page paper that addresses each of the four questions and indicates your level of participation in the group process.

> *Product (group):* Complete the "Group Process Form." Bring a poster to class that summarizes the experience.

Pilgrimage and Pilgrim's Progress Paper. Students will reflect upon the spiritual pilgrimage of Christian in *Pilgrim's Progress.* What parallels exist between you and Bunyan's account? And what do you see as places where your journeys differ? How adequately does the Hagberg and Guelich model describe Christian's spiritual development in *Pilgrim's Progress*? What are the lessons you take away from reading Bunyan and reflecting on your own spiritual journey?

Leading Lives That Matter Essay. What did you see as the general themes of Tolstoy's *The Death of Ivan Illyich* and how have these impacted your understanding of what you should do and who you should be? (i.e., What have you taken from your experiences and this book and how will it be applied in your life?)

Statements of Personal Intention

In these experiences students are asked to state their intention to embark or continue on a beneficial path. Students are invited to use a basic strategy of positive change—making a clear commitment to a beneficial pattern. Through stating a clear intention students indicate to themselves and others they are going to do something different or continue a healthy pattern with renewed intentionality—simply put, they make a pledge. In its most basic form a teacher may simply tell the class "to do well in this class you will need to learn the new vocabulary words every day and . . . if you are willing to do that I'll see you on Wednesday." Some professors opt to write a "Course Ethos Statement" to intentionalize their desire for cultivating a positive class atmosphere and to emphasize the importance of a prosocial orientation. Making personal intentions is a powerful device in promoting change. A significant way to signal this intention is to create a simple ceremony or pledge that marks the commitment.

Course Ethos Statements. I agree to: a. Show respect for class members and support their learning even when disagreements arise; b. Come on time to all seminars, workshops, field assignments, and lectures. I understand that tardiness and lack of preparation indicate lack of planning on my part and disrespect for fellow classmates; c. Come to seminars, labs, and workshops with readings and written work thoughtfully prepared, and actively participate; d. Complete assigned work carefully and by the due date; e. Complete a self-evaluation and faculty evaluation by the end the term.

Accountability Groups. Accountability groups help Christians stay faithful in their walk with Christ and help them overcome patterns of sinning. It provides a context to live out James 5:16, "Therefore confess your sins to each other and pray for each other so that you may be healed."

> **Guidelines:** The emphasis in these groups should be on grace-based accountability. Holding members accountable is the first priority, but this must be done with a clear realization that this is not a spiritual self-improvement program because the gospel tells us that not only are we dearly loved by God but that we will never be good enough, and while we're sinners, and we'll always sin, we are to be of good cheer because grace can heal and transform. These groups must be "safe containers" for honest confession and need to be judicious in including both support and challenge.

Process: Small Group Participation. Form a small group (same gender) for the explicit purpose of encouraging faithfulness in the practice of a spiritual discipline or avoiding defeating patterns of disobedience. The group should appoint an informal moderator who is the contact person and keeps the group on track. The small group meeting time should be approximately fifty percent prayer and fifty percent discussion/accountability on the "contracted issue." You should meet once each week for sixty minutes.

Product: Record your meeting times and have each member complete the "Commitment and Personal Engagement Evaluation Form."

Spiritual Practices

Spiritual practices and disciplines are a central part of the Christian devotional and community life. These sacred rhythms provide a context for receiving spiritual sustenance and learning to imitate Jesus. When fostering these practices we need to remember Jesus' words on the necessity of new wineskins (Luke 5:37–8). When spiritual disciplines are practiced from a legalistic framework then a legalistic lifestyle will ensue, but when they are placed in a context of faith and love, then a spiritually vital lifestyle is fostered. These assignments are intended to encourage students to learn to practice spiritual disciplines in an intentional and reflective manner. These may be related directly to the course content (e.g., practicing fixed hour prayer in a history class when monasticism is studied) or support a learning outcome (e.g., keeping a gratitude journal in a class seeking to engender compassion for the oppressed). Often these will be carefully designed individual projects, but sometimes students are guided through a group spiritual experience.

Lectio Divina. A structured process of reading and meditating (literally "divine reading") on a sacred text. The students are encouraged to establish a pattern of meditating on Scripture or a spiritually enriching text that includes slow and thoughtful reading, meditative pauses to mull over the text, times of prayer based on the text and a quiet waiting before God. Some highly structured patterns of practicing *lectio divina* have been developed. For the first-time meditator we suggest something less structured to keep the focus on the joy of being before God and his truth rather than on mere technique.

Holy Leisure/Sabbath keeping. Observe the Sabbath by refraining from labor (studying, housekeeping that can be done another day), distracting entertainment, and by positively using this time for hospitality, service, and leisurely spiritual activities. Seek to keep the Sabbath by grace and not legalistic rationalizations. Use Eugene Peterson's guidance to inform your choices of activities: "We could do anything, but nothing that was necessary. We would play and we would pray. Anything under the category of play was legitimate; anything in the category of pray was legitimate."[37] Record the activities of each Sabbath and compare your energy level and restfulness with previous experiences of non-Holy Leisure Sunday life.

Prayer Projects

These projects are intended to encourage students to incorporate prayer into their study of the classroom subject. The Bible calls believers to pray always and prayer should permeate the Christian student's academic life. With some of these projects the aim is not so much to cultivate new patterns of prayer as much as it is to foster a new dimension in one's prayers.[38]

Formational prayer. Spend thirty minutes praying over your notes from the readings. Reflect on the readings; talk to God about them. Then listen to what God says to you about what you've read. What nudgings or impressions do you get from the Holy Spirit about the relevance of what you've read for your life? Report on what God reveals to you about himself in this regard, the content of the reading, and about your own growth, teaching, and professional identity. Hand in two-page prayer reports on specified due dates.

Fixed Hour Prayer. For one week (five days out of seven) follow a pattern of morning and evening prayer. Select a prayer book and stay with it for the week. The most accessible ones are the *Book of Common Prayer* ("Daily Devotions for Individuals and Families" p. 137ff), *A Diary of Private Prayer* by John Baillie, *The Divine Hours* (book or on-line at explorefaith.org/prayer). Keep a log of when you prayed and write a one-page reflection.

Journaling and Discernment

These assignments encourage students to keep a journal related to the course material. We have found that journaling is one of the most common integrative assignments. Desired outcomes include: fostering self-reflection, documenting student engagement, providing the grist for discernment activities, and encouraging the development of intellectual virtues such as gratitude.

Gratitude journal. Every evening for three weeks write five things you are grateful for each night before bedtime. Look for things during the day for which you are grateful and give particular attention to those things that are gifts—good things that you received and enjoyed but did not cause. Submit this journal with all entries dated and with a brief reflection on what you learned from doing this.

After reading *The Wounded Healer* by Henri Nouwen aloud as a group, do the following exercise. Nouwen uses the descriptor "wounded healer" to describe the minister of Christ and in a sense the ministry of Christ to this world. How is this descriptor further unveiled when looking at the life, death, and resurrection of Jesus? How does this impact your understanding of what it means to be his apprentice, his disciple?

Read the following passage out loud as a group: Phil. 2:1–11 (everyone should have the passage in front of them as it is read). Take ten minutes and quietly sit with this passage allowing your time of meditation to be guided by this question: "How is Christ the model of a wounded healer?" After your time of meditation, dialogue together considering, "What are the sufferings/wounds of your time (personally and globally) and what does it involve to serve as Christ in this world?" or "How is it that in your own woundedness you become a source of life for others?"

Awe-Evoking Experiences

These projects are intended to encourage students to be open to awe-inspiring dimensions of their academic work. The experience of awe can occur at any point in the curriculum. In some cases it will be evoked through the study of Christian themes, for others, the grandeur and mystery of nature will be the precipitating factor, while still others will come to experience awe through beauty and aesthetics. These experiences are designed to help students process these experiences and see their formative value as they contribute to an appropriate diminishing of the ego.

Search for Convergence. A daily God Hunt to encourage finding "sightings of God's activity."[39] Keep a journal in which you record unusual convergences (e.g., a check in the mail when funds are most needed, seeing an old acquaintance when reconciliation is needed). Convergence of events (and recurrent events and thoughts) may reflect God's movement in a person's life. We will discuss what we have found in class.

Overcome by awe. Our studies and subject matter should lead us to times of being overcome by awe or mystery. Make note of times when the course material (this could be a reading, a lab experience, or a new perspective provided in the class) has given you an awe experience. An awe experience often has two sides: 1. An emotional element that variously combines amazement, deep respect, dread, veneration, and wonder, and 2. A feeling of personal insignificance or powerlessness in the face of this awesome person/object/theme. Be prepared to give a brief oral account in class of your being awestruck.

Identity Formation

In college, students begin to take on a professional and adult Christian identity. These projects are intended to help students reflect on their priorities and values, probing for what the students are coming to love, for the presence of Gospel virtues in their lives, and for the identity of their mentors and heroes.

Sacred Stories. Telling your story with an eye on discerning how God has been at work in your life. A large portion of our class is given to telling and listening to our stories.

I want you to practice the art of telling a story (you will be able to use your journey paper "theme" as a foundation and guide). Do not simply read your journey paper. Each student will have twenty minutes to share. Due to the size of the class I will have to be strict with time so please plan your sharing appropriately. Weave your own personal story through your internship experience. Viewing your internship as your most recent bookend, share also your prior life history, struggles, discoveries, growth, as well as future plans. I want you to practice the art of listening—a time of questions and prayer will be offered for each student after they have shared. I want you to view this as a creative experience in storytelling. The use of props, power point, video, music, overheads, etc. is suggested as tools to draw us into the story you are telling. I want you to view this experience as an act of worship (both as presenter and as listener).

Best Practices

Another beneficial assignment has been the position papers we write in Senior Seminar. It is so rewarding to finally explore things that I have always wanted to know more about. . . . Those are two assignments that have really impacted my faith and walk with God. They allowed me to search more about myself and the things I am interested in.
—Camie, student

In encouraging the use of soul projects, we are standing in the long tradition of Christian spiritual teachers who made spiritual practices part of their actual teaching. From these long-established practices we can find some persistent patterns that can be identified as best practices in this area. These best practices describe the framework for introducing these projects and concrete suggestions on how to structure them.

In asking faculty members who regularly employ soul projects about lessons learned, we were told: Be clear in your directions, tie them directly to course content, and suggest a venue. Students have been well socialized to know what it means to write a paper, but they are not as certain when it comes to something such as a soul project and consequently they will benefit from clear directions. Clarity does not need to be constricting and while these teachers all praised clarity they also underscored the benefits of allowing students to personalize assignments. We have found it helpful to present the project to the student with these three headings: project (title and brief description); process (what the students need to do including time and venue); and product (what the student needs to turn in as evidence of having done this). Soul projects are about fostering time before God and others, so it is critical that the experiential component is exceptionally clear. Course evaluations will yield some useful information about how students interpret assignment directions. As part of incorporating spiritual activities into a class, students need to be directed to make connections between the class materials and these activities. In other words, do not take for granted that a prayer assignment in a Biology course will lead the student to pray about what she is learning in the course. Make your expectations clear. The connection may be explicitly tied to a reading or assignment, or one may ask students to make the connection between their spiritual life and the course materials.

More than one professor reported being bemused when a student innocently let slip the venue for practicing a soul project (i.e., fast food restaurant, in a noisy dorm lounge where they were interrupted). Helping students understand the connection between setting and reflective practice is an important aspect of these projects. Suggested venues can be given in the general directions or by designating a specific location such as a chapel or building. Sometimes it is important to suggest a venue for a given assignment (e.g., "for this assignment find a spot where you can comfortably journal without interruptions for ninety minutes. In seeking to foster an awe-receptivity, you will need to do this assignment in a natural setting that you have found to be 'awe-inspiring.'") Asking students to report where they did their projects helps make them aware that they are expected to show intentionality in their choices.

Perhaps the most important variable that students bring to these projects is intentionality. Do they intend to just check off a task? Do they intend to make themselves better through focused self-discipline? Do they want to use their participation to impress the teacher? Participants in these projects need to be reminded that they should affirm their intentions of meeting before God and being open to his grace at the beginning of every project. There are a myriad of ways to do this. Some instructors provide a prayer of intention suggested for use by students before they begin a project. Others suggest a pattern of quiet and watchful breathing during which they become more attentive to God.

One of the tough judgment calls in using soul projects is balancing support and challenge. Students will not benefit significantly if all the projects are practices with which they are familiar and experience with some regularity. On the other hand, if students are expected to take on unfamiliar practices without directions and clear expectations they may feel challenged to the point that they become defensive or less than enthusiastic. A scale we have found helpful is "comfort, stretch or stress."[40] We want participants to feel stretched by the assignment (appropriate challenge in a supportive environment), but not so much that they become stressed and non-engaged (too much challenge). Personal communication and feedback from students provides one of the best ways of fine-tuning assignments.

One participant at a conference presentation related to soul projects recommended that soul projects in some way be connected to the local church. Perhaps instructors can state that soul projects are not a substitute for the church, and that the individual spiritual experience emphasized in many soul projects has its necessary counterpart in community expressions of worship. Scripture suggests that the community of believers includes an array of spiritual gifts so that personal experiences can be tested and either affirmed or questioned. The gift of distinguishing between spirits seems particularly relevant in this regard (1 Cor. 12:10), although the context of this passage implies that such discernment is as much a corporate activity as it is the result of personal gifting. The local church connection to soul projects deserves further exploration, as students could share their spiritual experiences with mature parishioners as part of their projects. It may also be that special services could provide a distinctive context for soul projects, such as a Taizé service, special church year services, or a midweek prayer meeting.

Evaluating Soul Projects

Evaluation can take place in several possible ways, using both quantitative measures and qualitative analysis. Students are not well served by merely giving an A for effort. Careful attention to the context and outcomes of the project can make evaluation more effective. Students should be asked to report on the time spent, date, time of day, location and ambiance of the setting, and how they construed their time (i.e., began with a prayer of intention, began with a time of quiet reflection). They may self-report on the degree to which they believe they followed the assignment, their preparation for the project (i.e., suggest practical items such as adequate sleep to prevent drowsiness, having all needed material at hand) and their perceived sense of engagement with the assignment (we suggest using a Likert scale where students mark their engagement level). John Coe adds that effort and proficiency in relation to other developmental indicators also should be assessed.[41]

Student allegations of subjectivity in grading can probably be diminished with clear standards. Here is an example of expectations for one specific soul project of a written nature:

> For each class after the first week you are to bring a written description of your participation in a soul project. The instructions for each activity tell you what to do and then how to write this up. The reports are graded on quality. A high-quality report provides thoughtful, sincere, complete responses to the assignment according to the instructions. A low-quality report gives brief, less thoughtful, sketchy, incomplete, irrelevant, trite, or phony responses to the assigned activity, or does not conform to the instructions. The key to writing high-quality reports is to approach the activity with informed enthusiasm, to give yourself time to reflect on the assignment prior to writing it up, and to really put your heart into writing about it. Reports should be typed, but need not follow a particular, formal writing style.

Evaluation in the form of a number or a letter grade is always an oversimplification of what a student accomplishes, and that seems particularly acute when it comes to evaluating an aspect of spirituality. Summative evaluations of this sort reflect product more than process, and clearly the latter is more crucial in soul projects. Students should be encouraged to describe the experience, not just the results, and explore the multidimensionality of soul projects in their narratives. Again, describing rich spiritual experiences in the form of narrative is admittedly reductionistic, yet that description in itself can be valuable as the student attempts to label components of what is, hopefully, an encounter with divinity that is beyond words. Even reducing the experience to accurate theological designations cannot be said to be adequately isomorphic to what was experienced—indeed this is its own kind of reductionism—but it can be beneficial to attempt such a representation. Rather than a comprehensive description, perhaps a tentative, partial convergence between event and the linguistic description should be the goal.

The following is an extended sample report form. Please note, the sample is more detailed than the typical report form so that a number of possible components can be explored here that might not be relevant to every soul project.

Sample Student Project Report Form

You were to select a quiet place that would allow for a time of undisturbed reflection.

1. Where did you do this? To what extent did this space work for you?

2. What did you do to structure your space and time so that it would be beneficial to you?

3. What other things did you do to prepare for this experience?

4. How long were you engaged in the experience? How much additional time did you spend reflecting before doing this report?

5. Outline specifically, in your own words, what you did during the time. (one paragraph)

6. Describe the internal, personal experience that resulted from this activity. (one paragraph)

7. What do you feel you learned through the experience? (one paragraph)

8. If someone not taking this class expressed an interest in doing this activity, would you recommend they do so? What adjustments to the instructions—if any—would you recommend?

9. I think I would:

( ) like to do this activity again in the near future

( ) possibly repeat this activity at some point in the future

( ) probably not consider doing this activity again

10. How much effort did you give this activity?

( ) a great deal ( ) a moderate amount ( ) minimal

11. What was the level of authentic involvement in the activity?

( ) highly engaged ( ) generally engaged ( ) somewhat distracted ( ) very distracted

12. I feel the intensity of the experience was:

( ) high ( ) moderate ( ) low

13. The degree of personal ownership of the experience was:

( ) high ( ) moderate ( ) low

14. The experience was:

( ) comfortable ( ) a bit of a stretch ( ) very much a stretch
( ) stressful

15. How valuable was this experience?

( ) very enriching ( ) somewhat helpful ( ) uncertain
( ) not helpful

16. Reflecting upon the above criteria, pray for two minutes, asking God to show you what grade you deserve for this soul project. At the conclusion of your prayer and reflection, what grade do you believe should be given?

Of the sixteen questions listed (some of them involving more than one answer), ten can potentially contribute to the grade given to the student (items 1–7, 10, 13, and 16). Responses to many of the items, but particularly the first five, attempt to determine if the student followed the instructions provided. Yet they also indicate the degree to which the student felt free to personalize the experience, which may or may not facilitate the activity, a factor the instructor may want to take into consideration in providing a grade. The length of time for the experience and subsequent reflection (item 4) may be another way of getting at the degree of engagement (items 11 and 13).

It should be noted that multiple measures—in this case fixed options as well as open-ended questions—may reveal consistency in student response, and thus at least some degree of reliability. One might question whether item 6 should be included in determining a grade. The assumption made is that the internal experience might be positive or negative: while a positive experience is desired by the instructor, a negative reaction might indicate a high level of authentic involvement as much as a positive reaction. Likewise, item 7 implies that the student can learn from any soul project, and by the same token that learning may not always be what was intended. Perhaps it is not too much to assume that a highly motivated person can learn something from any experience.

Depending upon the instructor's inclination, it may be that item 16 would carry a disproportionate amount of weight in assigning a final grade for the project. Yet that item carries with it—as indeed does the entire report—the assumption that the student actually carries out the project, and does so in the manner described. Some items that do not directly contribute to a grade may provide insight that will help in evaluating other items, and thus indirectly contribute to the grade. To say, for example, that the experience was "very much a stretch" (item 14) may imply that effort (item 10) be considered to a greater extent than personal ownership (item 13) for a given student.

The best evaluation—in the present time-space continuum at least—includes written comments and dialogue as a complement to grading. Ideally words could be at least a partial replacement for grades, preferably both written and dialogue in person. Evaluation in the form of a portfolio is a possibility to be considered, as well as the formal or informal paper. Group and peer evaluations of a written nature or checklists are also possible. But the perfect evaluation does not exist, and perhaps that should be admitted to students. This is but the human condition.

Conclusion

Soul projects are to be encouraged within the classrooms of Christian higher education in order to promote the spiritual and character formation of students. A search of foundational theories from the fields of philosophy, education, sociology, psychology, and business has provided a basis for the discussion and exploration of soul projects. Soul projects weave adaptations of Christian practices into the class-rooms and assignments for the purpose of promoting spiritual experiences and formation within the context of a specific academic curriculum and study. Major categories, best practices, and assessment were described. For each category, examples from our experience are shared in hopes that the reader might consider using these and/or adaptations in his/her classroom.

The work of soul projects is ongoing and feedback would be most welcome. Because the vision is to have soul projects used within all disciplines across the college campus, tested examples of soul projects used in other departments (i.e. law, science, history, engineering, medicine, and mathematics, etc.) would expand the ongoing discussions. Additionally, questions have been raised as to how soul projects might be adapted for the teaching ministry of the church. There may eventually be other contexts into which these general ideas could be exported, as a desire to promote the spiritual and character formation of learners grows beyond the formal realms of Christian higher education. Such work would most effectively and naturally evolve through the ministry of graduates who have, during their years as students, been spiritually transformed though the incorporation of soul projects in their learning experiences.

Chapter 12 Notes

[1] This chapter was first published as "Spiritual Formation Goes to College: Class-Related 'Soul Projects' in Christian Higher Education" in the *Christian Education Journal* 7 (Fall 2010): 401–422. It is reprinted here by permission of the *Christian Education Journal*, which holds the copyright to this article.

[2] On this theme, see, for example, Cornelius Plantinga, *Engaging God's World: A Christian Vision of Faith, Learning, and Living* (Grand Rapids, Mich.: Eerdmans, 2002); Nicholas Wolterstorff, *Educating for Responsible Action* (Grand Rapids, Mich.: Eerdmans, 1980); Steven Garber, *The Fabric of Faithfulness: Weaving Together Belief and Behavior during the University Years* (Downers Grove, Ill.: InterVarsity Press, 1996).

[3] Arthur Holmes, *Shaping Character: Moral Education in the Christian College* (Grand Rapids, Mich.: Eerdmans, 1991), 1, 58–72.

[4] Tim T. Clydesdale, *The First Year Out: Understanding American Teens after High School* (Chicago: University of Chicago Press, 2007), 4.

[5] Sharon Daloz Parks, *Big Questions, Worthy Dreams: Mentoring Young Adults in Their Search for Meaning, Purpose, and Faith* (San Francisco, Calif.: Jossey-Bass, 2000), 71–87.

[6] William Deresiewicz, "The End of Solitude," *The Chronicle of Higher Education* 55, no. 21 (January 30, 2009).

[7] On this theme, see especially Mark Edmundson, "Dwelling in Possibilities," *The Chronicle of Higher Education* 54, no. 27 (14 March 2008); or Maggie Jackson, *Distracted: The Erosion of Attention and the Coming Dark Age* (New York: Prometheus Books, 2008).

[8] Plantinga, *Engaging God's World*, 125.

[9] St. Augustine, *The Soliloquies of St. Augustine*, trans. Rose Elizabeth Cleveland (Boston, Mass.: Little, Brown, and Co., 1910), 1.2.7 & 2.1.1.

[10] Alasdair MacIntyre, *After Virtue: A Study in Moral Theory* (Notre Dame, Ind.: University of Notre Dame Press, 1981), 175.

[11] Craig Dykstra, *Growing in the Life of Faith: Education and Christian Practices* (Louisville, Ky.: Geneva Press, 1999), 70.

[12] Kathleen A. Cahalan, "Three Approaches to Practical Theology, Theological Education, and the Church's Ministry," *International Journal of Practical Theology* 9 (2005): 63–94.

[13] Craig Dykstra and Dorothy C. Bass, "A Theological Understanding of Christian Practices," in *Practicing Theology: Beliefs and Practices in Christian Life*, eds. Miroslav Volf and Dorothy C. Bass (Grand Rapids, Mich.: Eerdmans, 2001), 18. See also Craig Dykstra and Dorothy C. Bass, "Times of Yearning, Practices of Faith," in *Practicing Our Faith: A Way of Life for a Searching People*, ed. Dorothy C. Bass (San Francisco, Calif.: Jossey-Bass, 1997), 5.

[14] John Coe has served as a catalyst to our thinking about soul projects. See Coe, "Intentional Spiritual Formation in the Classroom: Making Space for the Spirit in the University," *Christian Education Journal*, 4NS (2000): 85–110. On the theme of service learning, see Mark Radecke, "Service-learning and Faith Formation," *Journal of College and Character* 8, no. 5 (July 2007).

[15] Parker J. Palmer, *To Know as We Are Known: A Spirituality of Education* (San Francisco, Calif.: Harper & Row, 1983), 69.

[16] Dykstra, *Growing in the Life of Faith*, 22.

[17] On these themes, see especially George Marsden, *The Soul of the American University: From Protestant Establishment to Established Nonbelief* (New York: Oxford University Press, 1994); Julie A. Reuben, *The Making of the Modern University: Intellectual Transformation and the Marginalization of Morality* (Chicago: University of Chicago Press, 1996); Jon H. Roberts and James Turner, *The Sacred and the Secular University* (Princeton, N.J.: Princeton University Press, 2000); and David P. Setran, *The College "Y": Student Religion in the Era of Secularization* (New York: Palgrave Macmillan, 2007).

[18] Wolterstorff, *Educating for Responsible Action*, 13–14.

[19] James W. Sire, *Discipleship of the Mind: Learning to Love God in the Ways We Think* (Downers Grove, Ill.: InterVarsity Press, 1990), especially 97–113.

[20] John Dewey, *Experience and Education* (New York, N.Y.: Macmillan, 1938), 42–50.

[21] Ibid., 33–50.

[22] Wolterstorff, *Educating for Responsible Action*, 3–6.

[23] Erik H. Erikson, *Childhood and Society*, 2nd ed. (New York: Norton, 1963). Also James E. Marcia, "Development and Validation of Ego-Identity Status," *Journal of Personality and Social Psychology* 3 (1966): 551–558.

[24] Parks, *Big Questions, Worthy Dreams*, 71–87.

[25] See especially Keith R. Anderson and Randy D. Reese, *Spiritual Mentoring: A Guide for Seeking and Giving Direction* (Downers Grove, Ill.: InterVarsity Press, 1999).

[26] Howard Gardner, *Multiple Intelligences: The Theory in Practice* (New York: Basic Books, 1993).

[27] Arnold H. Buss, "Temperaments as Personality Traits," in *Temperament in Childhood*, eds. Geldolph A. Kohnstamm, John E. Bates, and Mary Klevjord Rothbart (Chichester, N. Y.: Wiley, 1989), 49–58.

[28] M. Robert Mulholland Jr., *Invitation to a Journey: A Road Map for Spiritual Formation* (Downers Grove, Ill: InterVarsity Press, 1993), 57–73.

[29] Peter M. Senge, *The Fifth Discipline: The Art and Practice of the Learning Organization* (New York: Doubleday/Currency, 2006), 150–155.

[30] Chris Argyris, "Teaching Smart People How to Learn," *Reflections* 4, no. 2 (1991): 4–15.

[31] Keri Wyatt Kent, *Listen: Finding God in the Story of Your Life* (San Francisco, Calif.: Jossey-Bass, 2006).

[32] Jean Piaget, *Six Psychological Studies*, trans. Anita Tenzer, ed. David Elkind (New York, N.Y.: Random House, 1967).

[33] Dana R. Wright, "James Edwin Loder, Jr," in "Christian Educator's of the 20th Century," Talbot School of Theology, accessed October 16, 2006, www.talbot.edu/ce20/educators/view.cfm?n=james_loder.

[34] Bo Lozoff, *It's a Meaningful Life—It Just Takes Practice* (New York: Viking, 2000), 23–24.

[35] Michael Quinn Patton, *Qualitative Research and Evaluation Methods*, 3rd ed. (Thousand Oaks, Calif.: Sage, 2002), 457.

[36] H. Richard Niebuhr, *Christ and Culture*, expanded ed. (San Francisco, Calif.: HarperSanFrancisco, 2001).

[37] Eugene Peterson, "Eugene Peterson: That 'Good-for-Nothing' Sabbath," interview by Sandra Glahn, Aspire 2 Thinking that Transforms, weblog entry posted June 11, 2005, http://aspire2.blogspot.com/2005/06/eugene-peterson-that-good-for-nothing.html.

[38] One could possibly add activities using the imagination, including the use of Christian symbolism, structuring time through class celebrations of the church year or Old Testament calendar. See Chapter 6 of Alister E. McGrath, *Christian Spirituality: An Introduction* (Oxford, U.K.: Blackwell Publishers, 1999).

[39] Karen Burton Mains, *The God Hunt: The Delightful Chase and the Wonder of Being Found* (Downers Grove, Ill: InterVarsity Press, 2003).

[40] M. J. Ryan, *This Year I Will . . . : How to Finally Change a Habit, Keep a Resolution, or Make a Dream Come True* (New York: Broadway, 2006), 109. This scale resonates with Lev Vygotsky's concept of a "Zone of Proximal Development" in his book *Thought and Language* (Cambridge, Mass.: MIT Press, 1962).

[41] Coe, "Intentional Spiritual Formation," 103.

TOUR GUIDES, TRANSLATORS, AND TRAVELING COMPANIONS

How Faculty Contribute to the Spiritual Formation of Students

Greg Carmer

"What does the doctrine of the Trinity have to do with my modern history class?" It was an earnest question from an excellent faculty member, one who is a contributor to his field and is committed to the development of his students. The context was a faculty workshop on spiritual formation and I had just made an argument for the role that all faculty members play in the spiritual formation of our students, and our mutual responsibility to nurture them in the resources of the Christian tradition. He was having difficulty imagining appropriate ways to connect course material with the rich language of our theological heritage.

It is a good question and one that reveals one of the challenges Christian faculty members face in contributing to the spiritual growth of their students. For many of our institutions, helping students grow in their spiritual lives is central to our mission, yet obstacles in a variety of forms can prevent faculty from having the influence they desire to exercise.

In this chapter I will outline some of the common challenges faculty face in addressing the spiritual lives of students and suggest some strategies that are fitting for the classroom and for collaborating with residence life and campus ministry staff. In particular, I will offer three metaphors to suggest constructive ways of understanding the roles that faculty play in contributing to the spiritual formation of students. But first, it is important to understand a few challenges.

The Challenges of Contributing to Students' Spiritual Formation

It would be right to argue that, within Christian understandings, the shaping, development, or formation of the human person is work that belongs properly to the Holy Spirit. Whether understood as responsiveness to the call of God, conformity to the image of Christ, or demonstration of the fruits of the person, spiritual growth is always a matter that goes beyond human striving. Without the quickening involvement of God's Spirit within us, we have no hope of becoming creatures that reflect the glory for which we were created.

However, it is also true that our thoughts, behaviors, and dispositions play a significant role in cooperating with God's transformative work within us. So cultivating those thoughts, behaviors, and dispositions is a vital part of growing spiritually. Christian faculty members hoping to encourage students in ways that contribute to spiritual growth face several common challenges. We may organize these challenges according to several categories: *personal limits, institutional practices,* and *limiting perspectives.*

Personal limits may include factors such as: the demands placed upon one's time and attention in staying on top of teaching loads and contributing to one's professional guild; a sense of incompetence or personal discomfort in discussing spiritual matters with students; a sense of competition between the requirements of one's research and teaching career and the value of investing in the personal development of students held by one's institution; or a calendar so filled that one has little time to participate in special departmental events, let alone events sponsored by other divisions or non-academic departments.

Institutional practices which may present a challenge to faculty engagement with the spiritual lives of students include: large class sizes; core or general education classes being taught by part-time or adjunct faculty; a chapel program perceived to be disconnected from the activities of the classroom; and having academic advising conducted by personnel other than the teaching faculty.

Finally, a few perspectives which limit faculty members' effectiveness in aiding spiritual growth among students may include: a belief that matters of students' spiritual lives should be left to the chaplain's office or student development professionals; the belief that if one attends faithfully to the accreditation requirements of one's own department and to the acquisition of the discipline-specific content and skills by one's own majors, that the general intellectual, moral, and spiritual growth objectives of the school will somehow be met through other programming; that students are capable of making mature and integrative connections between course material and other areas of their lives with little or no help; or the notion that spiritual formation happens only through explicitly pietistic activities or religious practices.

Acknowledging the difficulties that all these challenges present, and with a full appreciation of the many pressures faced by faculty members, I would argue the following:

- The spiritual formation of students is the responsibility of all faculty (not a matter to be left to chaplains and student development staff).
- All faculty possess some ability to contribute positively to students' spiritual growth.
- The classroom affords a fitting and appropriate context in which that contribution can be made.
- Collaboration with student ministry personnel and participation in activities of the chapel office can multiply one's influence on students' spiritual lives.

Rather than addressing each of these directly, I would like to suggest several metaphors for the faculty member's role in students' spiritual journey that will help bridge the academic project of the classroom with the general aim of assisting students on their journey of a deepening spiritual life.

Metaphors for Faculty Influence in Student Spiritual Formation

Perhaps it is a phrase that is employed on your campus too; this little term students use derisively to suggest that campus culture is too provincial for their tastes and that community standards of conduct, in effect, raise a membrane of isolation and segregation between the student body and the real world. The term, as you may have guessed, is "bubble" and it is used in sentences such as "I have to escape the campus *bubble*!" or "People are so naive here in the *bubble*."

What students do not realize, however, is that campus life is typically a hotbed of ideas and activities, and that while they remain students, every week brings with it new people, places, ideas, authors, relationships, experiences, and insights capable of challenging their assumptions and revolutionizing their world. Compared to the pedestrian lives of the working masses who daily travel the same roads, watch the same entertainment, and interact with the same relatively small circle of friends, life on a college campus is more akin to a major air-hub connecting places, people, and cultures from all around the globe. Rather than living in a bubble, the vibrant life on campus is better compared to Grand Central Station which launches voyages to a thousand different worlds, and which has architecture comprised of a thousand windows with vistas into the universe. Of course, it is on the basis of what they see through those windows and experience on those voyages that they look back with contempt on the humble platform that launched their journeys. Perhaps it is only with time that they begin to appreciate the fact that the greatest gift of that bubble was the expansion of their horizons.

On the journey of enlarged vistas and expanded horizons which take students further out and deeper into the world, faculty play key roles, facilitating their passage from small worlds of self-referenced concern to the wonders of the worlds of history, science, literature, and art—a passage from the dimness of ignorance to the light of understanding. Likewise, on the spiritual journey toward greater apprehension of new life in Christ, faculty fill critical roles in aiding students on their way. The following metaphors suggest what those roles may offer: *tour guides*, *translators*, and *traveling companions*.

Tour Guides

A significant part of spiritual formation is finding answers to life's big questions: *What is life for? Who am I? What should I do? Where do I place my trust?* Yet with the specialization and division of labor that is a necessary part of contemporary campuses, these big questions can suffer neglect while faculty and staff focus on their particular areas of responsibility. Spiritual formation can be taken for granted, especially on Christian campuses, as a task shared by everyone but tended to by none. ("This is a Christian school, and we are all believers—of course students will grow spiritually!") Conversely, faculty members may abdicate responsibility and leave matters of spiritual formation to the professionals. ("My job is to teach math—the chaplain and student life staff take care of spiritual issues.") Both attitudes can encourage faculty to approach spiritual formation in a haphazard fashion, responding to opportunities to discuss spiritual matters only occasionally as they arise. However, faculty have an opportunity to serve as hospitable tour guides, helping students raise the big questions, connect the dots, and catch a glimpse of their place in the broader landscape—all factors which help students clarify a sense of identity and purpose.

We know that educational environments are not spiritually neutral.[1] Rather, the ways in which courses are offered, differences engaged, theories evaluated, grades assigned, learning assessed, furniture arranged, interaction facilitated, and reflection encouraged all contribute to a student's understanding of herself, the world, and her place in the world. The ways in which one class is related to another, and the academic project is related to the rest of one's life, communicate to students a great deal about how one is to navigate the world and understand one's obligation in the world.

Unfortunately, many of us have inherited, and work within, educational structures that owe more to the Carnegie Units model of measuring class time than to what makes good educational sense. From a distance, an outsider may be justified in assuming that the best learning model we have come up with consists of leading students from one fifty-minute lecture in a discrete discipline to the next within a series of seemingly incoherent requirements, all in a framework that is fairly disconnected from the interests, obligations, and exigencies of community life and personal identity. Yet few of us would point to such a strategy as typifying the moments of our most significant, life-shaping learning. Still, meeting the requirements of accrediting boards, keeping up with the expectations of one's professional guild, and providing educational opportunities packaged in a fashion readily recognized by prospective students tend to keep traditional structures in place.

Within this challenging environment, though, faculty members have opportunities to impact the structures that shape the educational project. Specifically, faculty may use their influence to encourage the incorporation of elements within the curriculum that have been demonstrated to contribute to the spiritual formation of students. Much like a tour guide articulates the highlights a city has to offer, a faculty member can highlight the vast resources within each student's grasp—resources or practices that intentionally aid in his or her spiritual formation. Such practices include: study abroad, service-learning, philanthropic giving and community service, interdisciplinary studies, leadership training, self-reflection, and contemplative practices.[2] These practices should be incorporated as much as appropriate in general education and core requirements.

In addition, the architecture of the four-year experience is also important in facilitating students' grasp of fundamental questions. Issues such as: how core classes are arranged and presented; whether capstone courses are offered, and whether opportunities for reflection and connection are promoted in those capstone classes; how one's major connects, or fails to connect, with other disciplines; and how general learning outcomes are assessed and interpreted, can all contribute to students' sense of who they are and how they should live. Similar to hospitable tour guides, faculty not only know and plan the journey, but can also explain the terrain, why certain elements are present and how they relate to one another.

The institutions and practices that shape the educational experience must be suited to general educational outcome goals as well as to the demands of individual disciplines. Well-designed structures ought to embody the qualities we identify in our general learning outcome goals for students: a sense of coherence, a view of the whole, congruity between cares and competencies, and a sense of purposeful relevance. One may ask if the rhyme and reason or coherence that exists within education requirements is intelligible to students, or accessible only to general education committees and chief academic officers. Are students given an opportunity to see the big picture, or are they left to wander among the trees of requirements and electives without catching a view of the whole forest? Faculty can help transform a sequence of required classes into a more coherent course of study rather than a checklist of obligations to be gotten out of the way. They can also help reinforce inter-departmental collaboration and connections between co-curricular activities and a student's major course of study. In a word, faculty have the opportunity to craft the four-year (or three-to-five year) curriculum in a way that exhibits our hopes for our graduates: a clear sense of identity, congruence, conviction, and purpose. Where there is a lack of continuity between the shape of the curriculum, on one hand, and the questions of who students are becoming and what they ought to do, on the other, educational institutions can easily neglect the cultivation of character along with other dimensions of students' inner lives. Indeed, this has been the trajectory of many schools that once took spiritual formation as a chief concern and have gradually lost interest in the inner lives of students over the past 150 years.[3]

By making time within the classroom for asking some simple questions and offering what may appear to be obvious observations, faculty can function as hospitable tour guides, helping students grasp the contours of the journey they are on and make sense of the territory in which they travel. Do your students understand where the courses they are taking fit in the institution's educational and spiritual goals articulated in college documents? Do they have an opportunity to consider how general education or core classes advance the mission of the school? Opportunities for reflecting on such questions may be built into classroom exercises as well as in evening discussions on topics relevant to students' academic experiences and their places in the wider world. Moreover, faculty can contribute to the general educational outcome goals and students' spiritual growth by creating opportunities to connect the meanings and values celebrated in chapel programs and co-curricular ministry opportunities (such as service to local communities and Bible study groups) to the learning and language of the classroom. Imagine the value of asking a student to employ concepts, perspectives, and theories of a course in reflecting on a novel read for a general education course or on their involvement in voluntary community service or a missions trip. Such an assignment would help the faculty member take greater ownership of the general developmental outcomes and assist students in gaining a greater sense of how their studies and activities relate to a coherent sense of self and purpose.

Translators

Translation is primarily about interpreting concepts and ideas from one system of meaning to another. Sometimes, this is made possible by a one-to-one correspondence between the words and meanings in one language with words and meanings in a second language. More often, however, it involves the use of a middle term that bridges the gap between one discourse and another. Successful use of such middle terms does not substitute or dissolve the meanings and values of one discourse into those of another. Rather, middle terms make points of connection that suggest the relevance, importance, and significance of elements within one discourse for that of another, thus enlarging both and catching both up within a new horizon broad enough to encompass both.

In the case of providing translation between the academic project and spiritual formation goals—that is, of connecting the content and quotidian activities of the classroom with the students' spiritual growth—there are such middle terms. Between sectarian definitions of spiritual formation ("becoming like Jesus"; "being transformed into the likeness of Christ"; "exhibiting the fruit of the Spirit") and the broadly generic ("openness to the transcendent"; "inner strength"; "moral orientation towards others"[4]), there lies a set of cognitive habits and affective orientations which are both deeply rooted in a Christian understanding of self and world, and broadly applicable to all educational settings. They are more *Theo-* than *Christo*-centric, which contributes to their wide applicability and allows for layering with biblical and theological language.

Here I offer three sets of cognitive habits and their accompanying affective orientations and suggest some of their importance to spiritual formation and relevance to the classroom. The cognitive habits—*paying attention, acknowledging dependence,* and *accepting responsibility*—may be taught through classroom exercises and assignments. The affective orientations which accompany the habits—*expressing wonder, exercising gratitude,* and *affirming hope*—however are not so much lesson-plan material but have more to do with "how teachers comport themselves"[5]; that is, how faculty engage the material and respond with their lives.

Paying Attention and Expressing Wonder

Perhaps no other habit is quite as fundamental to the inner development of the self as is the ability to train one's attention in one direction long enough for true insight to arise. Paying attention requires neglecting distractions to focus on a limited horizon. It is marked by focused eagerness, but is not so task-driven that it is closed to the unexpected. It requires care but is not self-interested. Paying attention takes a stance of receptivity, but is not passive. It not only opens oneself to receive *what is*, but also honors what *may be*. Paying attention may be marked by the tension of concentration, but is free from anxiety. In its purest form, paying attention loses all concern other than the quest for understanding.

Albert Einstein is rumored to have quipped: "It's not that I'm so smart, it's just that I stay with problems longer." More than ever it is important that we help students learn to pay attention to both their inner and outer worlds. Attending is a skill—a meta-skill, if you will—that could comprise the better part of learning.[6] And it is best taught, perhaps, by example. Simple classroom practices—such as asking questions and allowing for moments of silence—can open space for students to practice paying attention, but students are more likely to learn the habit if they see role models demonstrate it. I fear that we professors spend too much time asking to be paid attention to, and too little time practicing for our students the art of carefully paying attention. We are perhaps more comfortable playing the role of the one who knows than with modeling for students the act of coming to understand.

Paying attention, however, opens us to the world around us and within us, making the deliberate exercise of freedom possible. It may also open us to new experiences of God's presence. Simone Weil, who was as influential in political movements as she was insightful in spiritual matters, writes:

> If we concentrate our attention on trying to solve a problem of geometry, and if at the end of an hour we are no nearer to doing so than at the beginning, we have nevertheless been making progress each minute of that hour in another more mysterious dimension. Without our knowing or feeling it, this apparently barren effort has brought more light into the soul. The result will one day be discovered in prayer. Moreover, it may very likely be felt in some department of the intelligence in no way connected with mathematics. Perhaps he who made the unsuccessful effort will one day be able to grasp the beauty of a line of Racine more vividly on account of it. But it is certain that this effort will bear its fruit in prayer. There is no doubt whatever about that.[7]

An affective orientation that is naturally paired with the habit of paying attention and which contributes to spiritual formation is that of expressing wonder. Wonder differs from curiosity in that curiosity is often tied to simple insight or technical mastery, whereas wonder entails a disposition of the spirit. Curiosity is satisfied with understanding; wonder compels one towards a response. Curiosity leads to an insight which one may possess; wonder acknowledges the presence of something which is beyond possession.

Famously, in the *Theaetetus,* Socrates states that wonder is the beginning (or principle) of philosophy.[8] Wonder is both the vehicle and fruit of moving beyond the horizon of our immediate concern to contemplate what is. Ever transcending the self and simultaneously affirming the self as a member of the great family of *being,* wonder places one in conscious awareness of the constantly receding horizon between the known and the unknown and seeks understanding for its own sake. Wonder places one in relation to what is, not as a consumer or master or user, but as a sibling in creation. It celebrates what is and accepts that what is grasped is always surrounded by what is not understood. Not that we avoid thematic, conceptual explanation, but that the ever-receding background of our focal knowledge is a field of mystery, like black velvet against which our small diamonds of knowledge shine as stars in a vast sky of the unknown. It is not just that in wonder one is impressed by how much one does not know (that is a well the bottom of which will never be plumbed), but that what is known places claims upon the knower—claims that evoke a response of awe, reverence, respect, and care and which may convey a sense of the "harmonious wholeness"[9] Merton wrote about. Scripture also provides us with passages of wonder growing out of attention to the natural world and one's relation to it. Psalm 8 and 139 offer beautiful examples of this.

Helping students find their way into wonder may involve helping dislodge them from the mundane habits of viewing the world through utilitarian, consumer, or expressivistic lenses. It may also include occasioning some cognitive dissonance. However, the unsettledness of wonder is quite unlike the distress of lost paradigms of meaning. Provoking one to wonder is the opposite of seeking to deconstruct frameworks of understanding, because wonder expands frameworks rather than destroying them. The assumption that students are foreclosed fundamentalists can lead faculty members to assume the responsibility of disassembling the structures that have helped make possible a student's belief in the meaning, purpose, and goodness of life. Certainly, students come with frameworks that need to be expanded, altered and, in some cases, abandoned altogether. However, offering a new perspective (that the books of Scripture are historic documents and can be studied as such), or challenging a firmly held belief (that the universe is only six thousand years old) can be done in different ways. Faculty can undermine a student's belief that his or her religious tradition has something very important to say about things that really matter, *or* can affirm the importance of big questions and patiently offer a new platform from which students may experience a deeper sense of wonder, awe, and respect. As we practice with students the habit of paying attention and model for them the expression of wonder, we help cultivate in them spiritual awareness and response.

Acknowledging Dependence and Exercising Gratitude

Closely connected to a disposition of wonder is the acknowledgement of dependence and the posture of gratitude. Acknowledgement of dependence and interdependence is perhaps not a common objective on course syllabi, but it is relevant to every discipline we teach. Of course, we hope for all our students that they will be able to think for themselves and exercise the autonomy of judgment necessary for individual responsibility. But to cultivate spiritual maturity we must also help them acknowledge dependence and respond in gratitude. The culture of competition and critique to which faculty are socialized during graduate school is of limited value in advancing the spiritual formation goals of a liberal education. Perhaps our dependence is so obvious that we think it unremarkable. From the language we use, the concepts we employ, and the methods we practice, to the facilities we occupy, the readings we assign, and technology we depend on, in all these things our dependence and interdependence is profoundly evident. Yet by being mindful of our dependency in these ways, we have an occasion to help awaken students to one of the deepest spiritual and existential truths: that we are who we are only, ever, and always in relation to others and are radically dependent upon forces beyond our control.[10] Acknowledgement of dependence is concomitant with the sense of inner-connectedness that marks spiritual awakening.[11]

Students may come to us with an adolescent understanding of dependence and interdependence as a form of social contract which might run something like this: "For me to experience the freedoms of expression and security I wish to enjoy, I need to honor your desire for security and self-expression too; in this way we rely upon one another to respect the other's rights." Such an understanding is consistent with the categories of rights and tolerance and may form a minimal requirement for a pluralist, liberal democracy. It is not, however, the stuff of deepening spiritual identity. A social contract model of social identity is entirely compatible with the notion of selves conceived primarily as consumers and free self-expression as the greatest virtue, whereas appreciation for our interconnectedness and the claims placed upon us by our fellow humans and the rest of creation requires a deeper appreciation of our radical dependence with its concomitant responsibility.[12]

Parker Palmer argues that how professors interact with course material and how students are encouraged to engage the material has considerable impact on how students' inner lives are shaped. Our epistemology—the ways we view, use, and promote knowledge—holds our power for "forming or deforming human consciousness." "We shape souls," he writes, "by the shape of our knowledge." He states his thesis simply:

> I do not believe that epistemology is a bloodless abstraction; the *way* we know has powerful implications for the *way* we live. I argue that every epistemology tends to become an ethic, and that every way of knowing tends to become a way of living. I argue that the relation established between the knower and the known, between the student and the subject, tends to become the relation of the living person to the world itself. I argue that every mode of knowing contains its own moral trajectory, its own ethical direction and outcomes.[13]

When critique, competition, and objectivism are core features of the classroom, acknowledgement of dependence and the expression of gratitude yield to the delusions of autonomy and arrogance. In contrast, acknowledgement of our primal dependence upon the factors that have led to our existence and a response of grateful acceptance are central to spirituality. Cicero wrote that gratitude is the highest of all virtues and the source of all others.[14] We are commanded in Scripture to give thanks in all things[15] and the Apostle Paul reminds us that ingratitude is the ground of all types of wickedness and depravities.[16]

As with wonder, Christian professors are given the opportunity to model a posture of gratitude in response to our dependence. In a consumer-driven economy, gratitude is an easily neglected attitude. Discontentment fuels production and consumption as we are daily encouraged to covet our neighbors' cars, clothes, close friends, and teeth color. While commercial culture entices us to "compare up" (imaging how blessed is the apparently perfect life of the guy in the pharmaceutical commercial) and desire more, the classroom presents an opportunity to direct attention outward towards the issues of resource stewardship, care of neighbor, and inter-generational responsibility, and inward towards the source of our appetites, desires, disappointments, and true longings.

Exercises that ask students to identify ways in which they, as students of a particular discipline, are recipients of undeserved gifts and enumerating what they have to be grateful for within that field can help establish habits of mind and cultivate dispositions of heart that will yield spiritual fruit. In particular, such exercises assist in affirming one's identity as a member of the community of being. In the language of the New Testament, followers of Jesus may walk in greater awareness of themselves as members of Christ's body—"the fullness of him who fills everything in every way."[17]

Accepting Responsibility and Affirming Hope

Attentiveness that leads to wonder and acknowledgement of dependence accompanied by gratitude are both bound up with and push toward the acceptance of our inescapable responsibility as stewards of God's creation. Again, Psalm 8 (vv. 3–9 RSV) weaves together these elements of wonder, gratitude, responsibility, and hope in wonderful poetry:

> *When I look at thy heavens, the work of thy fingers,*
> *the moon and the stars which thou hast established;*
> *What is man that thou art mindful of him,*
> *and the son of man that thou dost care for him?*
> *Yet thou hast made him little less than God,*
> *and dost crown him with glory and honor.*
> *Thou hast given him dominion over the works of thy hands;*
> *thou hast put all things under his feet,*
> *all sheep and oxen, and also the beasts of the field,*
> *the birds of the air, and the fish of the sea,*
> *whatever passes along the paths of the sea.*
> *O Lord, our Lord, how majestic is thy name in all the earth!*

A sense of identity is never far from a conviction of purpose, both of which are central to the formation of the spirit. For knowledge is never without responsibility; the condition of our freedom is the commission of our stewardship. Bonheoffer, in his *Ethics*, makes explicit the connection between identity, purpose, and responsibility as he defines *calling*. "Vocation," he says, "is responsibility, and responsibility is the whole response of the whole person to reality as a whole."[18]

Inviting students into an embrace of responsibility may seem as frightening as it is daunting; it can be unsettling to imagine entrusting the future to those who currently have trouble managing course registration and class assignments! However, we can aid students in appropriating an identity of responsibility through mindfulness about which metaphors we allow to shape our understanding of education.

When education is imagined as a commodity that is sold to consumers, it is easy to assume that its purpose is to enrich the lives of those who are privileged enough to possess it. However, when education is cast as the process of preparing the next generation to grow into the responsibilities incumbent upon them as free persons, then different questions become important:

Who are you? not *What do you possess?*
What ought you do? not *What can you do?*

What responsibilities do students have for understanding the world and their impact within it? What responsibilities accompany the things they learn in our classrooms? What responsibilities do we have as professors—not only to department chairs and accrediting boards, but to our students, to truth, and to our local and global neighbors? How do our disciplines contribute to the protection and cultivation of our cultural and natural resources? What challenges and opportunities for contributing to the repair and development of our social and natural environments are emerging?

With the acceptance of responsibility comes one's spiritual stance towards that responsibility. Beyond psychological proclivities toward optimism and pessimism lie fundamental orientations of the spirit towards either hope or despair. Despair results from the belief that the ultimate meaning of life falls prey to circumstances beyond one's control: that meaning and purpose may be secured or lost depending upon the quality of what one suffers or accomplishes. Hope, on the other hand, rests in the conviction that the ultimate measure of meaning lies not in one's circumstances, but in a story much bigger than the vagaries of one's own life.

In the classroom we are afforded opportunities to help instill hope on a variety of levels. Some students need the benefit of an adult who communicates their belief in their ability to accomplish the necessary steps towards succeeding in a particular class. Others need to be reassured that through careful attention, perceptive intelligence, critical reflection, and wise deliberation, we are able to make progress on even the most difficult problems facing our local neighborhoods and the global community. All of our students may profit from the modeling of resilient hope that holds a steady belief in the good gift of life despite professional challenges and setbacks and personal disappointments and failures.

Hope differs from a similar sentiment readily found in academic settings: optimistic idolatry. Such idolatry is marked by exaggerated claims of a theory's, method's, or process's ability to deliver insight, explanation, control, or change. It will likewise grossly oversimplify complex realities and fail to acknowledge limits. Idolatry will call for sacrifices such as the neglect of certain areas of life, denial of competing interests, invalidation of marginal populations or experiences, and will ultimately fail to deliver on its promises. Hope, by contrast, readily acknowledges difficulties, aberrations, and conflicting interests, and yet continues to give itself to the quest for a fair and consistent solution. Where idolatry jealously insists on providing the only answer, hope acknowledges our current limits and trusts in a yet-to-be-revealed synthesis. Idolatry is always entangled with pride and the strong, even if hidden, aim of self-promotion. Hope acknowledges the contribution of others and a common fate for all. Idolatry says "I/we can build utopia" where hope prays regularly, "Your kingdom come, your will be done on earth as it is in heaven."

As translators, one exercise applicable in most classrooms is that of seeking to assess where one's discipline is vulnerable to idolatrous optimism and where it can honestly hope to make certain, if limited, contributions to the common good. Not only will such an exercise stimulate hope and foster a sense of responsibility, it will also reinforce the open nature of on-going investigation and our quest for understanding of, and fitting responses to, the world in which we live.

Traveling Companions

A third role that faculty have the opportunity of playing is that of traveling companions—ones who walk alongside students on their journey towards greater spiritual maturity. This may take the form of simple friendliness or the intimacy of one-on-one conversation with individual students concerning the challenges of their personal lives. In this role, we are granted access to how students view themselves: their sense of being at home in the world; their assessment of their ability to meet life's challenges; their sense of the transcendent; and meaning and purpose. In properly Christian categories, these challenges may be rearticulated as: believing that one is known and loved by God; that there is God-ordained work for them to do; and that the ultimate outcome of history is bound by God's righteousness.

It is a privilege (and sometimes a task) to walk with students through the emotional and spiritual vicissitudes that mark their journeys during the college years. Small challenges such as confusion about class scheduling, as well as major life crises such as the loss of a parent or sibling, often bring with them an occasion to interact with students in a very personal way. When such opportunities arise, faculty receive the gift of offering pastoral presence, empathetic support, and wise counsel which can provide the necessary encouragement to see students through difficult seasons and may effect deep and lasting change. In fact, according to research by Stella Ma, "working through a personal crisis or traumatic event" was reported by students as being second only to relationships with peers as a contributing factor to their spiritual growth while at college.[19]

Participating in co-curricular activities such as mentoring programs, small-group studies, or short-term service-learning and mission trips present excellent opportunities to get to know students in more personal ways. Better yet, such activities afford occasions for students to get to know their professors, their traveling companions, in more personal ways—a proven avenue of modeling spiritual paths of growth.

Concluding Note: The Value of Collaboration

The metaphors of tour guides, translators, and traveling companions offer suggestions for understanding the role of educators that rest as easily on the shoulders of campus ministry personnel and student development staff as those of faculty members. In the responsibilities and opportunities afforded by these roles, curricular and co-curricular distinctions blur. I believe firmly that as faculty and campus ministry staff, along with student development personnel, make a concerted effort to understand, support, and integrate each other's work with that of their own, the project of Christian education on our campus will come to reflect those traits we hope to see in our students: a deepening sense of identity and an empowering conviction of purpose. In turn, our students, too, will benefit from a greater opportunity to grasp the big picture of who they are and the life to which they are called.

Chapter 13 Notes

[1] Parker Palmer, "Community, Conflict and Ways of Knowing: Ways to Deepen Our Educational Agenda," in *Combining Service and Learning*, ed. J. Kendall (Raleigh, N.C.: National Society of Internships and Experiential Education, 1990), 22.

[2] Alexander W. Astin, Helen S. Astin, and Jennifer A. Lindholm, *Cultivating the Spirit: How College Can Enhance Students' Inner Lives* (San Francisco, Calif.: Jossey-Bass, 2011), 145ff. Also see: Alexander W. Astin, *What Matters in College: Four Critical Years Revisited* (San Francisco, Calif.: Jossey-Bass, 1993); Janet Eyler and Dwight E. Giles Jr., *Where's the Learning in Service-Learning?* (San Francisco, Calif.: Jossey-Bass, 1999); Barbara Jacoby and others, *Service-Learning in Higher Education: Concepts and Practices* (San Francisco, Calif.: Jossey-Bass, 1996); Sharon Daloz Parks, *Big Questions, Worthy Dreams: Mentoring Young Adults in Their Search for Meaning, Purpose, and Faith* (San Francisco, Calif.: Jossey-Bass, 2000); Robert A. Rhoads, *Community Service and Higher Learning: Explorations of the Caring Self* (Albany, N.Y.: State University of New York Press, 1997); and Eric O. Springsted, *Who Will Make Us Wise: How the Churches Are Failing Higher Education* (Cambridge, Mass.: Cowley, 1988).

[3] William C. Ringenberg, *The Christian College: A History of Protestant Higher Education in America* (Grand Rapids, Mich.: Baker Book House, 2006), 113; Springsted, *Who Will Make Us Wise*, 10; Michael L. Budde and John Wesley Wright, eds. *Conflicting Allegiances: The Church-Based University in a Liberal Democratic Society* (Grand Rapids, Mich.: Brazos Press, 2004), 14.

[4] Cf Astin, *Cultivating the Spirit*, 5.

[5] Nicholas Wolterstorff, *Educating for Responsible Action* (Grand Rapids, Mich.: Eerdmans, 1980), 111.

[6] "Although people seem to be unaware of it today" wrote Simone Weil, "the development of the faculty of attention forms the real object and almost the sole interest of studies." Simone Weil, *Waiting for God* (New York, N.Y.: G.P. Putnam's Sons, 1951), 105.

[7] Weil, *Waiting for God*, 106.

[8] Plato, *Theaetetus*, trans. Joe Sachs (Newbury Port, Mass.: Focus Publishing / R. Paullins Co, 2004), 155C. Aristotle makes the same observation in §2, book 1 of his *Metaphysics* (Ann Arbor, Mich.: University of Michigan Press, 1954).

[9] Thomas Merton, "Hagia Sophia," in *A Thomas Merton Reader*, ed. Thomas P. McDonnell (New York: Image/Doubleday, 1974), 506.

[10] This reality has been explored by social psychologists such as G. H. Mead from a behavioral and evolutionary perspective, and from a spiritual/existential perspective by Martin Buber and others.

[11] See, for example, Fowler's description of "Stage 6" faith: James W. Fowler, *Stages of Faith: The Psychology of Human Development and the Quest for Meaning* (San Francisco, Calif.: Harper & Row, 1981), 199.

[12] For a good critique of modern individualism, see Charles Taylor, *The Ethics of Authenticity* (Cambridge: Harvard University Press, 1991).

[13] Palmer, "Community, Conflict and Ways of Knowing," 107.

[14] Cicero, "The Speech of M.T Cicero in Defense of Cnæus Plancius," *XXXIII*, in *The Orations of Marcus Tullius Cicero*, trans. C. D. Yonge, Vol. 3 (London: G. Bell and Sons, 1913–21), 94.

[15] Cf. 1 Thessalonians 5:18.

[16] Cf. Romans 1:21.

[17] Ephesians 1:23, New International Version.

[18] Bonhoeffer, *Ethics*, in *Dietrich Bonhoeffer Works*, vol. 6 (Minneapolis, Minn.: Augsburg Fortress, 2005), 295.

[19] Stella Ma, "The Christian College Experience and the Development of Spirituality among Students," *Christian Higher Education* 2 (2003): 330. In Ma's research, eight of the top ten most significant influences on student's spiritual formation were non-academic, suggesting that what influence students may exercise in this arena, while non-systematic and occasional, may provide the opportunity for the deepest impact student's spiritual life.

IN PARTNERSHIP WITH COMMUNITIES

Spiritual Formation and Cross-Cultural Immersion

Cynthia Toms Smedley

He who does not see God in the next person he meets need look no further.[1]
—Gandhi

Se je pa wè, kè pa tounen (What the eye does not see,
does not move the heart.)
—Kreole Proverb

Like most freshmen, Kerri stepped onto campus flooded with a mul-titude of emotions: anxiety, fear, anticipation, readiness—all of which materialized as a small band of students helped to carry all her clothes, refrigerator, and even futon up four flights of steps to her freshmen dorm room. As she surveyed the area, she realized that the admissions office was not joking about size. All of her belongings in the overly-laden U-Haul truck would need to be reconsidered—only the essentials could remain. One item she decided must go was her full-length mirror. She did not realize the implications of foregoing this mirror, but the decision would later prove symbolic in her life.

In her third year, Kerri accepted an opportunity to serve in Calcutta, India for the summer. Her experience volunteering with Mother Teresa's home for the destitute and dying allowed her to uphold a culture of life by caring for the abandoned until their last breath. After a few weeks of service in this home, she observed something unique about her surroundings—there were no mirrors in Kalighat. No mirrors? Kerri was puzzled by this and located a sister to inquire the reason. The nun smiled at the student's sudden realization and informed her that Mother Teresa's home was intended to be a place without mirrors. "Without mirrors, we are forced to see our reflection through the eyes of others. Without mirrors, we must begin the process of allowing others to challenge us, mold us, and become integral factors in our vocational journey." Kerri's thoughts drifted back to her first days at Notre Dame when she abandoned her full-length mirror in her dorm room. A few years later, she delivered a speech to the incoming class at Notre Dame:

> The perceptive Calcutta nun's wisdom can be a challenge for all of us today. At this moment, it is tempting to stare in the mirror. Oftentimes, when fearful of new situations, we place shells around ourselves and turn inward, merely looking at our own perspective and reflection. However, we are called to action—to be doers—to allow the inspiring community around us to serve as a catalyst of our growth and development. This involves discarding our personal mirrors and looking to the eyes of others.

These words, born out of deep theological reflection, demonstrate Kerri's true encounter with otherness. The choice to travel to a different physical location and culture ultimately transformed her faith, her action, and her vocation.

As students encounter otherness, they gain a deeper understanding of themselves, their faith, and their world. Personal encounters with social challenges move students beyond the classroom walls to engage the lived experience of global communities. When carefully designed, deep and meaningful partnerships outside the campus fortress can become the essential ingredient for meeting the mission of faith-based education to form globally engaged citizens.

The potential for learning and transformation is not limited to undergraduate encounters. Leading a study-abroad program can also be one of the most exciting, rewarding, and pivotal experiences in a faculty member's career. However, for faculty, the host of details, planning, curriculum, and coordination that precede even the simplest of endeavors can quickly become overwhelming. From risk management assessment to cultivating local host contacts, the task can be both exhilarating and exhausting. Although most campuses offer support for each individual aspect of the physical set up, delivery, and re-entry from study abroad, there is little discussion concerning the spiritual journey and growth that inevitably occurs while encountering new cultures and paradigms. Thus, the most daunting and rewarding task for faculty is to see through the administrative cloud to construct and facilitate an environment of spiritual hospitality and mentorship.

This chapter will discuss the praxis of incorporating spiritual formative outcomes into cross-cultural programs, both in terms of pedagogy and the mentoring relationships that these programs engender. As Robert Mulholland writes in his book, *Invitation to a Journey*, "spiritual formation is the process of being conformed to the image of Christ for the sake of others."[2] Therefore, the pivotal role of faculty as mentors and catalysts in this encounter and transformation is one of both privilege and responsibility.

The Journey Inward:
Faculty as Mentors for Intellectual Emigration

Beyond physically crossing cultures, students must be pressed into intellectual emigration. Emigrating is defined as the act of moving away from the perspective of origin or leaving one's country or region to settle in another; it is often characterized by permanence. It is no mistake that I call on this concept, too, as movement away from origin of thought and ideology to a place of permanent intellectual hospitality. In order to do this, faculty must encourage students to create space—distancing them, as best they can, from their own culture. Miroslav Volf calls us to take this notion one step further into something he refers to as a kind of cultural cleansing for the sake of placing "identity and otherness at the center of theological reflection on social realities."[3] This space is not to be regarded as a threat or breaking down of faith, but rather a stance of hospitality in which students can comfortably stand and reflect on our attendant requirements to the human community.

As the winds of generational change blow upon the modern church, students must be prepared to interpret and internalize their place in it. Some of the loudest voices in political rhetoric and church leadership are still split on the role of the social teachings in Scripture.[4] Regardless of how we navigate the carefully regarded denominational language, at the heart of our mentorship, imitating Christ requires that we place others at the center of our faith. When Paul exhorts the Christians of Philippi to live a compassionate life with the mind of Christ, he gives a concrete description of what he means: "Do nothing from selfish ambition or conceit, but in humility regard others as better than yourselves. Let each of you look not to your own interests but to the interests of others" (Phil. 2:3–4). The message is no less relevant today as echoed by Richard Stearns, president of World Vision: "God asks us for *everything*. He requires a total life commitment from those who would be His followers. In fact, Christ calls us to be His partners in changing our world, just as He called the twelve to change their world two thousand years ago."[5]

Teachings about justice, however lucid, cannot fully take root until students encounter people affected by injustice. As students learn about social injustice and then encounter relationships with people who are suffering from their injustice, new questions arise that challenge their understandings of theology and their place in the world. The papal encyclical called *Spe Salvi*, translated from Latin as "Hope in Action," calls on teachings that are recognized in our heritage as a social reality. Indeed, the Letter to the Hebrews speaks of a "city" (cf. 11:10, 16; 12:22; 13:14)[6] and therefore of community, both individual and collective, in need of salvation. Consistently with this view, sin is understood as the destruction of the unity of the human race, as fragmentation and division. Hence redemption appears as the reestablishment of unity, in which we come together once more in a union that begins to take shape in the world community of believers. In this way, there is a communal component to salvation—and most importantly, a responsibility to care for one another.

In order to more effectively help students grapple with these questions, strategies such as theological reflection and social analysis must be employed. As Smith Shappell writes, "Pastoral theological reflection has its roots in the clinical pastoral education movement and envelops the concept of living human documents and recognizes people as the most forgotten source of doing theology."[7] Theological reflection offers a place where tradition and experience intersect, a place where experience and religious tradition converse with each other. Used in this way, faculty can mentor students through a framework that nurtures growth in faith by bringing life experience into conversation with the wisdom of the Christian heritage.

The Journey Outward:
Encountering People, Experiencing Theology

Insertion into communities offers students an opportunity to *experience* theology. Engaging people offers a communal element to spiritual formation by extending the principle of discernment from the personal realm to the social realm. By design, cultural immersions move explorations beyond traditional methods of studying theology and toward encountering people as "living human documents." Theology becomes more than texts and concepts as students experience the work of God through the lives of people who differ from themselves. By encountering God through the customs and patterns of life in different cultures, students begin to grasp a larger vision of God and how they relate to him.

The pastoral circle or the "circle of praxis"[8] has long been accepted as a means of bringing together these academic and pastoral approaches to social contexts. It offers the opportunity for students to practice "active" faith by aligning the pursuit of knowledge with the pursuit of justice through social analysis. Pedagogically, it presses students to apply traditional texts (Scripture, church documents, and classroom teachings) to real-world contexts while focusing on well-informed action as the final outcome. This see-judge-act[9] method focuses on four specific movements. The first, *insertion,* helps to locate the geography of our exploration in the lived experience of ordinary people's feelings, challenges, and circumstances. The second movement, *social analysis,* helps us to understand the experience through the richness of interrelationships. By examining causes, probing linkages, and identifying actors, we are able to understand the social forces shaping specific communities. The third movement, *theological reflection,* nurtures growth in mature faith by bringing life experience into conversation with the wisdom of the Christian heritage. It offers a standpoint of exploration—a place where tradition and experience intersect, a place where experience and religious tradition converse with each other. The Word of God brought to bear upon the situation raises new questions, suggests new insights and opens new responses. The fourth and final movement, *pastoral planning (or action),* focuses on the crucial aspect of decision and action. Through analyzing experiences and reflecting upon the social and theological implications, students can participate in an effective and carefully crafted response to social challenges.

In many ways, this method helps students align orthopraxy ("right action") with orthodoxy ("right knowledge" or "the authentic adoration and glorification of God"[10]). For students in Notre Dame's Migrant Experience Seminar, the pastoral circle has been an important method for deep learning and spiritual formation. Classroom sessions introduce students to the economic, political, and social issues surrounding the plight of migrant farm workers. Through class presentations, selected readings, and discussions, students develop a theology of migration and immigration. "As a call to cross borders and overcome barriers, migration is a way of thinking about God and human life and an expression of the Christian mission of reconciliation."[11] They interact with an immigration scholar, Father Dan Groody, C.S.C., who describes his theological method as:

> based on the Incarnation—the belief that God migrated to humanity so all of us in turn could migrate back to God. Broadly considered, these elements are woven together in a process that involves 1) immersion in

the world, especially into the life of the poor; 2) "interfluence," or the way in which the lived experience of Christian faith and the deposit of Christian tradition mutually influence each other; and 3) an interpretation of life that seeks to deepen our relationship with God and each other. This method is not just about retrieval and application, nor the gathering of new information for human formation. Rather it is a vision of life that leads to transformation and the construction of a new imagination.[12]

During the semester break, after weeks of theological reflection and discussion, students then travel to Immokalee, Florida to meet with migrant laborers, the families of migrants, the Coalition of Immokalee Workers, Catholic Migrant Farmworker Network, and a host of other agencies, schools, and advocacy groups working toward justice. Upon arrival to the community, many students are struck that such poverty and living conditions are present in Immokalee, Florida—just a short drive from Naples, Florida, one of the wealthiest metropolitan areas in the United States. One student wrote:

> In preparation for my trip to Immokalee, I read many articles informing me of the poverty and maltreatment of the workers in Immokalee and providing me with many statistics on the matter. I felt sufficiently informed when I left for the trip; I was convinced that I would know what to expect when I arrived. However, I was mistaken; I found that there were more complex issues that underlined the factors affecting the people of Immokalee than the ones that I read about. In just the week that I spent there, the most prominent social issues that I saw affecting the workers were: legal status, a lack of a decent wage or stable work, a lack of quality education, and a lack of a local government, which together affected the entire community.

Throughout the week, students utilize social analysis and theological reflection to gain a deep understanding of the challenges facing migrant workers. Following the immersion, students reflect on their experience and consider ways to move beyond awareness to faithful action and advocacy. As part of her final reflection, a student wrote:

> Through my experience in Immokalee, I was able to see first hand how unjust working and living conditions . . . affect . . . all aspects of life— mentally, physically, emotionally, educationally and religiously. Trying to connect Catholic Social Teaching with such unjust wages and lack of

benefits was very difficult in the beginning because it was difficult to find good in any part of the work taking place in Immokalee because it was so unjust. However after skimming back over Catholic Social Teaching principles, the parallels and applications between migrant work and Catholic Social Teaching seemed endless. Often it's the people without a voice that get treated unjustly and in the United States today, the undocumented migrant family/worker is one of the groups that is most vulnerable. These vulnerable, exploited workers need the voice of the Catholic Church and the social justice/action component to create better lives for migrant workers and their families. When a systemic change occurs with agricultural legislation it will improve the lives of many families and alleviate social service agencies of putting on the Band-Aids to the problems because people will be able to support themselves modestly.

As students are inserted in communities and into the experiences of ordinary people, their previous frameworks of faith and worldview are challenged. In most cases, the careful lines of theology that once seemed adequate must stretch to make meaning of new contexts. This skepticism, when well facilitated through a specialized curriculum, can assist students in delineating linkages among personal reflection, critical thinking, and faith in a global community context. This deeper and broader theological lens of the world seeks to understand the heart of the gospel message through a myriad of perspectives and it liberates and elevates all members of the global village. We cannot experience God unless we love our brothers and sisters, and we cannot love our brothers and sisters without experiencing God.

Translating the Experience: Home as a Guiding Metaphor for Crossing Cultures

The irony of study immersions is that we travel to distant lands in order to resurrect a pedagogy that "engenders an ethos of intimacy and affection."[13] In reality, crossing cultures is only the beginning of the journey and much is missed when we focus myopically on the orientation and immersion and give little attention to the re-entry. For most colleges, debriefing and re-entry from cross-cultural immersions consists of on-campus resources and program networks for future participation. However, we have neither done the hard work of plugging students into local community endeavors nor offered engagement opportunities for advocacy and action. To use a driving metaphor, we have revved the engine, driven onto the highway of discovery, and accelerated to top cultural speeds. However, we have not paid attention to the off-ramp—and in many cases, we may have forgotten to build one.

We must revise our programmatic infrastructure to reflect the reality that most students are just beginning to climb onto the arch of the learning trajectory when they arrive back to campus. We must not assume that students know how to exercise their newly developed convictions. In order to fully guide them through the transformation and growth process, we help them stand on wobbly legs of newborn activism, develop community advocacy skills, and support their intention to become civically engaged. In his 2011 book entitled, *Lost in Transition*, sociologist Christian Smith reports that, contrary to stories told in popular media, most emerging adults in America have extremely modest-to-no expectations for ways society or the world can be changed for the better, whether by volunteering or anything else.[14] Thus, our charge as faculty is to expand pedagogies to include aiding students as they translate their overseas experiences to local rootedness and a sense of place. "Love and seeing is never generic, it is never universal, it is always placed, timed and particular," write Bouma-Prediger and Walsh. "Just as we cannot love our neighbor 'in general,' but must always love *this* neighbor, here in *this* neighborhood, so also can we never love things in general or the world in general, or even creation in general, apart from a love, intimacy, knowledge and care for a particular place."[15]

I was recently struck by this notion as our departmental basketball team landed on the name, "Think Global, Hoop Local." Surely our skills on the court can barely be considered "hooping." However, we want our message that daily personal disciplines performed with people most closely in relationship to ourselves, such as local community initiatives, can help us.

The option of remaining locally active is not as trendy as continuing to look for more global experiences. Alternatively, experiences beginning and ending with local community organizations or opportunities to examine parallel issues within the local community help to begin our journey of physical emigration differently.

In his essay entitled "The Fate of Civilization and the Future of Study Abroad," Richard Slimbach reflects that:

> Our challenge as global educators is to *transcend* the artificial local-global division in order to *create* a 'third space' that emphasizes the interaction and mutual influence of 'multicultural' and 'international' perspectives and practices. Global learning can no longer be defined by the alleged

strangeness of geographically distant cultures. Especially in the great urban centers of North America and Europe, the wild mixing of peoples, values, and cultural forms has permanently reconfigured the very notion of what is ordinary and what is peculiar.[16]

Thus, the strategies discussed in these pages are intended for designing programs that expose students to the cultural other and move them toward cognitive dissonance, and ultimately spiritual formation and action as "glo*cally* engaged" citizens.

Beyond Student Learning Outcomes: Prolonged Engagement with Communities

"What happens if we allow homecoming to be the guiding metaphor for our educational praxis?"[17] Bouma-Prediger and Walsh pose this question in an attempt to remind us that education is not for upward mobility, but rather to gain skills to help in a hurting world. Their premise hinges on the reality that most education fosters a sense of displacement within students—a lack of rootedness that can eventually become destructive to creation, civilization, and even our own selves. Thus, our role as faculty and international education professionals is to backward design educational experiences from outcomes focused on active and engaged faith that responds to the needs of a suffering world. We must be concerned with fostering intimacy and a sense of place. However, this tension places us in juxtaposition between two seemingly opposing outcomes. As Rich Slimbach notes, "On the one hand we advocate for immersed and immediate experiences of 'place' within cross-cultural settings as indispensable to learning to see things as others do. On the other hand we participate in a historical process that favors what is new, fast, and transnational over what is deep-rooted, slow, and local."[18]

This tension, albeit difficult to navigate, offers faculty members a rare opportunity to demonstrate a model of prolonged engagement, both with the communities we visit and with the global Christian community. Prolonged engagement can be defined formally through community-based research initiatives that address social challenges[19] and include long-term goals and the strategies for action, ongoing evaluation and revision of those strategies, and can involve broad participation of various constituents in the community. However, prolonged engagement can also take the form of a mutually beneficial knowledge exchange between community partner and university. This engagement with communities places native cultures at the heart of educational endeavors. It elevates community partners to the role of teacher, peer, and co-laborer.

For far too long, universities have viewed communities as de-centralized petri-dishes for education and research agendas. This mantra only serves to divorce pedagogies of intimacy from the process of immersion. Furthermore, it reinforces an implicit belief system that power, knowledge, and resources (namely education and money) dictate one's ability to maintain agency. Consider the literature bias in other community-based fields such as service learning, where student outcomes assessment all but eclipses the small number of studies performed on community impact.[20] Moreover, most of us are in consensus and no longer believe that we have all the answers and nothing to learn from indigenous knowledge constructs. In the eloquent words of Lila Watson, aboriginal activist, "If you have come here to help then you are wasting your time. But if you have come because your liberation is bound up with mine, then let us work together." Prolonged engagement and mutuality with community partners ensures personal agency and power distribution—it also allows our students to witness a model of particular love and intimacy with place and people.

Henri Nouwen describes the community as mediator and reminds us that there is no individual Shalom, but rather that we should adopt a compassionate life together. In his book entitled *Compassion*, he talks about sitting down to a cup of coffee and hearing the local news blaring from the TV—so many tragedies, so much hurt. How can we possibly respond without the collective gifts and resources from a global Christian family? Nouwen writes:

> The Christian Community mediates between a suffering of the world and our individual responses to this suffering. Since the Christian community is the living presence of the mediating Christ (meaning, we are Christ's hands), it enables us to be fully aware of the painful condition of the human family without being paralyzed by this awareness. In the Christian Community, we can keep our eyes and ears open to all that happens without being numbed by technology stimulation or angered by the experience of powerlessness. . . . In community, we are no longer a mass of helpless individuals, but are transformed into one people of God who reveal themselves to the world in solidarity, servant hood, and obedience. In community, our gifts and energies are multiplied and delivered to a hurting world.[21]

Prolonged engagement (or investment) also requires that we assume a stance of solidarity with community. Solidarity reminds us that we are all part of one human family—whatever our national, racial, religious, economic, or ideological differences—and in an increasingly interconnected world, loving our neighbors has global dimensions.[22] It assists in answering Christ's call to move away from ordinary and comfortable places in order to take up residence in a hurting world. This discipline, referred by Henri Nouwen as voluntary displacement, helps us to "counteract the tendency to become settled in a false comfort and forget the fundamentally unsettled position that we share with all people."[23] In this space, we enter into relationship and bear the burden of common human brokenness and common need for healing.

Faculty as Flexible Counselors and Multi-Taskers

Focusing on one of the main learning objectives in study abroad programs, Engle and Engle identified two factors that most effectively lead to cross-cultural development: direct contact with the culture and "skillful mentoring which guides, informs, inspires, and stimulates the experiential learning process."[24] Effective programs provide opportunities for direct immersion in the culture, along with support for the students. A study abroad experience could be transformative or traumatic for students. Therefore, these programs need to be skillfully administered so students are appropriately challenged and also supported by the facilitators of the program.[25] As John Dewey reminds us, "Mere activity does not constitute [an educational] experience."[26]

However, the line between building up and breaking down is a thin one. In *Cultivating the Spirit*, Astin and Lindholm note that study abroad increases religious skepticism among undergraduates.[27] These findings are no surprise to faculty and staff on home-campuses welcoming students back from their study abroad experience. Students ask questions differently as a result of their exposure to a wide range of religious believers and non-believers in other countries. This skepticism, when well facilitated through a specialized curriculum, can assist students in delineating linkages among personal reflection, critical thinking, and faith in a global community context. During this critical time, the role of the faculty mentor becomes more than a trip planner and administrator; it becomes a hybrid between campus minister, academic expert, cultural connoisseur, and administrative wonder.

Conclusion

For many students, the journey of spiritual formation begins the day they arrive to campus. However, some of the most transformative experiences result from a physical and intellectual emigration away from comfortable dorm rooms, familiar methods of learning, and language and cultural constructs.

In his opening forward to the book *Transformations at the Edge of the World*, Ken Bussema, VP of the Council for Christian Colleges and Universities (CCCU), notes a poster that states "Find yourself somewhere else." The slogan is a simple and subtle reminder that the wanderlust of youth—coupled with the unique opportunities available in the collegiate environment and life of the mind—can offer the most critical and informative learning a student may encounter during the college experience.

One trap that we fall into is a myopic focus on the immersion—the actual trip—as the primary means of transformation. What if we were to flip this traditional perspective on its head? What if we were so bold as to consider the homecoming—or home—as the guiding metaphor for the educational experience? As faith-based universities, our missions require that we are kingdom workers and world changers.

For many educational institutes, study abroad and domestic cultural immersion accomplish similar education goals. Cultural immersion can take place in any region or culture where the economy, language, or worldview is completely foreign. These experiences are still based in the context of "other," and require students to adopt a hospitable stance toward culture and language. However, they offer a more sustainable, affordable, and transferable experience for students; and the immersion requires considerably less administrative prowess. Notre Dame's Center for Social Concerns sends students to communities in Arizona, Florida, and Chicago to gain a greater understanding of obstacles facing immigrant communities from Latin and South America. In doing so, students encounter real faces and stories in a context that allows them to consider their own long-term engagement in policy, education, and outreach that directly affects these communities. Furthermore, some in the field of experiential education and education abroad believe that the future of study abroad and domestic service learning, whose scholarship and pedagogies closely mirror one another, will merge to provide students a continuum of experiences where intercultural skills are developed domestically, expanded internationally, and transferred for the good of local U.S. communities in which most students will live out the balance of their adult lives.

When these methods are successful, students return to their campuses and communities with new eyes. In *Compassion*, Henri Nouwen and Fr. Don McNeil write: "Compassion means going directly to those people and places where suffering is most acute and building a home there."[28] Our encounters of otherness now reflect learning that forms deep understanding of people, communities, and solidarity—and we are most effective in our own backyards.

Chapter 14 Notes

[1] Mahatma Gandhi, quoted in Donald Posterski, *Enemies with Smiling Faces: Defeating the Subtle Threats That Endanger Christians* (Downers Grove, Ill.: InterVarsity, 2004), 57.

[2] M. Robert Mulholland Jr., *Invitation to a Journey: A Road Map for Spiritual Formation* (Downers Grove, Ill.: InterVarsity Press, 1993), 12.

[3] Mirslov Volf, *Exclusion & Embrace: A Theological Exploration of Identity, Otherness, and Reconciliation* (Nashville, Tenn.: Abingdon, 1996), 17.

[4] Associated with the teachings of Thomas Aquinas, the Catholic Social Tradition, and originally attributed to a Jesuit priest in 1840, the term *social justice* has become a versatile and yet polarizing term.

[5] Richard Stearns, *The Hole in Our Gospel: What Does God Expect of Us? The Answer that Changed My Life and Might Just Change the World* (Nashville, Tenn.: Thomas Nelson, 2009), 1.

[6] Benedict XVI, *Spe Salvi*, Vatican Website, 2007, http://www.vatican.va/holy_father/benedict_xvi/encyclicals/documents/hf_benxvi_enc_20071130_spe-salvi_en.html.

[7] Andrea Smith Shappell, "Reflection as a Means of Discovery: Where Is God in the Experience?" in *Transformations at the Edge of the World: Forming Global Christians through the Study Abroad Experience*, eds. Ronald J. Morgan and Cynthia Toms Smedley (Abilene, Tex.: Abilene Christian University Press, 2010).

[8] Joe Holland and Peter Henriot, *Social Analysis: Linking Faith and Justice* (Maryknoll, N.Y.: Orbis Books, 1986). The concept of praxis was first developed by Paulo Freire in his seminal work, *The Pedagogy of the Oppressed*, trans. Myra Bergman Ramos (New York: Herder and Herder, 1970). This method has also been called the hermeneutic circle.

[9] Cardinal Joseph Cardijn, a Belgian priest and the founder of the Young Christian Workers Movement, proposed the 'see,' 'judge,' 'act' method as way to read and respond to the signs of the times. Acting upon Cardijn's inspiration, Pope John XXIII incorporated the "See—Judge—Act" method into Catholic social teaching and practice through the *Mater et Magistra* in 1961.

[10] Cardinal Ratzinger, "Eucharist, Communion and Solidarity," lecture to the Bishops' Conference of the Region of Campania in Benevento, Italy, June 2, 2002, available online at Catholic Online, http://www.catholic.org/featured/headline.php?ID=2066.

[11] Daniel C. Groody, "Crossing the Divide: Foundations of a Theology of Migration and Refugees," in *Theological Studies* 70 (2009): 638.

[12] Daniel Groody, "Theology of Migration: A New Method for Understanding a God on the Move," in *America Magazine* 204, no. 3 (7 February 2011).

[13] Steven Bouma-Prediger and Brian Walsh, "Education for Homelessness or Homemaking? The Christian College in a Postmodern Culture," *Journal of Education and Christian Belief* 8, no. 1 (Spring 2004).

[14] Christian Smith et al., *Lost in Transition: The Dark Side of Emerging Adulthood* (New York: Oxford University Press, 2011).

[15] Bouma-Prediger and Walsh, "Education for Homelessness or Homemaking."

[16] Richard Slimbach, "The Fate of Civilization and the Future of Study Abroad," unpublished manuscript.

[17] Bouma-Prediger and Walsh, "Education for Homelessness or Homemaking."

[18] Slimbach, "The Fate of Civilization."

[19] Mary Beckman, Naomi Penney, and Bethany Cockburn, "Maximizing the Impact of Community-Based Research," *Journal of Higher Education Outreach and Engagement* 15, no. 2 (2011): 83.

[20] Randy Stoeker, Elizabeth Tryon, eds. with Amy Hilgendorf, *The Unheard Voices: Community Organization and Service Learning* (Philadelphia, Pa.: Temple University Press, 2009), 4.

[21] Henri J. M. Nouwen, Donald P. McNeill, and Douglas A. Morrison *Compassion: A Reflection on the Christian Life* (Garden City, N.Y.: Doubleday, 1982), 53.

[22] John Paul II, Sollicitudo Rei Socialis, (Vatican Website, 1987).

[23] Nouwen, McNeill, and Morrison, *Compassion*, 61–62.

[24] Lilli Engle and John Engle, "Assessing Language Acquisition and Intercultural Sensitivity Development in Relation to Study Abroad Program Design," *Frontiers: The Interdisciplinary Journal of Study Abroad* 10 (2004): 219–36, 232.

[25] Steven Kortenhoeven, "Students' Experiences of a College Short-Term Mission Trip: A Phenomenological Study," (doctoral dissertation, Azusa Pacific University, 2011), 43.

[26] John Dewey, *Democracy and Education: An Introduction to the Philosophy of Education* (New York, NY: The Free Press, 1916).

[27] Alexander W. Astin, Helen S. Astin, and Jennifer A. Lindholm, *Cultivating the Spirit: How College Can Enhance Students' Inner Lives* (San Francisco, Calif.: Jossey-Bass, 2011).

[28] Nouwen, McNeill, and Morrison, *Compassion*, 25.

CONTRIBUTORS

Keith R. Anderson is the President of The Seattle School of Theology and Psychology where he also serves as Professor of Spiritual Formation. He holds an MDiv from Bethel Theological Seminary and a DMin from George Fox Evangelical Seminary. Author of several books, he co-authored *Spiritual Mentoring: A Guide for Giving and Receiving Direction*, published by InterVarsity Press. Keith and his wife, Wendy, who have three married adult children and six precocious grandchildren, live on an island in the Pacific Northwest.

Cary Balzer currently serves as the Director of Faculty Development at John Brown University. He also holds the J. V. McGee Chair of Theology and serves as an assistant professor. A graduate of Seattle Pacific University, he received an MDiv from Asbury Theological Seminary and both an MTh and a PhD in theology from the University of Manchester, England. His first book, *The Devotional Wesley*, was published in 2009. Cary and his wife, Tracy, lead student trips to England, Ireland, or Scotland every year. They live in Siloam Springs, Arkansas with their youngest daughter, Langley. Their older daughter, Kelsey, and her husband live in South Korea.

Greg Carmer serves as the Dean of the A. J. Gordon Memorial Chapel at Gordon College, a position he has held since 2002. He also directs the Christian Vocation Institute, a collection of programs—including the Elijah Project—which help students explore the theological underpinnings and practical out-workings of vocation. Prior to assuming the responsibilities of dean, he served as the Director of

Service-Learning and Missions. Greg holds an MA and a PhD in philosophical theology from Boston College, and a BA in philosophy and the social sciences from Spring Arbor College. He lives with his wife, Laura, and their three boys in Beverly, Massachusetts.

Perry Glanzer is an associate professor of Educational Foundations at Baylor University, where he has been working since 2002. He graduated from Rice University, received his masters in Church-State Studies from Baylor, and earned a PhD in Religion and Social Ethics from the University of Southern California. He then traveled to Russia, where he taught philosophy for a year at a prominent national university and also at an experimental Christian educational institution, the first of its kind in Russia. Perry's writing and research cover the relationship between religion, education, and politics. He and his wife live in Hewitt, Texas with their two sons, Bennett and Cody.

Daniel Haase earned both his BA and MA from Wheaton College in the Christian Formation and Ministry Department where he now serves part-time as Adjunct Professor and Internship Coordinator. He teaches in the areas of discipleship, spiritual guidance and discernment, and ministry calling. For the past twelve years he has lived in an underclassman dorm on campus with his wife, Kathleen, who is the Residence Director. Dan's full-time job is as a homeschool father to his two young Padawan sons (Chris, twelve, and Ben, ten). He has a marvelous dog, a long-haired miniature dachshund, named Bunny.

Steve Harper currently serves as Professor of Spiritual Formation and Wesley Studies at the Florida-Dunnam Campus of Asbury Theological Seminary in Orlando. He received his Bachelors's degree from McMurry University, his MDiv from Asbury Theological Seminary, and his PhD from Duke University. He is the author of thirteen books and co-author of another eleven. He is married to Jeannie, and they are the parents of two children (John and Katrina) and grandparents of Zoe and Isaac. In addition to his ministries as a United Methodist clergyperson and seminary professor, he and Jeannie enjoy traveling in their pop-up camper.

Steve Moore currently serves as the Executive Director and CEO of the M. J. Murdock Charitable Trust in Vancouver, Washington. He is also the Senior Program Fellow for A Foundation for Theological Education. Steve has served at Texas Tech University, Seattle Pacific University, Asbury Theological Seminary, and Baylor University prior to his current leadership role. He and his wife, Thanne, have three children: Madison, Maegan, and Mollie.

M. Robert Mulholland, Jr. is Emeritus Professor of New Testament at Asbury Theological Seminary. He received a BS in Electrical Engineering from the U.S. Naval Academy, an MDiv from Wesley Theological Seminary, and a DTh from Harvard Divinity School. He served United Methodist churches in Maryland, Massachusetts, and Texas, and presently serves the Shirley Community Church in Shirley, Maine. For seventeen years he was the Vice President and Provost of Asbury Theological Seminary. He is the author of *Shaped by the Word, Invitation to a Journey, The Deeper Journey,* and *The Way of Scripture.*

Rod Reed has served as University Chaplain and Dean of Spiritual Formation in two Christian universities since 1997. He is a recognized authority on spiritual formation in Christian higher education, serving as chair of the Campus Ministries Commission of the Council of Christian Colleges and Universities from 2005–2009. Rod has also visited fifteen Christian universities in the role of peer reviewer for institutional approaches to spiritual formation, and has researched spiritual formation practices on nearly thirty Christian university campuses. He is currently finishing his PhD dissertation entitled "Shaping the Whole Person: A Contextualized Theology of Spiritual Formation in Christian Higher Education."

Susan Reese, Associate Professor of Spiritual Formation at Souix Falls Seminary, is committed to supporting students in discerning their call and spiritual life as well as developing their ministry skills. Her commitment to teaching and student development began in her undergraduate degree and professional work at the University of Sioux Falls. She received her Master's in Counseling from Sioux Falls Seminary and her EdD in Adult and Higher Education from the University of South Dakota. Her dissertation is entitled "Student Affairs Practitioners Implementation of Spiritual Development Programs in the CCCU." Susan is married to Randy Reese and together they love their son Liam and the prairie life of Sioux Falls, South Dakota

William P. (Bill) Robinson is President Emeritus of Whitworth University in Spokane, Washington, after serving as president from 1993–2010. He currently works full time speaking and consulting with universities, businesses, and churches. In 2010, a second edition of Robinson's book *Leading People from the Middle: The Universal Mission of Mind and Heart* was released. His second book, *Incarnate Leadership,* was published by Zondervan in February 2009. Robinson earned his bachelor's degree from the University of Northern Iowa, his master's degree from Wheaton College, and his PhD from the University of Pittsburgh. Bill and his wife, Bonnie, live in Spokane, Washington. They have three married children, Brenna, Ben, and Bailley. Bill entertains himself with sports, art, music, and taking orders from his grandchildren.

Linda Rozema has recently served as research assistant for the Christian Formation and Ministry Department of Wheaton College. She received an AA degree in nursing from Cattonsville Community College, a BA in Human Services from Judson College, and an MA in Christian Formation and Ministry from Wheaton College. Linda is married to John and they have three children and four grandchildren. She enjoys traveling to visit family, especially the grandchildren, and she is involved with women's ministry, gardening, and quilting between trips.

David Setran is Associate Professor of Christian Formation and Ministry at Wheaton College, where he teaches courses related to the history and philosophy of Christian education and ministry with college students and young adults. He holds a PhD in History of Education from Indiana University. His first book, *The College "Y": Student Religion in the Era of Secularization*, was published in 2007. David enjoys running, playing tennis, and spending time with his wife, Holly, and their four children.

Cynthia Toms-Smedley is an assistant director at the University of Notre Dame's Center for Social Concerns. Prior to this position, Cynthia taught cross-cultural immersion skills at Peking University in Beijing, China, and was the assistant director of the Uganda Studies Program located in Mukono, Uganda. She received her master's degree from Boston University and is a PhD candidate in Higher Education. Her dissertation research focuses on the impact of international service learning on developing communities. She is co-editor of the recent book, *Transformations at the Edge of the World: Forming Global Christians through the Study Abroad Experience.* Cynthia resides with her husband, Michael, and two sons in South Bend, Indiana.

James Wilhoit is Scripture Press Professor of Christian Education at Wheaton College. He is the author of *Spiritual Formation as if the Church Mattered* and co-editor of *The Dictionary of Biblical Imagery (IVP)* and, with Leland Ryken, *Effective Bible Teaching.* In his time away from school he enjoys being with his family, gardening, running, and wasting time with God.

Bob Yoder currently serves as Campus Pastor and Assistant Professor of Youth Ministry at Goshen College. He received his BS in Biology from Eastern Mennonite

University, an MDiv from Associated Mennonite Biblical Seminary, and a DMin from Western Theological Seminary. Bob is an ordained pastor in the Mennonite Church USA and has served in congregational, camp, conference, and college ministry settings. Author of several essays and articles in the areas of biblical lament and adolescent faith development, he recently co-edited *Youth Ministry at a Crossroads: Tending to the Faith Formation of Mennonite Youth* and is editing another book on the history of Mennonite Youth Ministry set to be published by the Institute of Mennonite Studies. Bob and his wife, Pamela, have two children, Josiah and Mira. A recent highlight for them was running the original route marathon in Greece from Marathon to Athens.

CPSIA information can be obtained at www.ICGtesting.com
Printed in the USA
LVOW13s0422240614

391392LV00001B/1/P